For Mom and Dad

for your continual understanding, support,
and ability to raise three sons with a sense of decency

WATERFALL ICE
Climbs in the Canadian Rockies

March 1997

To Ashley,

Here's to more days in rain and hopefully more days on the summits (not to mention some fine single malt)!

Good Climbing

Joe Josephson

Joe Josephson

Front Cover: The author takes on an interesting variation on the otherwise normal Good, Bad and The Ugly. Photo by François Damilano.
Back Cover: Richard Ouairy on Echo Madness. Photo by Brad Wrobleski.
Title Page: Barry "Bubba" Blanchard enjoys Coire Dubh with Yamnuska behind. Photo by Brad Wrobleski.

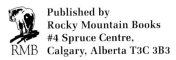

**Published by
Rocky Mountain Books
#4 Spruce Centre,
Calgary, Alberta T3C 3B3**

© Joseph Josephson, 1994
2nd printing revised 1995

Printed and bound in Canada by
Kromar Printing Ltd., Winnipeg

The Publisher wishes to acknowledge the assistance of Alberta Culture and Multiculturalism, The Alberta Foundation for the Arts and the department of Canadian Heritage in the publication of this book.

ISBN 0-921102-33-X

Canadian Cataloguing in Publication Data

Joseph Josephson 1967-
  Waterfall ice

  First-2nd eds. by Albi Sole
  Includes index.
  ISBN 0-921102-33-X

  1. Snow and ice climbing--Rocky Mountains, Canadian
(B.C. and Alta.)--Guidebooks. 2. Waterfalls--Rocky
Mountains, Canadian (B.C. and Alta.)--Guidebooks. 3.
Rocky Mountains, Canadian (B.C. and Alta.)--Guidebooks.*
I. Sole, Albi, 1953- II. Title.
GV199.44.C22R63 1994   796.5'22'09711   C94-910764-6

CONTENTS

Climbing Areas

ACKNOWLEDGEMENTS

Albi Sole pioneered Rockies ice and the guide-book over fifteen years ago. I am forever in-debted to him for his vision, continued support and for allowing me to carry on in his footsteps.

Alex Taylor started me in this crazy busi-ness of ice climbing and Bruce Hendricks showed me a new vision of pursuit—without either of you I could not be the ice climber or person I am today. This book goes out to you.

Many people contributed to the final prod-uct, some in a way they may never realize. To all of you I am grateful and hope I can someday repay the favour .

Mike Balfour of the Rampart Creek Hostel deserves a special thanks for providing a 'home-away-from-home' for me and countless others. He made our days along the Banff-Jasper enjoyable and something to look for-ward to. This is from all of us Mike.

A special appreciation goes to those who went out of their way to provide desperately needed information and support—the incom-parable Barry Blanchard for his inspiration and writing of the Foreward; Scott Backes and Tim Pochay for their profound friendship; Margo Talbot for filling in my ignorance as I panicked about certain areas I could not get to myself; Larry Stanier for writing most of the avalanche section; Glenn Reisenhofer and Jeff Everett for their information, enthusiasm, and great new routes; Kirt Sellers for digging up previously unknown information about the Columbia Valley and Golden areas and getting it to me at the last minute; Dave Thomson and Dave Chase for sharing the wonders of Icefall Brook; Cyril Shokoples for his sense of hu-mour and letting me liberally use information from his Mini-Guide to David Thompson Ice; Jean Walters and Rick Yeoman of The Dry Ranges fame; and finally for the support and enthusiasm of The Ice Connection of François Damilano and Godefroy Perroux.

Thanks to Don Serl and Kevin McLane for permission to use information about the Abalakov Sandwich.

I send kudos to others who contributed infor-mation and put up with my continuous has-sling–Tim Auger, Barry Blanchard, James Blench, Andrew Brash, Carlos Buhler, Joe Buszowski, Frank Campbell, Rodger Debeyer, Jim Dodich Jr., Keith Haberl, Eric Hoogstraten, Michael Kennedy, Troy Kirwan, Brent Kozachenko of Waterton National Park, Guy Lacelle, Allan Massin, Karl Nagy, Paul O'Byrne, Murray Toft, Marc Twight and Terry Willis of Yoho National Park.

I am indebted to Don Serl and Alex Taylor who went the extra nine yards when proof-reading, and finally woke me up to my slaugh-tering of the English language. Others crucial in the task of proofing various text versions are Nancy Geismar, Bruce Hendricks, Guy Lacelle, Tim Pochay, and Ken Wylie.

As I fall into the 'point-and-shoot' crowd of photographers, the great selection of photo-graphs in the book would not have been possi-ble without the help and expertise of Patrick Morrow. Thanks Pat for answering my igno-rant questions and letting me commandeer your light table and laser printer.

The generosity of many photographers who supplied images is also greatly acknowledged. Thanks to Peter Amann, Tim Auger, Scott Backes, Barry Blanchard, Frank Campbell, Greg Cronn, François Damilano, Jim Dodich Jr., Kevin Doyle, Jeff Everett, Tom Fayle, Keith Haberl, Bruce Hendricks, Eric Hoogstraten, Troy Kirwan, Jeff Lakes, Karl Nagy, Jeff Nazarchuk, Paul O'Byrne, Commander Bill Pelander, Godefroy Perroux, Philippe Pibarot, Glenn Reisenhofer, Dave Shakatko, Kirt Sell-ers, Larry Stanier, Grant Statham, Alex Taylor, Dave Thomson, Ty Trand, Marc Twight, Brian Webster, and Brad Wrobleski.

Others who assisted in a variety of ways are Jay Honeyman, Nathalie Martin-Jarrand, Greg McAuley, Martha McCallum, Biaba Morrow, Geoff Powter and Jim Swanson.

Photos on previous pages:
p.6 Joe Josephson on the first ascent of Virtual Reality. Photo David Shakatko
p.7 Snivelling Gully. Photo David Shakatko
p.8 The right side of Louise Falls. Photo Pat Morrow
p.9 "The Poch" in profile on the first ascent of Red Man Soars. Photo Barry Blanchard

"Have you heard from Jo-Jo yet?" It was a common question for Troy Kirwan to ask me, or me him, around about Thursday during the winter of 92/93. "Ya, he called me at 11:37 last night, and Whipper (Grant Stratham) at seven Tuesday morning". "He's twitching man". "Ya, Big Time". Troy, Grant and I live in Canmore and were spending much of our weeks climbing and skiing. Jo-Jo was in Calgary supervising sewing machines, drinking too much coffee, and growing anxious over the weekend ice climbing plans. He'd call us when the ice anxiety and quadruple espressos eroded a hole in his psyche. We developed the "Jo-Jo Factor"–the outrageousness of that weekend climb varied inversely with the timeline of Jo-Jo's "hey, what are the conditions doing?" phone please. The earlier in the week that we heard from him, the higher the grade and wilder the climb that weekend. I got a call one Monday, Troy Tuesday and Whipper Wednesday. That Saturday Jo-Jo and Scott Backes created *Acid Howl*—a truly twisted concept: link-up a thousand feet of gossamer ice as best you can—a real adrenaline treat. By Friday the next week we still hadn't heard from Jo-Jo and we realized that we worried more about him, not hearing from him; we called him, and true to the "Jo-Jo Factor" he was going out with an old friend to cruise some mellow ice, he was even drinking decaff.

"What's happening with conditions Whipper? I'm stuck in this butt-hole of a city and I don't know spit". It was Wednesday; our world was back to normal. In true traditional fashion we called a meeting of the "Social Climbers Club" whose function is to ensure that the four of us, and whoever else is going ice climbing, start the day right with a solid triple bypass breakfast at the Fireside Inn, Canmore. We're talking about the kind of food that'll still be with you after one hour and fifty seven minutes of skiing like a Swede and postholing like an elk—read: bacon and eggs, hashbrowns, stacks of toast, pots of fully caffeinated black coffee, and lots of ice climbing talk. Talk about the ice, is it free of snow and, therefore, camouflage, has an arctic high left it slate grey and as brittle as Belgian crystal, or has the Chinook wind coaxed it to the point of Plasticine—we can go hook those daggers in space and go for the one-arms, Grr! Is the avalanche hazard restricting us to the front ranges, or is it safe enough to plow up to the French Maid out above Yoho's west gate. Has anyone been into the Ghost lately? Is it drivable? Who's been climbing what" how fast? And in what style? What's the dirt? Plans for the winter, plans for the Greater Ranges, plans for the day…

That day the wind spiked my hair into my eyes with the force of a tattooing needle. Jo-Jo climbed with true panache, legs wrapped around the pillar, tools scratched into the window pane of ice, body fighting to keep from barndooring in the wind. Whipper and Troy were across the valley working on their own survival. The trees thrashed–some snapped, and snow grains bounded across the gravel flats to compact into dirty drifts of boilerplate, or disappear in sublimation. High overhead the Chinook's claws had opened the sky and it bled long incisions of stretched grey cloud.

Wild, outrageous, high-end "Jo-Jo Factor" … Canadian Rockies ice climbing; it's never the same twice, always an adventure, Harding's words twinkle around in my skull: "I guess that I climb because I'm mad… but it's a fine kind of madness". Grab your ice tools, Jo-Jo's guidebook, and get on out there and have some fun!

Barry Blanchard, Canmore, 1994

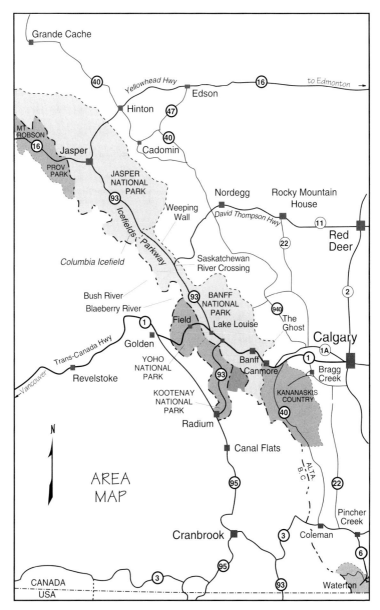

AREA MAP

This book covers the greatest geographic area of just about any climbing guide in the world. This results in the monumental task of trying to make sense of over 30,000 square kilometres –not a problem when talking to locals or those intimate with the range, but desperate for those new to the area.

Climbers from France once told me about their first visit to the Rockies. They were so overwhelmed by the vastness of the range that it was all they could do just to find the most obvious routes. After several weeks of battling warm Chinook conditions and 'hidden' climbs, they cut their trip short and returned to France, depressed. Indeed, as you drive west from Calgary on a clear day, an endless sea of peaks stretches on the horizon.

Providing you can follow a road map and understand the basics of a topographic map, this book will give you the necessary landmarks and information to find your desired routes.

As with any project of this size, inaccuracies are inevitable. Years of experience, effort and rewriting were required to get all the details correct. Every attempt has been made to give information that represents the usual or typical conditions you will find on the ice climbs and approaches. Remote and obscure routes are conjecture and require that a liberal translation of the description be applied. Corrections and updates are gladly welcomed and should be sent to the author in care of Rocky Mountain Books, see page 34.

Do not immediately flip to the page of the famous route(s) that you want to tick off. Like a good novel, this guide is meant to be read in its entirety so you can understand really what the route descriptions are telling you.

The introduction to each area includes a brief description of the flavour of the climbing, how to get there and what to or not to expect. Following the introduction is a description of roads and access into the area, any useful facilities and the most convenient way to reach the closest emergency personnel. Emergency phone numbers are listed on page 272.

The route descriptions run in a south to north fashion. Other areas that branch off the main spine of the Rockies are included as they are encountered. The key to understanding the layout and geography of the range is to determine where the major highways are. Then, everything else falls into place.

Maps

A number of sketch maps based on 1:50000 and 1:200000 topographic maps are used. Dots indicating the location of the climb(s) are placed onto the map. Combined with the detailed verbal description you should be able to gain a better understanding of the Rocky Mountain geography and hopefully spend a minimal amount of time looking for your chosen route(s).

A list of the relevant topographic map sheet(s) to the area is included with each section. The six digit grid references given in the route descriptions are all taken from the 1:50 000 National Topographical Series. These can be obtained from private sources such as climbing shops, book stores or the ACC Clubhouse in Canmore, or by writing:

Canada Map Office
615 Booth Street
Ottawa, Ontario
Canada K1A 0E9

The grid reference for a climb is the approximate location *of the base of the route*. Occasionally the grid reference of a prominent landmark or other object is also included. On the right-hand border of each National Topographic Map you will find instructions on how to use the Universal Transverse Mercator Grid System to locate the specific position on the map. It is wise to buy and learn how to use a compass.

Distances and Signs

Every attempt was made to give accurate road distances as measured by an automobile odometer. The distances are measured from a prominent intersection or other landmark. Various road and trail signs make good indicators but can be knocked down or changed.

References

There is a growing amount of literature published about winter climbing in the Rockies. Whenever it is appropriate, references are included. These references give you additional or background information about a particular route or the general area. They also make for good reading (or fire starter) during those extended Arctic fronts.

Travel Information

The plain and simple fact is that, to have a good ice climbing trip in the Rockies, you need a vehicle. Public transportation is poor to nonexistent. The routes are spread out over such a huge area that it takes a *full day* just to drive from end to end.

Arriving By Air

Calgary and Edmonton both have large international airports. You can fly directly to either city from within North America, and from Europe or Asia.

Bus

Regularly scheduled Greyhound buses service the Trans-Canada Highway (#1) areas stopping at Golden, Lake Louise, Banff, Canmore and Calgary. Scheduled buses also travel Highway 16 between Edmonton and Jasper. Phone Greyhound Bus Lines, or Brewster Transport (762-6767) in Banff for further information.

Car Rentals

The usual car rental companies are at the airports but there are better deals to be had, so check the Yellow Pages on arrival and shop around. You may want to rent a four-wheel drive in case you want to go to an area like the Ghost River, but don't tell the rental agent that! Car rentals from the major international chains (Hertz, Avis, Tilden, etc.) are also available in Banff, Jasper, Golden, and Invermere.

Highways described in this book are all in excellent condition and are usually well-maintained in winter. Recorded winter weather driving conditions are available out of Banff, Jasper and BC Highways. If climbing near a main highway, try to find a parking place off the road as high speed snow-ploughs regularly maintain most highways. If a pull-out is not available, park in a straightaway so oncoming snow-ploughs will have ample time to see your vehicle.

Car

From the US, a number of routes are available. When coming from east of the Continental Divide, the best route is via US Interstate 15 north of Great Falls, Montana. The Sweetgrass/Coutts border crossing, open 24 hours, is about three hours drive from Calgary. The Carway/Peigan border crossing on US Highway 89 near Glacier/Waterton Park is open in winter for limited hours. Highway 89 is very scenic but the driving can be slow.

Several highways lead north out of western Montana and Idaho. US Highway 93 comes from Kalispell, Montana. Access from the Spokane, Washington or Couer d'Alene, Idaho area is via US Highway 95. Both Highways 93 and 95 lead to the Columbia Valley and Radium, BC. With good travelling conditions, Radium is five hours from Spokane. If driving from the west coast, get on the Trans-Canada Highway (#1) near Vancouver, BC and take that all the way to Banff; nine to ten hours.

Where to Stay

Calgary and Edmonton are large metropolitan cities with a countless variety of hotels, hostels, restaurants, galleries, bars, high and low life. The major Alberta mountain towns mentioned in this guide are Pincher Creek, Sundre, Nordegg, Canmore, Banff, Lake Louise, Jasper and Grand Cache; in BC, Field, Golden, Radium and Invermere.

Most climbers base out of the towns of Canmore, Banff, Lake Louise or one of the hostels along the Icefields Parkway. These communities all have the facilities of larger towns with many hotels, bed and breakfasts, restaurants and pubs offering a number of dynamic alternative activities ranging from nightlife, hot pools, movies, galleries, festivals, downhill and cross-country skiing to excellent coffee shops. It's highly recommend you check out the cultural and artistic happenings at The Banff Centre and the Whyte Museum of the Canadian Rockies in Banff.

Pincher Creek, Golden and Invermere are also large full service towns. Many other communities mentioned in the guide can accommodate you as you stop over while climbing or travelling through the nearby areas. Relevant specifics are given in the Facilities section in the introduction to each climbing area. Further tourist information can be obtained by calling the local Chamber of Commerce, see p. 265, or by writing:

Alberta Tourism
3rd Floor Commerce Place
10155 - 102 St.
Edmonton, Alberta
Canada T5J 4L6
Phone 1-800-661-8888

Tourism BC
Parliament Buildings
Victoria, BC
Canada V8V 1X4
Phone 1-800-663-6000

Most climbers are on a limited budget and look for more modest accommodation than the high priced hotels /motels found in most tourist towns. Both the Alpine Club of Canada and the hostel associations offer affordable accommodation that is popular with climbers.

Alpine Club of Canada

The *ACC Clubhouse,* just outside Canmore, is the most popular facility for climbers, offering dormitory style beds for about 60 people, a library, complete kitchen facilities, sauna and a bar. Follow the 1A Highway east from Canmore to Indian Flats Road, 1.2 kilometres east of the Trans-Canada Highway overpass. Turn north here and follow the signs to the clubhouse. Alpine Club members receive a discount (international memberships recognized). 1994 prices are $11 / night for members; $19 / night for nonmembers. Memberships are available at the office. Bookings can be made through the main ACC office by writing or calling: Box 2040, Canmore, Alberta, Canada T0L 0M0, Phone 403-678-3200.

Another attractive facility is the *Canadian Alpine Centre and International Hostel at Lake Louise* owned and operated in conjunction between the ACC and the Southern Alberta Hostel Association. This modern facility has over 100 beds, a restaurant, library, lounge and self-serve kitchen. Phone 403-522-2200 for reservations. The ACC also owns and maintains several *backcountry huts* that make ideal base camps when climbing in certain areas. They are completely equipped with foamies, cooking utensils, stoves and lanterns. Normally no custodian is present and the huts are locked with a combination lock. Booking at the main ACC office is a simple matter of exchanging a Visa or Mastercard number for the combination lock number. Huts in areas described in this book are:

Elizabeth Parker Hut (Lake O'Hara)
Stanley Mitchell Hut (Yoho Valley)
Sydney Vallance Hut (Fryatt Creek)

Hostels

The *Southern Alberta Hostel Association (SAHA)* and the *Alberta Hostel Association (AHA)* operate a number of moderately-priced hostels which are extensively used by ice climbers. Many are conveniently located in the heart of popular ice climbing areas. Most have saunas that are the perfect remedy for cold, aching bodies after a long climb. 1994 prices are $9/night for hostel association members; $14/night nonmembers. One- and two-year memberships are available at the hostels. For information and/or reservations write or phone:

- **SAHA**
  #203, 1414 Kensington Road NW
  Calgary, Alberta, Canada T2N 3P9
  Phone 403-283-5551
- The Banff Hostel (154 beds)
  Phone 403-762-4122
- Castle Junction (Trans-Canada (#1) and Radium Highway (#93) junction).
- Mosquito Creek on the Icefields Parkway near Bow Lake.
- Rampart Creek on the Icefields Parkway near Mt. Wilson/ Weeping Wall.
- Hilda Creek on the Icefields Parkway near the Columbia Icefields.
- **AHA** (hostels near Jasper /Nordegg)
  10926 - 88 Avenue
  Edmonton, Alberta T6G 0Z1
  Phone 403-433-5513 or 403-433-3139.
- Shunda Creek west of Nordegg on David Thompson Highway (#11). Phone 403-721-2140.
- Edith Cavell, ski access only near Mt. Edith Cavell off Highway 93A.
- Whistlers, 7 km from Jasper off the Icefield Parkway.
- Maligne Canyon, 11 km from Jasper off Highway 16.

Obtaining Supplies

Food, gear and other life maintenance supplies required while in the mountains can be obtained at all the main communities which have banks, groceries, bakeries, laundromats, post offices and assorted supplies. Be warned however, that some stores (Jasper and Lake Louise in particular) have very inflated prices. These towns also have a wide range of amenities geared towards the tourist industry such as book shops which sell maps and guidebooks. So support the local economy and make sure you buy a copy of this book for all your friends and family back home.

Climbing gear can be purchased in Calgary at the Mountain Equipment Co-op (269-2420), in Banff at Monods (762-4571) and in Jasper at Gravity Gear (852-3155). The other communities have outdoor/camping stores but mostly for hunting, fishing and snowmobiling. So if you need some extra climbing gear, "don't expect to find much in these parts partner".

Climbing guides and/or instruction can be obtained from The Association of Canadian Mountain Guides, Box 1537, Banff, Alberta, Canada T0L 0C0, or by looking under "Mountain and Ice Climbing Tours" in the local telephone book Yellow Pages.

Regulations

Most routes in this book are located in areas where backcountry use is controlled to some degree. Many climbs are within the boundaries of one of five national parks in the Rockies; Waterton, Banff, Jasper, Kootenay and Yoho, or are located within either a British Columbia Provincial Park (Elk Lakes and Mt. Robson) or Alberta's Kananaskis Country. Each area has similar backcountry regulations which are summarized here. Areas outside of these parks have few controlling regulations, but any peculiar to such areas are mentioned in their introduction.

Backcountry Use Permits

Backcountry use permits are required in the five national parks when spending *at least one night* in the backcountry and can be obtained at park information centres for $5 per night. At present, permits are not required for day trips.

Registration

A voluntary registration system is provided by the Park Service for potentially hazardous activities within the national parks. For years climbers have shunned the use of such a system. However, you are strongly advised to do so especially if travelling in remote or alpine areas. It is necessary to register in person during regular office hours at either park information centres or warden offices. Registering out is a contractual agreement requiring a signature. All overdue registrations are checked out. When registering:

• you must provide a reasonable estimate of your trip time to avoid unnecessary use of costly rescue helicopter flight.

• you **must** notify the Park Service upon completion of your trip by either dropping off the registration slip or by telephone. If you are late, phone at your *earliest* convenience. Failure to notify the Park Service of your return or cancellation of a trip is grounds for prosecution.

Rescue personnel exercise some discretion before commencing a search. Factors such as weather conditions, length of time overdue, assessment of the individuals' ability, number in the party etc. are considered. Therefore, you must be prepared to spend *at least one night out* before expecting help. Weather conditions and terrain may make outside help very difficult at best. It is recommended you travel with a strong idea of self-reliance and the understanding that SuperWarden may not arrive to whisk you off to safety if and when things go bad.

Vehicle Permits

All vehicles stopping in national parks must have a Park Motor Vehicle Permit which can be obtained at park information centres, or at the east entrance to Banff Park (Canmore), the west entrance to Kootenay Park (Radium), east and west gates of Jasper Park (Highway 16, at the north end of the Icefields Parkway (Jasper) and at the entrance to Waterton Park. One and four day or annual permits are available. If staying longer than a few days, the $50 (1995 price) annual permit is your best bet. Annual permits, expiring March 31 are the same price regardless of purchase date.

CLIMBING IN THE ROCKIES

Winter climbing in the Canadian Rockies can be an intensely rewarding experience. Combine the immense beauty and wildness with the quantity and quality of the climbing, and you have a place few can match. Climbing in the Rockies can also be very sobering—the mountains are big, the hazards and challenges are many. Patience is the greatest skill you can bring to (or learn from) the range. Weather and conditions don't care who you are or how far you have travelled to get here and both can stay bad for weeks at a time. This is not meant to scare you but to educate you and make you think. There are so many routes here—with prudence and appropriate route selection, you can safely climb on a different route just about every day the entire winter.

Choosing Routes

For routes of any and all difficulties, an understanding of the full grade is crucial. Despite the changing nature of ice, great attempts were made to create a consistent grading system. Don't get caught up in the numbers game—remember that each route has been given a particular grade for a reason. Either know or quickly learn your own abilities and level of acceptable risk and commitment. And don't forget that for every route regardless of the grade, the crux will be finding and placing adequate protection. Safe leading of ice climbs is for experts only.

Season

Much to the chagrin of local rock climbers, the ice climbing season often lasts seven months! Depending on the year, some routes are doable in early October and may continue to be climbable into late April. *Slipstream* has been climbed in July and the low altitude *Professor Falls* in May. Realistically, the season is in full swing by early November and lasts until the first week of April with many south-facing routes falling apart in late March. One of the best times for Rockies' ice is in November to mid-December, particularly in the front range areas like Kananaskis, The Ghost, The David Thompson and parts of The Bow Valley. Early season also finds a higher concentration of first ascents as people get out to climb those newly-formed smears before getting scooped. Some south-facing or low elevation routes may not come into shape until mid-season or after a cold snap.

March is the most friendly month. Longer days mean warmer temperatures, softer ice, later starts for the day, and donkey trails leading to the popular routes, but there really is no perfect time to come to the Rockies. Arctic fronts and big snowfalls are the two biggest factors that dampen an ice climbing trip and can occur at any time.

Unseasonably warm temperatures can occur in any month. If you have particular routes in mind, especially difficult and more alpine ones, plan your trip for at least a month. Even then there is no guarantee that conditions will come into shape. Call the sport shops for conditions. Melt-freeze conditions are not common in the Rockies and most routes will either form or not form at the beginning of the season. If they don't form you are usually out of luck for the remainder of the season, but remember, even in a below average year there are more than enough routes to go around.

Avalanches

Avalanches are **THE** single biggest hazard to ice climbers throughout the Rockies. The majority of the climbs in this book are at least partially threatened by avalanches. However, with experience, good judgement and patience you can greatly reduce the risk of being involved in an avalanche and still get in lots of climbing.

This section is intended as an introduction to avalanche hazard awareness as it applies to ice climbing in the Canadian Rockies. IT IS NOT, however, a substitute for experience. I recommend that all climbers participate in a recognized avalanche course and develop snow stability evaluation skill. Re-read *Avalanche Safety for Skiers and Climbers* by Tony Daffern at the start of each season and make full use of information available through public avalanche forecasts. It is important to talk to local climbers and skiers to obtain information on snow conditions.

Winter in the Canadian Rockies is generally characterized by shallow snowpacks and extended periods of dry, cold weather. These factors contribute to the formation of significant weak layers in the snowpack such as depth hoar, facets, and surface hoar that can persist throughout the winter. Left to themselves, these weak layers simply make for poor travelling conditions. When 'loaded' through additional snowfall, wind or the weight of a climber, avalanches up to the entire depth of the snowpack are possible. Be aware of large settlements of the snowpack as characterized by a 'whumpfing' sound. If this is happening on the flats during an approach you should be wary of conditions higher up. Furthermore, cracks may run across terrain and trigger slopes around you. This is especially of concern in approach gullies.

Remember that avalanche forecasting in the Rockies is much trickier than in more maritime regions. Climbers travelling here from other areas may have to readjust their thinking. For example, the old adage of letting snow settle for 48 hours after a storm is usually rushing things in the Rockies.

Snow Stability Evaluation

- **Avalanche activity**. The most significant sign of snow instability is recent natural avalanche activity. Note the aspect and elevation; similar slopes will have similar conditions, but be aware that instability may be widespread.

- **Precipitation.** Any amount of new snow is significant. With intense snowfall rates, wet snow, or in combination with wind, as little as 5-10 cm can trigger an avalanche cycle. Rain, which can be expected any time throughout the season, can rapidly decrease snow stability.

- **Temperatures.** Direct solar radiation (i.e. sunshine) causing a rapid temperature increase is a **significant** avalanche trigger. This is especially true as the season progresses with longer days and higher daytime temperatures. High temperatures have been the main ingredient in ice climbing avalanche accidents in the Rockies. Climbers everywhere like to climb on warm days in the sun; a potentially deadly combination on ice climbs.

- **Wind.** Light winds (20 km/hr) can move large volumes of snow into soft or hard wind slabs on lee slopes. This snow movement can create both very localized and widespread condi-

tions. Seemingly calm days in the valley may have dangerous winds aloft, creating cornices and loading slopes above your intended route. Look for plumes blowing off the ridge tops and check the weather synopsis for wind speeds aloft.

- **Terrain.** Slab avalanches generally start on slopes between 25 and 50 degrees. On steeper slopes, snow usually falls off as spindrift which can gather into a serious mass, enough to knock you off or even bury you. Be concerned not only with the terrain you are on but also the area above the approach and the climb. Learn to recognize starting zones and avalanche paths. Often, huge slopes are hidden far above the intended route and avalanches can rocket down even when the area around the climb appears safe.

- **Snowpack information.** In the Rockies, snow conditions today may depend upon what happened months ago. A report of general conditions is available from National and Provincial Parks and The Canadian Avalanche Centre (see page 272). Use these sources as a basis for your evaluations, but be prepared for rapidly changing conditions and areas that defy the forecast. Use your common sense and be prepared to turn around. Take pride in your decisions to come back and climb another day.

The nature of ice climbing creates some **special problems**:

- Many ice routes follow gully systems for part or all of their length. Gullies can act as lee slopes, as they are often sheltered from the wind and slabs may develop on either side. Secondly, gullies generally have large bowls or collection zones above. Avalanches starting anywhere in these areas will likely follow the natural drainage down the gully, leaving climbers directly exposed. Finally, gullies are serious terrain traps. A small slide that may be insignificant on a large slope can easily bury someone when the debris is confined to the gully and you have nowhere to hide. Likewise, a small slide may be enough to 'catch' you and carry you over a cliff.

• Ledges and low angle sections of a climb can collect enough snow to cause significant avalanches on otherwise safe routes. You should consider belaying across or climbing around these areas.

• A few 'modern' routes are formed by glacier runoff and are in the fall-line of seracs. These hazards defy all forecasting. When a serac goes, despite what some people believe, it has nothing to do with temperatures or the time of day. If you choose a route under a serac, move fast–don't be surprised if something awful happens.

• As more waterfall routes are climbed in alpine areas above treeline, cornices become a bigger issue. Be wary of any cornice anywhere over the climb. Even if a small chunk comes off, it can trigger loaded slopes below and create a large avalanche (for example, this is the single biggest danger on the popular route *Slipstream*). Cornices can fail at any time; there is no evidence supporting when a cornice will go. Also, a route does not have to be on a high mountain face for cornices to develop. Any relatively flat area around the top of the route that is exposed to prevailing or local winds will likely build a cornice. Keep an eye open.

In the event of an avalanche accident, the victims best hope for survival lies with themselves and the other members of their party. If outside help must be called in, it is usually too late. Know the basics of avalanche rescue. Although not a common practice amongst climbers, it is highly recommended to carry a shovel, transceiver and an avalanche probe and to learn how to use them. The standard frequency of avalanche transceivers in Canada is 457 kHz. Old 2275 kHz units should be replaced.

Reference Books and Courses

Avalanche Safety for Skiers and Climbers, Tony Daffern, 2 ed., Rocky Mountain Books, Calgary, 1992.

Available in most outdoor/book shops. An in-depth, easy-to-read text with lots of information based on experience in the Canadian Rockies.

Information on backcountry avalanche courses is available from:

The Canadian Avalanche Association Training School, Box 2759, Revelstoke, BC, V0E 2S0, Phone (604) 837-4624.

The American Association of Avalanche Professionals, P.O. Box 34004. Truckee, CA 96160, Phone (916) 587-3653, Fax (916) 587-4313.

Other Hazards

Aside from avalanche there are a number of other hazards, large and small that when overcome, are part of what makes ice climbing such a rewarding if not sometimes miserable sport. They include, but are not limited to the following:

Cold

The Rockies are legendary for extended Arctic fronts. Temperatures can plunge within a few hours to minus 30°C and stay there for weeks. Down coats are standard equipment most of the season as are additional pile layers and extra mitts in case you drop one or they get soaked. Carry a Balaclava in your pocket to put on at the belay. Be familiar with cold injuries and guard against the onset of frostbite and hypothermia. Eat and drink well the night before and during the climb and take a thermos with something hot to take the big chill off at belays.

Sun

The sun can turn a low avalanche hazard into extreme in just a few hours (see avalanche section). Particularly later in the season, the sun can warm a climb drastically to increase the amount of running water and melt screw placements. Icicles may fall and even whole climbs can collapse.

Darkness

Headlamps are standard gear for every route. The few times I haven't taken one, as luck would have it, I've needed it. You can't start a climb too early, but so often, too late.

Running Water

Many climbs have copious amounts of surface water. Surface water has its advantages in that it usually makes the ice fairly soft with good tool placements. Too much water is very uncomfortable and can make you feel like you're getting a body enema. Some routes can be wet in temperatures of minus 30°C or below and this is especially dangerous as a soaked climber stands a high chance of hypothermia and gear can get dangerously frozen. It is advisable to avoid soaking climbs in cold temperatures.

No matter what the glove manufacturers say, your hands will get wet. I sometimes put a plastic bag like a bread sack between my mitt liners and shell or better yet, put on a dry pair of mitts part way through a climb, it does wonders for your comfort level.

Another factor is running water underneath the climb. It is common on steep pillars, to have a hollow straw with water gushing through it. This can form spooky transparent plates through which the water is visible. Be careful of these, for if they collapse you will be in big trouble. Try to spread your body weight out by stemming across these sections and climb gently.

When rappelling, be certain to pull the ropes immediately after the last person is down. Ropes can freeze surprisingly fast particularly when the ice and the ropes are wet, even on warm days.

Fixed Rock Anchors

The repeated freeze/thaw cycles of the Rockies and the dubious nature of local limestone can and will loosen fixed pitons and corrode bolts and hangers. Be suspect of any fixed anchor you come across and check pitons to insure they are still well driven and the rock around them is not loose. Do not pound on bolts for this weakens them; rather, visually inspect the placement and the hanger. Rappel slings should be beefed up or better yet replaced if they are at all faded, frayed or just look old and weak.

Cut off the old slings and take them with you. One 50 m pull of a rope through a rappel sling weakens that sling by up to 25%. Never rappel/belay off a single anchor piece. This also goes for single rappel rings which are common. Make sure the slings to each piece are equalized in the direction of pull. Each sling should be independently connected to each piece so that if one section of sling or anchor should fail, the integrity of the entire anchor is not compromised. A frightfully common sight is the 'death triangle' where one sling is tied between two pieces and the rope fed through this one sling—an all-or-none proposition. Just because there is a fixed anchor doesn't mean it is solid or that the person(s) putting it in knew what they were doing.

Falling Ice and Wearing Helmets

It was once said that you don't need to ice climb with helmets because if you have good style, you won't expose yourself to icefall from your partner. Even though it is a good practice to find sheltered belays in caves or under overhangs etc., **all climbers should use helmets** to protect from icefall generated by your partner leading above you, from your own ice tools and from naturally occurring icefall. With improved technique and experience, you will knock off less ice than the neophyte, but even the best climbers will clean a reasonable amount especially on difficult or early season ascents.

When placing your tools beware of dinner plates and icicles falling onto your face. If your placement looks like it will knock off a sizeable chunk, duck your head and let the helmet take the brunt of it. When you arrive at the base of the climb or cliff; put your helmet on right away; ice and rock can fall before you start the climb. The use of helmets is not a style issue (contrary to recent trends); it is an issue of necessity. Some routes have large icicles hanging off the sides or above your intended line so be wary of these potential skewers, especially if it gets the sun. I once saw a major portion of *Transparent Fool* fall off shortly after we ran away. It still gives me the willies.

Rockfall

A hazard not usually considered while ice climbing is rockfall. The Rockies are loaded with piles of loose junky rock that need no more than a whisper to set them off. Sun, melting snow and ice and wind can start a trundle, and it occurs surprisingly often. A fatality on *Cascade* in 1993 was due to a single, albeit large, rock hitting a climber standing near the base of the route.

Remoteness

Remoteness is a serious factor in the Rockies. One hour approaches are considered normal and two to three hours are not uncommon. Even the easiest routes take on major proportions in case of an accident. What are you prepared for and capable of in case of complications or even a rescue? Getting lost is a real possibility for darkness, heavy snowfall and/or thick bush can disorient you in no time at all. Carry a compass.

Other Climbers

Other climbers are potentially the biggest danger on an ice climb. On a crowded climb the standard joke is, "Lets leave before we have to rescue someone". Other climbers will knock off ice, invariably be slower than you (remember they are saying the same thing about you) and generally slow things down for the day. If there is lots of time and room for several parties and you are not too concerned with looking at the watch, it can be an enjoyable and social time; otherwise, there are lots of other routes to do. *Cascade Waterfall*, *The Weeping Wall*, *Louise Falls* and *Professor Falls* are notorious for big crowds so get there early and don't let others get on your case to hurry up or get out of the way as this may compromise **your** safety. Tell them to relax, try another climb or to get out of bed earlier. Stand your ground; absolutely **no one** has the right to put you in danger. If rappelling, do so safely in consideration of others who may be below you.

Conduit trash from the Upper Weeping Wall.

Karl Nagy

Abalakov Sandwich

This is not a new energy bar for ice climbing, but rather an anchor system that, in the last four years, has revolutionized the way people descend and back-off ice climbs. The traditional method in the Rockies started with lengths of ski poles placed in the ice. This evolved into the use of sawn-off sections of electrical aluminum conduit. Despite the inherent weakness and finicky nature of conduit, it became the standard ice rappel system for over 15 years. Fortunately, the use of conduit is now obsolete with the advent of the Abalakov Sandwich.

Vitaly Abalakov was the Soviet Union's most distinguished mountaineer. After an early career of hard ascents in the '30s he had to give up climbing for nine years to recover from the loss of one-third of his left foot and parts of most of his fingers to frostbite during the third ascent of Khan Tengri in 1936. Intense, focused exercise allowed him to resume mountaineering after the second world war, and he wracked up major achievements in the Caucasus, Tien Shan and Pamirs over the next fifteen years. He worked professionally monitoring athletic performance and developing equipment for mountaineering and other sports. His eccentric rotating protection devices led directly to the Lowe Tri-cams and to Friends, while on ice he developed a simple, strong method of setting a rappel anchor: The Abalakov Sandwich, also called the V-thread or ice hourglass.

The Abalakov Sandwich can be constructed on just about any ice surface, whether horizontal or vertical. Create a small starter hole and turn the first screw in roughly at 60° off the perpendicular. The closer to perpendicular, the more ice you will displace and generally the stronger the anchor, however, don't make the angle too great, as this will create problems in intersecting the second hole. The game is to make the holes as widely and deeply spaced as possible. Many folks partially extract the first screw as an alignment sight for the second screw. Start the second hole 15-20 cm (6-8 inches) angled back across the first at about the same angle. Once done, the resulting V-shaped hole is threaded with a 40-100 cm length of rappel sling by using a length of bailing wire or coat hanger to snare the end. This is then tied into a sling with a fisherman's knot. With 7 mm cord, these anchors have been field tested to over 909 kg (2000 pounds) force making it an strong, multi-direc-

tional and easy to make anchor that can be placed almost anywhere.

Reference

"Ice Anchor Review", Joseph Josephson, *The Canadian Alpine Journal*, Vol. 76, 1993, pp. 66-67.

"The Abalakov V-Thread", Don Serl and Bruce Kay, *The Climber's Guide to West Coast Ice*, 1993. pp. 24-5.

"Getting Down on a Shoestring", Murray Toft and Joseph Josephson, *Climbing Magazine,* No.124, Feb/March 1991, pp. 100-103.

"The Ice Hourglass. A Safe and Environmentally Friendly Anchor for Ice Climbing", Murray Toft and Joseph Josephson, *Explore Magazine*, No. 49, Winter 1990, pg. 41.

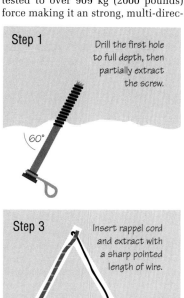

Step 1 — Drill the first hole to full depth, then partially extract the screw.

60°

Step 3 — Insert rappel cord and extract with a sharp pointed length of wire.

30-40cm required.

Step 2 — Drill a second hole to intersect with the first.

←15-20cm→

Leave in position for an alignment sight.

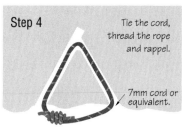

Step 4 — Tie the cord, thread the rope and rappel.

7mm cord or equivalent.

Graphic courtesy of Kevin McLane, Merlin Productions Inc.

ENVIRONMENT & STYLE

The Rockies are historically a place of ambivalence. Climbers have been able to perform and behave just about however they like, and have taken pride in the fact that there are few 'ethical' debates that plague many other areas. In the past this has created few problems due to the relatively low numbers of climbers. But increasing pressure from many fronts including number of climbers, increasing land development, wildlife impact, national and provincial park regulations is creating a situation that requires some foresight and discussion.

Environment

A heavy mantle of snow seems to protect the land from the travelling ice climber. But as the number of climbers escalates every year, some areas are seeing the effects of increased use.

Trees

An increasing common sight is small uprooted trees at the bottom of a climb. Crampons have a large impact on the shallow soil and fragile vegetation around trees so be sensitive to scampering around on tree roots or in places where there is little snow; you could be killing your anchor.

Nature's Call

I doubt many of us would defecate in a stream during the summer months. When you respond to a call of nature in the middle of an ice climb or at the base, think about what you are doing. Even though everything is frozen, it still means that you are dumping into a flowing stream. On popular climbs this can add up to quite a cesspool. Try to use out of the way places in the surrounding forest. If the next pitch is particularly scary and you absolutely must go, look for a ledge to traverse out on and get away from the main avenue of travel. The rest of us really don't want to belay on a ledge next to a big pile. Remember to carry a lighter and burn your toilet paper.

The ground around popular climbs and practice areas can look like gardens littered with countless 'snow flowers'. When urinating, don't be lazy. Walk a little farther from the base and try using a tree well or some place where you are not going to leave a trail of yellow stain. It is really offensive.

"Butts"

More than once I have come to a ledge only to find numerous cigarette butts. I even once found a filter purposely stuffed into a small air pocket halfway up a pitch. This is another offensive act that should not be tolerated. If you just cannot be bothered to put those butts away into a pocket, be a real man or woman; use filterless.

Access

Most of the climbs in the Canadian Rockies are within national or provincial parks or in public (Crown) lands that have already been used for mining, water diversion or logging. As a result, the Rockies have few of the access problems that are continually escalating in the US.

Private Land

Parts of the Columbia Valley and the Front Range areas on the eastern slope are privately owned or have approaches through private land. Most areas are remote and have historically had open access, so at the present time, only one area warrants mention, the Bow Valley. The land east of Banff National Park is under increasing residential and industrial development. Presently there are few climbs in the area so few problems are likely. Approaches to many of the climbs may change over the next few years. If in doubt inquire with local climbing shops or the Town of Canmore Administration Office. Only one incident is required between climbers and land owners to create problems for everyone else.

Road Closures

Perhaps the biggest issue affecting ice climbers, mountaineers and skiers in the Rockies is the closure of highways. Some closures are important to protect wildlife corridors but most are due to park service budget cuts. Waterton National Park has had several road closures over the years and at least one of those roads will not be reopened in the foreseeable future. The biggest tragedy would be the closure of the Icefields Parkway between Lake Louise and Jasper. Every year there is discussion about it remaining closed for the winter. Imagine what it would be like if suddenly the approaches became two to three days in length instead of 10-60 minutes. A large number and a diverse range of people use this highway during winter—let's hope it stays open. If you are concerned, and you should be, write a letter to the Chief Banff National Park Administrator. See page 265.

Finally, be smart, be safe and be self-sufficient. Believe it or not, there are people who would like to see climbing regulated if not banned; let's not give them fuel for their fires through increasing rescue expenses.

Style

Now that you are environmentally and politically correct in your thinking about ice climbing, how about your style?

Free versus Aid

The local ethos on ice climbing has evolved strongly toward free ascents. A free ascent is defined if protection is placed without hanging onto equipment with climbers holding themselves by muscle power, using a free hand to place protection. You can only hang on a belay after having placed the first anchor in this manner. Any other form of progression such as resting on an ice tool or a screw is considered to be artificial aid.

Standards in the Rockies have risen to a point where using artificial aid or 'hanging' is not considered an option, but then neither is falling. You must know or quickly learn your limits and what you are capable of. If you must hang to divert disaster, that is considered better style (and a lot smarter) than falling. Forget the ethics police and style; falling on ice climbs is a serious business and avoid it with all the powers of your being.

Aid climbing on rock to reach ice is acceptable style and many new routes are being done in this way, providing they follow a natural line. Remember that some climbs just aren't meant to be done—forcing an unnatural line for the sake of a new route is frowned upon.

Control

The final issue regarding style is one of control. One of the most frequent ways in which ideas of style are evaded is by completing a climb at the expense of safety. How safely an ascent is made is a subjective matter. Unlike the use of direct aid, for example, this sort of evasion is easily concealed. Tools popping out of the ice, dropping gear, needlessly bombarding your belayer with ice, poorly placing protection or generally shaking your way up a climb are all regarded as very poor style. Regarding a safe and in-control climb as a more stylish ascent is a much more honest approach than glorifying the addition of another tick to the 'Hit List'. Obviously, this approach to style has a strong value of promoting safety.

GRADING ROUTES

The grade of a route is the combination of length, commitment required, technical difficulty and seriousness. Most people focus solely on Technical Grade; however, ice climbing in the Rockies involves many variables, many of which are unique to the area. Few areas can match the combined factors of remoteness, sustained cold, poor snowpack, size and quantity of ice.

This book introduces Technical Grade or Degree 7+ (*Sea of Vapors*). Degree 7+ is strictly a comparison to other routes in the range, particularly *The Reality Bath*, *Riptide*, and *Gimme Shelter*. *Sea of Vapors* has a Commitment Grade of V, whereas the other routes have one of VI (*The Reality Bath* is given a VII). Although, *Sea of Vapors* has one very thin, technical pitch, the rest of the route is considerably easier (WI 6+). The other routes, however, are very sustained with multiple pitches at their stated Technical Grade and thus have a higher commitment. They should probably be considered harder overall.

Rather than downgrade routes, it is better to continue the scale upward (see below under Technical Grade). But this is a moot argument, for at the extreme levels of difficulty and seriousness it doesn't really matter; they are all hard. There is so much more to 'the grade' of a route than just its Technical Grade. Don't get caught up in the numbers game; it is one reason people die.

All grades in this book are determined by comparison between routes in the Rockies. Little or no thought is given to routes outside the range.

Commitment Grade
(Roman Numerals I to VII)

Also called Engagement Grade, the key factors here are the length and difficulty of approach and descent, length of the climb itself, the sustained nature of the climbing, and the objective hazard. Modern routes are progressively thinner and on more fragile features. In some climbing areas, these qualities are included in the overall Commitment Grade. However, due to the added factor of severe remoteness of many Rockies routes, this notion is hard to include in a Rockies Commitment Grade. Thus, this book adds a Seriousness Grade to be discussed later.

Please note that the Commitment Grades stated in this guide in no way compare to those given to rock routes or alpine mountain routes as found in *Selected Alpine Climbs in the Canadian Rockies* by Sean Dougherty. Commitment Grades are specific for frozen waterfalls and alpine routes that are considered as waterfall ice routes.

I. A very short and easy climb within minutes of the car. No avalanche hazard and easy descent by fixed anchors or walking off. Very little commitment.

II. A route of one or two pitches within easy reach of a vehicle or emergency facilities, little or no objective hazard. A quick descent by rappel or walk off.

III. A multi-pitch route at low elevation or a one-pitch route with an involved approach (one hour or more and/or no trail) on foot or ski demanding good winter travel skills. The route may take from several hours to most of a day to complete. The approach and/or the climb are subject to occasional winter hazards including avalanche. Descent usually by rappelling and may require you to make your own anchors.

IV. A multi-pitch route at higher elevations or remote regions, more subject to weather patterns and objective hazards, primarily avalanche. May require several hours of approach on foot or ski requiring a greater knowledge of mountain travel and hazards. Descents may be on hazardous terrain and/or require construction of your own anchors.

V. A long climb that requires a competent party and all day to complete. Usually on a high mountain face or gully ending above treeline. Subject to sustained climbing and/or avalanche hazards with a long involved approach on foot or ski. A high level of climbing experience and winter travel skills are needed to climb safely. Descent involves multiple rappels from your own anchors.

VI. A long waterfall with all the characteristics of a large alpine route. The climbing will be very sustained for its given Technical Grade. Only the best climbers will complete it in a day. Often requires a ski and/or glacier approach with a difficult and tiring descent. Objective hazards will be high, which may include avalanche, falling seracs, high altitude, whiteout, crevasses and/or remoteness. An extraordinary degree of fitness and experience is required.

VII. A route that has every characteristic of a Grade VI but is considerably longer and harder, both physically and emotionally. The climbing will be technically very difficult for many pitches and may take days to approach and climb. Objective hazards will be very high such as large avalanche bowls and/or active seracs. A 50-50 chance of getting the chop.

Technical Grade (Degree 1 to 8)

This part accounts for the pure nature of the climbing on the single most sustained technical feature of a route. The predominate features accounting for this Technical Grade are length of a pitch, its overall steepness and the usual characteristics of the ice which may include blue plastic ice, chandelier mushrooms, thin plate, and/or overhanging bulges. In this guide, it is designated by the acronym WI, which stands for 'Water Ice'. Technical Grade can also be summarized as the Degree of a route, in order to distinguish from its Commitment Grade.

Despite attempts by Bugs McKeith to create an open ended system and the introduction of the two part system, including a Commitment Grade and a Technical Grade, many routes have been packed into a few grades. The system became once again closed ended with great resistance to WI 7 and above. This created a wide disparity in the difficulty within each Technical Grade. Therefore the Technical Grade system has been broken as follows; 2, 3, 4, 4+, 5, 5+, 6, 6+, 7, and so on. This is primarily to open it up and distinguish between the middle grades that are traditionally filed into WI 4 or WI 5.

If looking at leading a WI 4 + pitch such as the upper pillar on the left side of *Louise Falls* you must understand; in a good fat year or after the chandeliers have been knocked off by previous parties, the pitch may be WI 4. Whereas in a lean year or after weeks of sun leaching, or even after a large amount of traffic has created overhanging sections, the route may be WI 5. Granted, ice climbs are very difficult to attach fixed grades to due to the differences from year to year and week to week. However, most climbs have general characteristics to them and can be lumped around a 'usual grade'. But in reality, few people refer to the following parameters when rating the technical difficulty of a route. Rather, the yardstick is a comparison against established climbs that have a consensus grade. Herein lies the difficulty–experience levels, overestimation of steepness and length and egos add an immeasurable subjective factor to those comparisons.

1 A frozen lake or stream bed. No one has had the audacity to claim a first ascent of a WI 1 in the Rockies.

2 A pitch with short sections up to 80 degrees. Good possibilities for protection and anchors.

3 Sustained ice up to 80 degrees. Requires adeptness at placing protection and belays. May have short sections of steeper ice but will have good resting places. The ice is usually good.

4 A sustained full pitch of off-vertical or a shorter length (10-25 m) of vertical ice. The ice may have some technical features like chandeliers and may have long runouts between resting places.

5 A long strenuous pitch. May be a full ropelength of 88°-90° on good ice with few, if any, resting places or a shorter (20-40 m) pitch on bad featureless ice. Adequate protection requires excellent technique.

6 A full 50 m pitch of dead vertical ice or a shorter length of nasty proportions. Few, if any, resting sites. Protection is put in while standing on front points or in awkward situations. Ice quality is variable and climbing technical. Technique and efficiency are at a premium.

7 A full pitch of near vertical or vertical ice that is very thin or a long overhanging technical column of dubious adhesion. Both require diverse and creative techniques to climb and hopefully find protection. A very physically and emotionally draining pitch.

8 These routes do exist. We should never say the pinnacle of technical possibility has been reached. What is needed is the proper vision to see these lines and an adequate sense of the requirements, both technically and in terms of the hazards involved.

Seriousness Grade

Any waterfall ice climb can be as run out as the individual wants it to be. Depending on experience, ability and style of ascent almost any route can be sewn up or desperately run out.

Some routes can be seriously thin and unprotected due to underlying rock or air. Others are incredibly small and fragile. These latter routes are generally free standing pencils and require a great amount of care and ability to climb safely. Similar to these fragile 'cigars' are thin shields of ice that often form over high volume waterfalls. To my knowledge, no accidents have happened to date on such a climb; (i.e. 2nd pitch of *Takakkaw Falls*), however, it is my opinion that these fragile plates of ice pose huge hazards for the uninitiated. Obviously not all climbs will be found with these designations.

R. Reserved for very thin routes. This is similar to the runout designation given in many rock climbing areas. Depending on the season and the time of year, particularly early season, many routes may fall into this category and then fill out to a safer thickness later in the year. The R designation should be reserved for those routes that are traditionally very thin even in the best of years. On these routes a party will be faced with long runouts with difficulty and/or creativity required to find adequate protection from the ice and/or the rock. Many mixed routes may fall into this category.

X. These are very fragile routes that stand a possible chance of collapse while climbing them. By definition these routes are usually runout as well. Therefore all the caution reserved for an R climb should be noted here.

Again, an early season ascent can place a steep pillar into this category and then later in the year it may fill out to be quite solid.

Rock Grades

More and more routes are including rock pitches to link patches of ice (mixed climbing). When a pitch is given a rock grading, this means that major portions are on rock but may have sections of verglass, moss or snow. Rock climbing is graded on the YDS system from 5.0 to 5.10 and up. However, these pitches usually involve crampons so direct translation is very sticky indeed. The rock grade is generally how difficult the pitch 'feels'. With rock shoes and a chalk bag in the sun it will undoubtedly be easier, but it still means you must be competent at the stated grade.

Aid climbing grades, A1-A3, would be the same as they are found anywhere else. But remember local limestone usually requires a bit more gumption and nailing than a straight-in granite crack.

Length (in metres)

Understanding the length of climb is important in estimating its overall difficulty and your ability to safely complete the route. In this book, length is usually estimated by the culmination of how much rope is payed out on each pitch. For longer routes such as *Polar Circus* and *Slipstream* it is difficult to assess because they have long easy sections. In this case, length means the total vertical gain from the bottom of the route to the top. Specific details will be found in the route description.

Stars ✱✱✱

This guide sees the introduction of a quality or star rating, indeed a difficult and very subjective endeavour. It is based on three stars. High star ratings are not confined to the hard routes like we find in most rock climbing guides. Great effort was given to create an even distribution of stars across all grades of difficulty and types of routes; whether they be easy WI 2, WI 6 test pieces, fat plastic cruises or thin hooking nightmares. Stars are to be used in conjunction with the aesthetic location and route description of the climb, not just the technical difficulty. Less attention was given to the length of approach and more to the quality of the line. Some of the best routes in the range are three to five hours from the car. Zero stars does not mean that the route is worthless. There are, in fact few ice routes that would not be recommended given good ('good' being another subjective description) conditions. Stars given for obscure or rarely climbed routes are pure conjecture, based on the given description.

Directions

Left and right descriptions apply as if the climber is facing inwards, towards the route on the approach, the ascent and the descent.

RECOMMENDED ROUTES

Twenty All-Time Classics
Blue Angel
Bourgeau Left-Hand
Bourgeau Right-Hand
Bow Falls
Carlsberg Column
Cascade Waterfall
Curtain Call
Expert's Choice-all lines
Hydrophobia
Kitty Hawk
Louise Falls
Nemesis
Pilsner Pillar
Polar Circus
Professor Falls
Slipstream
Sorcerer, The
Takakkaw Falls
Weeping Wall (Lower and Upper)
Whiteman Falls

Alpine Routes
These routes are generally considered to be 'alpine' due to their length, position and/or objective hazard.

Aggressive Treatment
Ambivalence Falls
Arctic Dream
Borderline
Coire Dubh Intégrale
Drip at the Centre of the Universe, The
Elderly Man's Day Out, An
Gentleman's Day Out, A
Gimme Shelter
Reality Bath, The
Senior Project
Slipstream
Striving for the Moon

Low Avalanche Hazard

The following routes generally have low avalanche hazard. Beware; many routes may have low-angle sections that can collect enough snow to produce significant sluffs that can knock off a leader or even bury someone. Others may have slopes that will be hazardous only during one of those hideous 50-100 year avalanche cycles. Have a good read of the detailed route description for more information. Remember, any slope below tree line that doesn't have large trees on it, is usually that way for a reason.

Aerial Boundaries
Balfour Wall, The
Bow Falls
Bragg Creek routes
Canmore Junkyards
Cline River Gallery
Columbia Valley, The
(all routes except Nelson Creek Falls)
Dry Ranges, most of the area
Evan-Thomas Creek routes
Expert's Choice
Five Seven Zero
Ghost River, most of the area
Grotto Falls
Haffner Creek
Heart Creek
His and Hers
Johnston Canyon
Kicking Horse Canyon
(all routes except Lady Killer/I Scream)
King Creek Seepages
Louise Falls
Maligne Canyon
Murchison Falls
Nothing But the Breast
Panther Falls
Quick and Dirty
SARs on Ice
Takakkaw Falls, except the approach
Tangle Creek

Two O'Clock Falls
Vanilla Ice
Whimper Wall
Water Hole, The
Waterworks (Yoho)
Weeping Wall, (Lower and Upper)
Wet Dream
Whiteman Falls

Mixed Climbs

Routes in which much of the difficulty lies in thin ice or mixed/rock climbing. Such routes are rapidly gaining favour amongst more climbers.

2 Low 4 Zero (In lean years)
Anorexia Nervosa
Auto de Feu
Blessed Rage
Bountiful Drought
Bullwinkle
Christmas Present
Coire Dubh Intégrale
Day After les Vacances de Monsieur Hulot, The
The Drip at the Centre of the Universe
Grecian Formula
Irish Mist
Mixed Master
Mon Ami
Phantom Falls
Pipimenchen
Pitches of Eastwick
Political World
Red Man Soars
Ribbon, The
Sea of Vapors
Shampoo Planet
Snowline (In lean years)
Tease, The
Sliver, The
Touch Me if you Can
Twisted Sister
Wild Fire
Wolverine Falls
Woolley Creek Routes

The biggest factor in establishing new routes on ice is finding them. There are few of the so-called ethical debates that rage in the establishment of rock climbs. There are, however, a few things to keep in mind.

Many parties leave single bolt anchors on their routes. This is unacceptable. A brand new bolt that you've put in may be adequate for your rappel but in a year or two that same bolt can no longer be trusted on its own. The first ice climbing fatality in the range occurred on *Cascade Waterfall* when a single bolt anchor failed. As the numbers of climbers increase, it is fair to assume that more and more of these people will not have the experience to adequately assess the safety of fixed anchors. As long as a single bolt anchor exists, people will use them. This also goes for manky anchors with two or more pieces, or any other fixed anchor (see Hazards section, page 22). Some of the things I've seen people rappel from is appalling. Let it be considered negligent and plain ignorant to leave behind single piece or manky anchors. If you are forced to leave suspect anchors due to extraneous circumstances such as epics, please mention in your route report that the anchors need beefing up.

With the ever increasing popularity of safe ice anchors, especially the Abalakov Sandwich, see page 24, rock anchors are, more often than not, unnecessary.

If you're worried about others claiming your route, make sure to submit a complete detailed description.

Naming new routes is, of course, a privilege and one of the few rights a first ascentionist has. If you come across a route with obvious signs of being previously climbed and cannot find out who climbed it, try naming it yourself and crediting it to Unknown or as a first recorded ascent (FRA). Otherwise, we'll have dozens of routes called "Unnamed".

There are an astronomical number of short inconsequential steps and smears in just about every drainage from Waterton to the Yukon border. A surprising number of people have claimed 5-20 m new routes that are three to four hours away. As a result, all WI 2 climbs that are 25 m or less have been thrown out, unless it is very close to the road and has some value historically or as a practice area. If you're really interested in having that wilderness WI 2 experience, pick about any drainage you like and go for it.

In this book I have taken the liberty to put all first ascent names in alphabetical order, regardless of who lead what or whose idea it was. Climbing is a joint effort between two or more partners and if you're worked up over which name goes first or whose idea it was, then publish an article. If only one name appears, it was a solo ascent.

If you find and climb a significant or worthwhile new route please follow these guidelines for reporting it:

• Know the exact location. Most of the time spent in compiling this book went into trying to discover where the routes are. Learn how to read a map, give the map sheet number and the six digit military grid reference for the base of the route and any other major features used in locating the route.

- Name of the climb.
- Length from the bottom of the first pitch to the top of the last pitch (be realistic); if unsure, indicate the number of pitches you climbed.
- Grade; Commitment, Technical and Seriousness. Compare it with well established climbs that you've done.
- Date and names of first ascent party.
- Character of the climb; include any outstanding (or poor) features, good stories involved with the ascent and other miscellaneous information.
- Potential hazards, such as avalanche, seracs, rockfall, river crossings, etc.
- Detailed approach description, including where to park, is it visible from the road, time for an average party, terrain features, etc.
- Nature of the climb. Blow-by-blow accounts are not needed, just an idea of what to expect.
- Exact descent details.

Send information to:
Joe Josephson
c/o Rocky Mountain Books
4 Spruce Centre S.W.
Calgary, Alberta T3C 3B3
CANADA

CANADIAN ROCKIES ICE CLIMBING HISTORY

Since the sport of waterfall ice climbing took hold in the Canadian Rockies in the early '70s, it has progressed from an obscure diversion for a few fanatics to a common and popular winter pastime. The first waterfall to be climbed was *Cascade Waterfall* overlooking the east entrance into the Banff Townsite. No one seems to know who made the first ascent but Lloyd McKay and partner certainly got close to the top in the winter of 1965. Despite this prodigious effort with primitive gear and the already firm establishment of waterfall climbing in the US, it seems that few people ventured onto the vast number of frozen waterfalls that abounded until the winter of 1972-73.

That season, the terodactyl ice tool arrived in Calgary. Armed with the 'terrors' drooped pick, the assault was on and the accessible, easier climbs began

to fall. Standards rose quickly, culminating in the first ascent of *Bourgeau Right-Hand* over two days.

In the winter of 1973-74, charged with the success of the previous year, climbers began to look at the bigger waterfalls. After several attempts, the *Lower Weeping Wall* was climbed on Christmas Day by expatriates Bugs McKeith and Rob Wood. It was here that Bugs discovered his infamous aid technique, *"through my own lack of boldness"*.

"On two previous occasions faced by pillars of brittle vertical ice, and lacking the guts to frontpoint up them, I had attached aid slings to the shafts of both terodactyls and found that, even on vertical ice, I could relax and spend as much time as I wished clearing rotten ice and placing each axe alternately to my complete satisfaction."

It is with this technique that McKeith and Wood, along with Jack Firth and Canadians Tim Auger and teenager John Lauchlan pushed onto longer multi-day climbs like *Bourgeau Left-Hand* and *Takakkaw Falls*.

Having climbed these classics, climbers looked to find routes that offered a new level of difficulty. Firth and Lauchlan concentrated on the short nasty icicles around Field, like *Pilsner Pillar*. Meanwhile, McKeith looked toward a route he called *Nemesis*. Success on this long, exceptionally steep, unusually thin climb came after several months and a variety of partners.

Unaware that they were at the forefront of ice climbing development, the Canadians were criticized for their use of aid techniques. However, the big Rockies routes of the early '70s were of a length, steepness and remoteness unparalleled anywhere in the world. Even today with modern gear, techniques, and attitudes these routes have remained serious challenges.

Due to its size and uncertainty about the nature of the climbing, *Polar Circus* was attempted only once prior to December 1975. That month saw two teams head up only days apart. The Burgess twins, Bugs McKeith and Charlie Porter reached the top after eight days employing many fixed lines and aid techniques. As they were descending Eckhard Grassman, Mike Lailey and Laurie Skreslet completed the climb in five days with aid limited to one five-metre section on the final pitch. For several years *Polar Circus* remained the pinnacle of achievement for it was 700 metres, nearly three times the overall length of any other waterfall yet completed.

It was during the remainder of the decade that the Rockies waterfall scene really came into its own as a mecca for winter climbing. Publication in magazines, mostly by Bugs McKeith, put the word out and visiting Americans spurred activity as the old aid lines were cleaned up and skills were honed. Practices like the use of umbilical cords and carrying a third tool became standard. In 1977 Duncan Ferguson and Dave Wright freed the *Lower Weeping Wall, Takakkaw Falls* and *Carlsberg*. Things really heated up the following year when John Roskelly freed *Pilsner Pillar*, at the time the hardest single lead yet accomplished in Canada. The locals were also active that season with new free routes like *Teardrop* by Trevor Jones, Raymond Jotterand and Greg Spohr, a one and half day free ascent of *Polar Circus* by Jotterand and Lauchlan and speed ascents of *Takakkaw* which was climbed in a day from the road by Alan Burgess and Jim Logan. Then, only a week later, boldly soloed by Lauchlan.

With the end of the '70s came the end of an era that was marked by several strong achievements during the 1979-80 season. Jim Elzinga and John Lauchlan climbed *Slipstream* on the East Face of Snowdome. Involving glaciers, avalanche slopes, seracs and altitude, this route opened a new genre of alpine ice climbs. Later that season, James Blench and Albi Sole incorporated the steepest lines on the Lower and Upper Weeping Walls to create the *Weeping Pillar* which was easily the most difficult and sustained route in Canada. That same duo, teamed up with Lauchlan, later made the second ascent and an all-free climb of *Nemesis*.

In 1980, Albi Sole put out the first guidebook to Canadian Rockies ice called *Waterfall Ice*. But it wasn't just first-ascent glory that accounted for the following explosion in activity. In the boom years of the early '80s more people could afford the time and expenses of winter climbing. Gear and clothing technologies made large bounds and one could now stay warm, place gear quicker, and more easily find partners.

In the new route frenzy of the early '80s, some major venues were almost single-handily developed. Noted examples are the Ghost River which produced over 40 climbs mostly by Frank Campbell and The David Thompson Highway, the stomping grounds for Cyril Shokoples.

It took several years for the technical standards to catch up to the quickly rising skill levels with one exception– *Gimme Shelter*. Completed in April 1983 by Kevin Doyle and Tim Friesen, this still unrepeated route was years ahead of its time and was probably the hardest ice climb in the world.

It is important to note that aid climbing was virtually abolished by 1977. Few first ascents reported since have used aid techniques. This includes the act of hanging on your tools to place gear. Originally employed to prevent a dropped tool, umbilicals (cords attached from the ice tool to the waist) were sometimes used to support the climbers weight (i.e., hang) while they placed protection. By the end of 1980's, Rockies standards rose to the point where the top climbers no longer put umbilical cords on either tool and all placements and protection were supported by the strength and ability of the climber.

Although overall technical standards were slow to follow, activity was far from lackadaisical. The art of soloing became a more common endeavour. *Central* and *Right-Hand Weeping Wall, Pilsner Pillar, Polar Circus, Bourgeau Left-Hand* and *Slipstream* had all been quietly soloed by the mid-'80s. One of the landmark events of this era came in March 1986 with the same day solo of *Polar Circus* and the Weeping Pillar (first solo ascent) by Jeff Marshall. For training he earlier soloed the remote *Twin Falls* and climbed *Takakkaw Falls* with a partner in a single day.

Also in the mid '80s came the apex of the three genres of hard waterfalls that were established in the '70s. *Pilsner* was the first, but *The Terminator* is the ultimate in freestanding vertical pencils. This prize was claimed by Craig Reason and Jay Smith in January 1985, one of the finest seasons ever in the Rockies and to date the only year *The Terminator* has completely formed.

The standards in long, steep and thin routes like the classic *Nemesis* was taken to a new level with *Gimme Shelter* and firmly established with the ascent of *Riptide* in April 1987 by Jeff Marshall and Larry Ostrander. These are outstanding climbs in alpine environments that require large amounts of skill and experience to find protection and belays. Both routes are given a Technical Grade 7.

The 1980's era came to a quick close in February 1988 with *The Reality Bath* by Randy Rackliff and Marc Twight. This treacherous alpine waterfall on a large north face combined sustained difficulties guarded by active seracs and avalanche slopes. It is unrepeated and remains the only Engagement Grade VII in the range.

The second edition of Albi Sole's *Waterfall Ice* in 1988 proclaimed that routes fed (and threatened) by seracs are part of the future of ice climbing in the Rockies. Indeed, quite a few such lines remain unclimbed. Several routes like *Borderline, Arctic Dream* and *Ambivalence Falls* were climbed under seracs, but fortunately this style of route did not become popular. Instead ice climbers of the 1990's have become entranced by a genre of mixed waterfalls that offer a new level of difficulty and redefine the limits of possibility.

The first significant mixed waterfall in the Rockies was the ultra-classic *Mixed Master* by Joe Buszowski and Troy Kirwan in December 1991. The following season Joe set the standard again with Peter Arbic on *Shampoo Planet*. As *The Terminator* comes within 10 m of touching almost every year several people audaciously attacked it with the new attitude that, *"it doesn't have to be formed to be formed"*. Over two days in January 1993 Jeff Everett, with a variety of partners was the first to climb up behind *The Terminator* to the initial pillar which was aid climbed onto thicker ice above. Later that season Serge Angelucci and partner made the top in one push. Lead by Barry Blanchard and Joseph Josephson, over a dozen new mixed routes were completed by the end of the 1993-94 season.

Not all the activity centred around these 'futuristic' routes. Many gaps were filled as smears and drips across the range were systematically climbed. An unprecedented number of climbs (over 150) were reported in the early '90s with most being visible from the road. Many have become moderate classics while the number of desperates has grown from only 18 WI 6 or harder routes in 1988 to presently over 50. Stark proof of the increased number of active climbers and the higher level of standards.

Striving for the Moon by Barry Blanchard and Ward Robinson and *The Drip at the Centre of the Universe* by Keith Haberl and Larry Stanier were two major routes completed in the 1992-93 season. They were unique among alpine waterfall routes as they were taken to or near the summit of major mountains, not just to the top of a gully or an ice cliff.

In attempts to up the ante on the solo front, Richard Ouairy soloed *Ice Nine* (in WI 5 conditions), *Polar Circus* and all but the last pitch of the *Weeping Pillar* in 1992. Another significant solo enchainment occurred in January 1992 with the linking of the remote Ghost River climbs, *Hydrophobia* and *The Sorcerer* by Joe Josephson. *Nemesis* finally received this ultimate expression of climbing by Jeff Lakes in March 1991. The prolific Guy Lacelle made many difficult solos in the '80s and into the '90s including *Iron Curtain* and the first ascent of *Betty's Pillar*. *Polar Circus*, which has become a popular solo was climbed *intégrale* when Enzo Marlier soloed the rarely formed *Pencil* and continued to the top.

Perhaps the most impressive solo of the '90s was Bruce Hendricks solo first ascent of *Blessed Rage*, an audacious line involving hard mixed climbing and sustained ice with large objective hazards. Along with *Fearful Symmetry* and *Sea of Vapors, Blessed Rage* is part of the 'Hendricks Trilogy'. All three routes represented a new level of vision and boldness. Sporting exceedingly thin ice on a bulging, near-vertical wall, *Sea of Vapors* is technically the hardest and one of the most serious waterfall routes in the Rockies.

Paul O'Byrne

Lucifer. Blue Angel lies around the corner to the right.

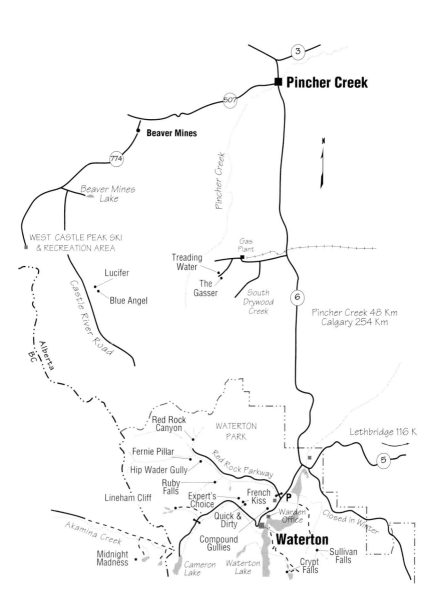

WATERTON NATIONAL PARK

Waterton National Park, the southern-most area covered in this guide, sees very little winter traffic despite offering above average ice climbing. The park and surrounding area are seasonally about five to ten centigrade degrees warmer than the Banff region and are influenced by frequent Chinooks. As a result, there is often little or no snow, and so lower than normal avalanche hazard. The flip side finds a shorter ice climbing season beginning in mid-December, running till mid-March. Call ahead to enquire about conditions.

Waterton is an ideal location for a weekend ice climbing trip. Several routes near the townsite and on Akamina Road can be done in a short day after travelling. A more involved route can then be done the following day. Undoubtedly many new, quality routes are hidden in the backcountry.

Getting There

Drive Highway 3 either west from Fort MacLeod or east through the Crowsnest Pass to Pincher Creek. The quickest route from Calgary is via Highway 2 south but a more scenic drive from Calgary is via Highway 22 south from Bragg Creek to Lundbreck and east to Pincher Creek. From Pincher Creek, drive Highway 6, 50 km south to Waterton Park, about three hours either route.

From Montana, the quickest access is via US Highway 89 on the east side of Glacier Park and Highway 2 to Cardston, then Highway 5 to Waterton Park. The Carway/Peigan Port of Entry is only open 9 am to 6 pm November 1 to mid-May. Chief Mountain Port of Entry on Montana Highway 17 to Alberta Highway 6 is closed in winter.

Facilities

Waterton townsite is largely boarded up in winter but a few motels are open year-round, and a grocery store is open three days a week. The town of Pincher Creek, 50 km north, offers many options for motels and food at better prices. Westcastle Peak Ski Area, near Pincher Creek, is an almost secret destination for great powder skiing. A picnic shelter and campground with toilets and garbage bins is located 3.4 km east of the Waterton townsite near Red Rock Parkway. The shelter is enclosed and has a supplied wood stove. Bring a lantern, a bucket for water (from the creek behind the shelter), and an axe (not essential) along with your camping gear and you will be set. The motels in town have reasonably-priced cafés for a breakfast and coffee before heading out for the day. Downright civilized!

Emergency

The warden office, 1.3 km east of town, is open Monday to Friday and has a voluntary registration form posted outside. If you sign out, remember to return your card at the end of the trip to prevent a needless and expensive rescue (at your cost!). Wardens are available during office hours for information on routes and approaches. Stop by for a chat before and after your climb; they are always interested in new condition reports and meeting park users. See page 272.

Maps

82 G/1 Sage Creek
82 H/4 Waterton Lake

Waterton Townsite

As you enter the townsite, one of the first things you'll notice is a blue flow of ice directly above the warden compound on the right. This is the right-hand and best of three separate gully climbs collectively called **Compound Gullies**. They face southeast and are subject to Chinook conditions. These gusty, warm winds can create sunny, plastic ice, high avalanche hazard (when there is enough snow), rock and icefall. The entire climb can disappear and form again several times a season.

Right Gully ** 300 m II, 3

Park at the Warden compound 1.3 km east of town and walk up the slope to the base in 15-30 minutes The route starts with several short pitches up a nice curtain of varied ice. Continue up several ropelengths of snow to a final steep column of ice. Rappel and downclimb the route. A downclimb in the trees left of the gully is also possible.

Centre Gully * 200 m II, 2

Park as for the *Right Gully* but walk left to the next gully. A short pitch of ice leads to snow and minor ice steps to where the gully forks. Either side offers good WI 2 ice for several pitches. Walk off left or rappel. Downclimb the route.

Left Gully 300 m II, 2

Continue past the warden station and park at the Information Centre (closed in winter), 0.7 km west. *Left Gully* is similar to *Center Gully*, with a single pitch of stepped ice at the top. Walk off left or rappel and downclimb the route.

Red Rock Parkway

This road begins just north of the bridge over Blakiston Creek on Highway 5. Red Rock Parkway is about 3.6 km east of the townsite (near the campground and picnic shelter). This road has not been plowed in winter for many years. Don't write it off, however. High winds and warmer temperatures often leave the road clean of snow. Take a mountain bike for quick and easy access to reach the end of the road (15 km) near Red Rock Canyon in about 45 minutes.

Ruby Falls * 60 m III, 3

Approximately 8 km up Red Rock Parkway (1 km past Crandell Lake trailhead), Ruby Creek comes down from the southwest (82 H/4 819426). *Ruby Falls* may be approached from Cameron Lake Road over Crandell Lake. It is 3 km to the Red Rock Parkway and gains only 100 m in elevation. About 1 km above the road, the valley forks. Exactly at the crotch of this fork, lies a pretty curtain.

Approximately 1.5 km west of Ruby Creek, two similar smears have been climbed. These are dubbed **Leaky Lucy** and **Drip Dry** due to their wet nature.

Hip Wader Gully 70 m II, 2

Located about 12 km up the road and 500 m past Lost Horse Creek (picnic site), it is visible across the valley to the left and is the right-hand of two minor drainages. The first ascentionists used hip waders to cross the creek and then up 70 metres of snow and a short ice step with more snow to the climb itself (82 G/1 183444).

Climb three short pitches with the third being the hardest and sometimes thin to start. Downclimb to the left.

Fernie Pillar * 90 m III, 5

Continue along the Parkway 15 km to the end of the road. Look south to the lower slopes of Mt. Blakiston in an area of blowdown to where this north-facing route should be visible. Cross the creek and walk up to the route in 30-45 minutes (82 G/1 169449). Give it a look, it could be one of the Rockies hidden gems waiting to be rediscovered.

Little is known about this climb but it is undoubtedly quite hard as the first lead is a full pitch of vertical strenuous ice ending on a tree belay to the right. A second, more moderate pitch rises up in three steps with some steep variations possible. Downclimb either side or rappel the route.

Red Rock Canyon ** 25 m III, 4+

From the end of the road to the north is a popular summer hiking trail up Red Rock Canyon. The top of the canyon is a short walk from the parking lot and at the last bridge, there is usually at least one very steep pillar pouring into the canyon. This makes an great top roping and arm-pumping playground.

Cameron Lake Road

This area offers some of the most accessible and highest quality ice climbing in all the Rockies. For now, this road will remain open in winter. As you enter the townsite take the first right (north) turn onto the Cameron Lake Road once known as the Akamina Highway.

The *Quick and Dirty* and *Expert's Choice* areas are very close to the road and get lots of sun. Avalanche hazard is usually not a problem due to minimal accumulations of snow as most of it gets melted away during Chinooks. But remember, these large slide paths are there for a reason; beware of big avalanche cycles. The routes have a short season and start falling apart during Chinook conditions, creating a hazard with falling ice and copious amounts of running water. With their southern exposure, the routes stay quite manageable, even during cold Arctic fronts.

Quick and Dirty *** 80 m II, 3

Drive up the Cameron Lake Road for 3.9 km and look for the first obvious route on the right side (north) through a short gap in the trees. Park in a wide section of road just past the creek bed and walk through the trees on the left side of the creek for no more than 30 minutes. *Quick and Dirty* is the right and biggest of three possible climbs in this tiny amphitheatre (82 H/4 854391).

The first pitch has ice up to 90° leading to a sloping ledge. A second, easier pitch leads to the top. This is an excellent climb that is hard for its grade and is enjoyable even when it is quite thin. From the top of the route walk right up the creek bed until it is possible to traverse left through the trees (another blue pillar of WI 3 can be seen above). Continue through the trees, staying away from the cliff edge until it is obvious that you can go down and traverse easily back to the base of the route.

French Kiss * 45 m II, 3

A one-pitch climb that is found several metres left of *Quick and Dirty*. Previously called **Unnamed**, the name was found in an old file at the Warden Office but I'm afraid to enquire how the name, *French Kiss,* was applied to the route.

This varied pitch fills out a good day when climbed with *Quick and Dirty*. A hard variation (WI 5+/6) exists between the two routes. It climbs a vertical pillar that is capped by hanging icicles. From

Close-up of Expert's Choice, Middle Route.

44 *Waterton National Park*

easier ground above the icicles make a mixed traverse left onto *French Kiss* and continue to the top. Walk left off the ledge or rappel from a large tree.

Expert's Choice

If this climb was farther north and closer to a higher population of climbers, it would be a world famous ice route, right up there with the Weeping Wall. Aside from being only 30-45 minutes from the road and south-facing, what more needs to be said! The climb is unmistakable on the right side 4.8 km up the Cameron Lake Road. Walk up the left side of the drainage. At the start of the walk, if in doubt, head up a steeper slope to the left instead of staying in the drainage bottom. It is easier in the long run. The *Left Side* forms every year as well one or both of the *Middle* and *Right Sides*. Each line offers a classic route for its grade. Rappel the route from fixed stations on the left side.

Left Side *** 125 m III, 4

The *Left Side* can form spectacular scoops and caves of ice as a result of the Chinook winds blowing the drips about. The first pitch is crux and ends after 40 m at a bolt belay on a ledge to the left. Another long pitch leads out and past an old bolt station (two rusted $^1/_4$-inch bolts) and climbs up to another ledge and a new beefy bolt station. The final easiest pitch turns right and climbs past huge caverns to the top, and an interesting piton belay.

Middle Route *** 130 m III, 6

A beautiful line right up the middle of the falls, *Middle Route* probably forms more often than the *Right Side*. The first 40-m pitch is sustained, technical and "just keeps coming at ya". Belay in a large cave on the left. The second, beautiful pitch starts out vertical then kicks back to a more reasonable angle and better ice. A final WI 2 pitch leads to the top. Traverse easily to the fixed station atop the *Left Side*.

Right Side *** 130 m III, 5

This is the far right side of the waterfall. When formed up well, the *Right Side* is similar to the *Middle Route* but the first pitch is considerably easier. Often it will be very thin with narrow pillars and icicles. Under these conditions the Technical Grade and seriousness level are definitely increased. Traverse to the *Left Side* and rappel that route. This may require a short fourth pitch to reach the fixed piton station.

Midnight Madness 110 m IV, 3

This remote climb is located in British Columbia, outside Waterton Park. Drive up the Cameron Lake Road to the end of the plowed section, 13.5 km west of the townsite. Ski 1.5 km up the road to the Akamina Pass Trailhead. Follow the wide trail for 1.6 km to the Park boundary and the Continental Divide. Follow the trail down past the Forum Lake Trail to the Wall Lake Trail (sign) and turn left to Wall Lake. Refer to *Ski Trails in the Canadian Rockies*. The route is to the northwest and is very wide with many variations. The route can be reached from BC. Snow machines are allowed on the trails leading up to the Divide from the BC side.

The route is climbed in three good pitches. Because it is located west of the divide, there is a lot more snow and a higher avalanche hazard. This route is subject to large cornices. A walk off 150 m right is possible but it is recommended to rappel the route.

Lineham Cliff Waterfall ** 125 m IV, 4

This is a very good route with an involved approach. Drive up the Cameron Lake Road for 9.3 km and look for the Lineham Creek Trail sign on the right (north) side. Ski or walk the trail 4.2 km to the base of the climb (82 G/1 151401). *Lineham Cliff Waterfall* is actually two parallel lines pouring off an impressive headwall and both have been climbed. This north-facing route has a higher chance of avalanche. Check with the wardens for conditions.

The left-hand route climbs 50 m with steep steps into a narrow section and more moderate ice to the top. The right-hand starts wide, finishes narrow and is easier than the left. Given an early start, they are both easily climbed in a day. Rappel the routes. A complicated descent is possible down the summer trail that traverses the cliff but it is exposed and loose; not recommended.

East Side-Waterton Lake

Crypt Falls * 155 m V, 4

A remote climb near the US Border on the headwall below Crypt Lake (82 H/4 921318). *Crypt Falls* is actually three separate flows. The first ascentionists climbed the central and longest of the three. From Highway 5 near the townsite, cross the lake at the Bosporous and ski up the Crypt Lake Trail. Beware of avalanche hazard. It is recommended to check with the wardens for updated conditions and exact approach details. The falls is 11.5 km from Waterton Lake and 700 metres of vertical gain so it is generally an overnight trip in a very beautiful valley.

Climbed in three long or four shorter pitches. The first pitch is the steepest, a classic WI 4. The rest of the climb is less steep but sustained. Rappel from trees right of the route.

Lineham Cliff Waterfall.

Sullivan Falls *** 230 m V, 5

Excellent climbing in a most beautiful basin makes this worth the long ski in. The climb is just visible with binoculars from Highway 5 near the park gates. Park at Marquis Hole 1.4 km east of the warden office and walk or ski across the flats to the Waterton River. Cross the river (hopefully frozen) and follow the Vimy Ridge Trail. Leave the trail where it turns southwest towards Vimy Peak and climb up onto the treed ridge on the west side of Sofa Creek. Stay out of the drainage bottom as long as possible; it is a horrible bushwhack. Once you get into the creek, continue up to the west side of Sampson Basin and the route (approximately 82 H/4 948337). Allow four to five hours to the base. The route is commonly done in a long day car-to-car. Check with the wardens regarding travelling conditions and ask to see the large print photo they have on file.

The first pitch leads up a massive and usually cracked freestanding curtain for 25 m to easier ice. A second narrower pitch on sustained 70-80° ice ends on a snow ledge. The wide tier of ice above is climbed in two excellent pitches. A shorter smear is found to the left. It is not known if it has been climbed. If worried about avalanche hazard, rappel the route. Otherwise, it is possible to climb down or rappel either side.

Sullivan Falls

Pincher Creek, 50 km north of Waterton National Park, is a small town with a lot of western character. The foothills and mountains west of Pincher Creek are floating on a pool of natural gas and, as a result are crisscrossed with numerous survey roads and cut lines. This makes the access easier and less restrictive than in the Waterton area. The Drywood Creeks and the Castle River are the only areas commonly known to contain ice routes. There is a good bet that countless others can be found—a perfect area for snow machine-assisted approaches. See the introduction to Waterton National Park for travel information.

Drywood Creek

From Pincher Creek, drive south on Highway 6 for 20 km. Just south of the railroad bridge over the highway is the paved Shell Plant Road. Turn west and follow the road for 9.1 km to the Shell gas plant. Continue past the plant to where the road descends to a little lake (82 G/3 137652). Turn left and follow the main road past two pumping stations (in 1993). The Gasser is obvious on the southeast side of the valley.

The Gasser ** 75 m II, 3

This is the main climb in the area. From the road, wade across the creek and hike up to the climb. Start on a short undulating pitch followed by a long and sustained ropelength on usually good ice. Rappel the route or walk east and scramble down.

Treading Water 40 m III, 3

This route is located 1 km past *The Gasser* on the northwest side of the road. It gets lots of sun and you don't need to cross the creek. Climb one pitch of moderate ice. Beware of cornice build-up along the ridgeline. Rappel the route.

South Drywood Creek

The following routes are a little more complicated to get at than *The Gasser*. Turn onto the Shell Plant Road as for the Drywood Creek climbs. Six kilometres west of Highway 6 turn left on Hastings Coulee Road. Follow the main road around and take the first right into South Drywood Creek. Follow the road 10 km to a gas pumping station. The climbs are located across the creek on the south side of the valley.

Easter Bunny ** 100 m II, 2

The first climb to come into view, *Easter Bunny* has a long season climb due to its northern aspect and high winds in the area making for interesting climbing. There is some avalanche hazard but there is rarely enough snow around. This climb has many variations on stepped bulges and good plastic ice. Walk off to the right.

Sunshine Corner * 90 m III, 3

Walk or drive (depending on the state of the road) past the pumping station to the second drainage on the south side of the creek. Cross the creek and continue up the drainage past a small seepage until the waterfall comes into view to the west. Climb two ropelengths of ice and then traverse right to another pitch and a half of easier ice. Rappel the route or hike up and traverse right into a snow gully which is followed down onto rock ledges. Traverse right from the rock ledges until finding a suitable place to climb down.

Windy Corner 45 m II, 3

Continue past the *Sunshine Corner* drainage for 1 km. *Windy Corner* is easily seen on the north side of the valley. Follow a gully up to the base and climb one pitch of undulating ice 75-90°. Continue up the gully for 150 m to a half pitch of similar ice. Rappel the top pitch then traverse right across scree to a snow gully which is followed to the trail.

Castle River

As you drive up the valley, there appears to be no suitable terrain for waterfall ice anywhere. Then, just as you come around a corner, you see two routes high on a southwest-facing cliff band. These spectacular routes are two icefalls well worth the long drive.

From Pincher Creek, follow Highway 507 west for 17.4 km toward Westcastle Peak Ski Area. Turn left on Secondary Road 774 and follow it for 15.1 km past the hamlet of Beaver Mines to a road leading to Beaver Mines Lake and campground. Turn left. Drive for 3.7 km and take the first junction on the right onto Castle River logging road. Follow this for 16 km until the climbs come into view on the left-hand side. Castle River Road is not plowed in winter. Try to go before December 1; hunting season is still open and hunters will be driving the road keeping it broken open. It may still be broken open after that date but if not, ski or snowmobile in. Hike uphill several hundred metres to the climbs.

Blue Angel *** 125 m IV, 4+

Blue Angel is the right-most of the three climbs and forms every year, sometimes by early November. The position of the route and the surrounding scenery make this a must visit for these outstanding climbs. This climb was immortalized on the front cover of the second edition of Albi Sole's *Waterfall Ice* and also with beautiful colour photos in Yvon Chouinard's *Climbing Ice*.

Start up an apron to reach steeper ice. Climb a harder-than-it-looks pitch with some steep sections and find a comfortable belay off to the side of the final pillar. Traverse out and climb the vertical pillar to the top. Rappel the route.

Lucifer *** 100 m IV, 4

This is another well-formed route found 50 m left (west) of *Blue Angel* and is easily climbed the same day.

Climb two long, sustained pitches on interesting and varied ice. As the climb is narrow in places there may be some entertaining stemming off the rock. The second pitch is slightly harder than the first, a beautiful route. Rappel the route.

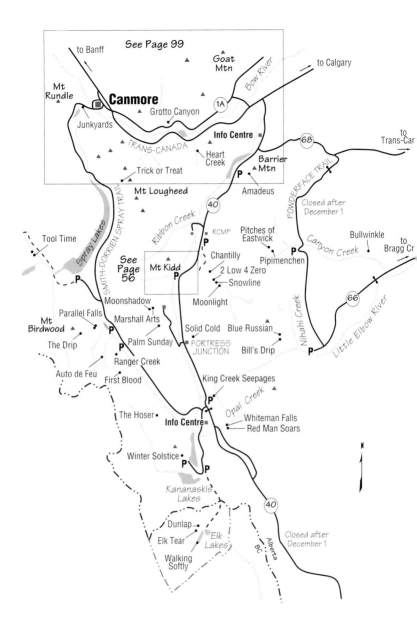

KANANASKIS COUNTRY

Kananaskis Country describes a vast area covering the entire front ranges south of the Trans-Canada Highway to Turner Valley. The four main ice climbing areas include Bragg Creek, Kananaskis Trail (Highway 40), The Smith-Dorrien Spray Trail, and Elk Lakes. Considering the size of the area, there are a surprisingly small number of routes but many are above average in quality. Much of the area is dry and very windy yet it still seems to produce a few new routes every year and is a great place to find early season (Oct.-Nov.) climbs. Frequent Chinooks and poor travelling conditions tend to destroy many of the climbs later in the season. Avalanche forecasts and stability reports are available from the Peter Lougheed Park Ranger Office. They are also posted at the Burstall Pass parking lot and Kananaskis Visitor Centres.

Getting There

Kananaskis Country is the closest climbing area to Calgary. The Bragg Creek area is reached via Highway 22 South from the Trans-Canada Highway turn-off 35 km west of Calgary. Kananaskis Trail is reached from the Trans-Canada 65 km west of Calgary or 45 km east of Canmore. The Smith-Dorrien Spray Trail can be reached from the Kananaskis Trial 54 km south of the Trans-Canada or by driving south from the town of Canmore past the Nordic Centre.

Facilities

Kananaskis Village, near Highway 40, has a high-class hotel with restaurants and pubs. Ribbon Creek Hostel is just up the road from the village. However, all the routes are easily climbed if you are based out of Banff/Canmore or Calgary. Refer to individual sections for specific facilities in each area.

Emergency

The area is administered by Kananaskis Country. In an emergency, contact Kananaskis Emergency Services. Ambulance and RCMP services are located 0.5 km south of the Kananaskis Village/Nakiska Ski Area turn-off, on Highway 40. 24 km from the Trans-Canada Highway. See page 272.

Maps

82 J/11 Kananaskis Lakes
82 J/14 Spray Lakes
82 J/15 Bragg Creek
82 O/3 Canmore

Bragg Creek Area

In the forested foothills west of Calgary lies the bedroom community of Bragg Creek. The 8-9000 foot- high mountains in the area are large munge piles of scree which hide disappointingly few waterfalls. For those willing to walk and explore, you may be rewarded with a hidden pillar or smear, but then again you may find nothing more than blisters and windburn. After November 30, most roads are closed for the winter. In a dry year, mountain bikes could be used. Be ready for cobble-strewn river beds, high winds, and little snow. Food, drinks, gas, and other amenities are available in Bragg Creek and Turner Valley.

Canyon Creek

Bullwinkle ** 90 m 5.10 WI 4+

This waterfall, possibly the closest one to Calgary, is only 30 minutes approach from the car. Follow Highway 22 south 10 km from Bragg Creek. Turn right onto Secondary Route 66. Stop at Elbow Ranger Station for information and a map–it could save hours! Continue past the Ranger Station to Canyon Creek and follow the road north to the Ing's Mine parking area. Walk north up Moose Dome Creek past a locked gate heading toward the Shell gas plant. Just before the crest of the first hill, turn northwest through the trees and up the steep slope to below the fall (82 J/15 550416). In recent years, the ice has never quite reached the ground. The climb starts about 20 m right of the hanging ice and below a shallow black corner.

Climb loose rock to the corner. Hard moves lead to good holds and blocky ledges on a traverse line to the left and a two bolt belay just right of the ice. The second pitch climbs onto the ice and past two vertical sections to a belay on blocks at the top of the ice. Traverse right along the ledge to a tree, rappel to the bolt belay and then to the ground.

Pipimenchen ** 100 m III, 5.6 A1 WI 4

As for *Bullwinkle*, continue down SR 66 to Powderface Trail. Turn right and follow the one-lane dirt road north for 14 km and park at a sharp bend at the bottom of a steep hill. If coming from Canmore, turn off the Trans-Canada onto Highway 40. One kilometre south of Barrier Lake Information Centre turn east on Sibbald Creek Trail (SR 68). Continue 14 km to the north end of Powderface Trail and follow this south for 20.5 km to the same big bend. Hike one hour up Canyon Creek. *Pipimenchen* is visible in the first small cirque to the north. Go 20 minutes upstream to the waterfall which is identified by an unlikely-to-form pillar topped by 50 m of ice (approximately 82 J/15 431404).

Start 30 m left of the pillar. Aid a shallow groove of good rock for 25 m (five bolts) that has a high probability for a free ascent. Another 25 m of 'alpine' 5.6 leads to the ice. Continue 50 m to the top and rappel first off a tree and then off bolts (50-m rope required).

Reference
Canadian Alpine Journal, Vol. 76, pg. 108, illus., 1993.

Pitches of Eastwick 140 m III, 3 R

Walk 20 minutes past and around the corner from *Pipimenchen*. The route consists of thin smears up east-facing slabs with scant protection considered to be "very alpine". Rappel the route.

Elbow River

Bill's Drip * 35 m III, 3

This climb was named in honour of the late Bill March. Continue past the Powderface Trail turn-off on SR 66 to the Little Elbow parking lot. Walk along the river to the Nihahi Creek trail then walk about 2.5 km north up the dry creek bed (90 minutes). *Bill's Drip* and *Blue Russian* are located on the left on Mt. Fullerton (82 J/15 462310).

Start with a 12-m pillar followed by easier steps to a tree belay on the left. More ice may form 30 m up slope. Rappel the route. It is possible to easily traverse to the top of *Blue Russian*.

Blue Russian * 45 m III, 4

100 metres right of *Bill's Drip* (82 J/15 460312) is *Blue Russian*. Climb thin steps of steep ice to the base of a 12-m freestanding pillar followed by two short steps. Rappel from trees.

Typical Bragg Creek terrain with Bill's Drip on the left and Blue Russian to the right.

Sheep River

Bob's Route 25 m II, 2

From Bragg Creek follow Highway 22 to Turner Valley or take Highway 2 south of Calgary to Okotoks, then turn west on Highway 7 to Turner Valley. Follow the Sheep River Trail (SR 546) to Sheep River Visitor Information Centre.

This is a short route found down snow slopes directly south of the ranger station on the far side of the Sheep River Gorge. It was named for Bob Oldham who was killed in an avalanche on Mt. Thompson in 1981.

Brewer's Droop ** 75 m III, 4

As for *Bob's Route*, continue on SR 546 to the junction with the Gorge Creek Trail (road is closed at Sandy McNabb Campground after Nov. 30). Drop down into the Sheep River and walk upstream for 40 minutes to the route on the left (82 O/15 655119). This climb offers a pleasant two-pitch route with a steep pillar to finish. Walk off to the right.

Kananaskis Trail
Highway 40

Due to its proximity to Calgary, this area is a popular playground. After November 30 the road is closed 54 km south of the Trans-Canada Highway. For access, this affects only the Opal Creek climbs. At the end of the road, you can turn right onto Kananaskis Lakes Road which passes the park office and connects with the Smith-Dorrien Spray Trail. Gas and limited grocery supplies are available at Fortress Junction. The Barrier Lake Visitor Centre, 11.7 km south of the Trans-Canada, is open in winter for limited hours and closed Monday (except holidays) and Tuesday. It has a pay phone near the entrance. The routes along Highway 40 are described from north to south.

Barrier Mountain

Amadeus *** 55 m III, 4+

This classic, testy climb sits high above Barrier Lake and rarely forms completely. Park next to a "Barrier Lake" sign 4 km south of the Barrier Lake Visitor Centre. Follow trails past the popular Yellow Wall rock climbing area and continue up the gully, across scree to the base (82 O/3 364551). Be ready for variable and thin ice conditions. When formed, *Amadeus* usually doesn't last beyond the first Chinook.

Begin with a short, unconsolidated pillar to a ledge. Another steep section leads to a good belay on the left. More sustained ice leads to the top and a bolt belay on the left. Rappel the route.

Bruce Hendricks working it out early in the season on Amadeus.

Evan-Thomas Creek

The following six climbs are located up the wide drainage opposite Mt. Kidd offering excellent climbing with an easy approach and zero avalanche hazard. Park at the Evan-Thomas Creek parking lot 16 km south of the Barrier Lake Visitor Centre on the east side of Highway 40. Ski or walk along the cross-country ski trail to a fork and take the sharp bend right and down the hill to the creek and a small bridge. All routes are found upstream from here.

Chantilly Falls * 100 m II, 2

Follow the creek upstream for a total of 2.5 km from the car to the climb on the right side in a small cleft (82 J/14 327374); one hour. The falls are named for the often lacy appearance of the ice.

This route is an easy climb with a ledge about halfway–a good beginner's route or a solo spin en route to *Moonlight*. Rappel from trees and downclimb (one rope adequate).

Moonlight *** 110 m III, 4

Approach as for *Chantilly*, upstream 1 km and 200 m uphill on the right (82 J/14 331365). Three routes are located 10 m apart. Some years none form, other years two or three independent lines form and rarely, one huge curtain forms. *Moonlight* is the left-hand line. An early ascent discovered deep baritone 'gonging' that sounded like an Indo-Chinese xylophone called a Gamelin, thus the alias 'Glass Gamelin'.

The first pitch climbs a long, often thin ice hose to a belay on the left of the crux curtain. Launch up the steep pillar 10 m to easier ice. Another short wall leads to the top. Rappel the route. You can walk left to a large chute in the cliff and make two rappels from trees.

Snowline ** 100 m III, 4

Approach as for *Moonlight*, a few metres to the right. *Snowline* is probably the most common line to form, but it can be only several inches thick. It is highly recommended in such conditions presenting exciting mixed climbing. When it's fat, it's a steal at WI 4.

Similar to its neighbour, start with a steepening slab (a bolt may be visible about 10 m up) and continue to a shallow corner where a protected belay is hard to engineer. Two old bolts may be found on the right after thirty metres. Continue up a steeper pitch to a ledge followed by a short step to the top. In very fat seasons, a difficult narrow icicle forms over the steep wall just right of *Snowline*. **The Pipeline** variation (WI 5) gives exciting technical climbing and is an alternative if the other routes are busy. Rappel off a tree to a second tree on the left of the climb just above an overhanging section (slings). A long 50 m rappel and a tiny bit of downclimbing brings you to the ground, or make an intermediate rappel. Be careful of rappel trees.

In 1993 a 20 cm-round tree with a bunch of rappel slings around it was found at the bottom of the climb. If there is enough ice, it's best to construct your own ice anchors.

2 Low 4 Zero ** 90 m III, 3 R

The right most of the three routes, 10 m from *Snowline* in a wide groove. Most often *2 Low 4 Zero* is an iced-up rock route but it occasionally forms up fat. It can offer some cool climbing.

Climb two full pitches. When in lean condition, a healthy rack of knife blades is recommended. Rappel as for *Moonlight* or *Snowline*.

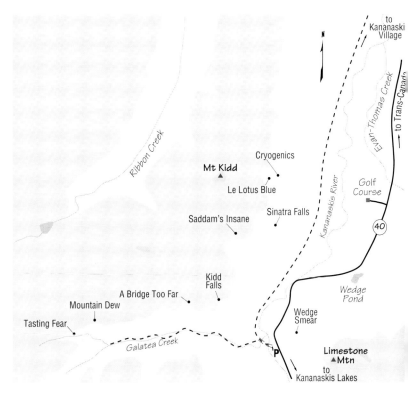

Combo Falls 50 m III, 2

Numerous short routes on generally good ice are found upstream from *Moonlight*. *Combo Falls* is situated 0.5 km upstream from *Moonlight* and 300 m up the southeast slope at the first side drainage to the right. (82 J/14 332361).

A smaller smear can be found 200 m up the canyon (82 J/14 5334363) on the opposite side of Evan Thomas Creek. Rappel off the trees.

Good H'evans Thomas 40 m III, 3

This climb is about 1.5 km beyond *Moonlight* and 0.8 km upstream of the canyon mouth where open water can be skirted on the left wall (82 J/14 341357).

Climb two 15 m walls followed by shorter steps. Rappel from the trees.

Mount Kidd

Across from Evan-Thomas Creek, a beautiful complex peak, Mt. Kidd, rises high on the west side of Highway 40. The next six routes all lie along its east and south sides and offer excellent climbing relatively close to the road. All routes are threatened by avalanche hazard in this area. The East Face could make an aesthetic winter alpine climb. The following routes are described from south to north (left to right) and are best accessed from the Galatea Creek parking lot, 21.5 km south of the Barrier Lake Visitor Centre. See map page 56.

A Bridge Too Far * 300 m IV, 4+

Follow the Galatea Trail west about 2 km. The climb is visible up the slope to the right at the fifth footbridge (82 J/14 266364). Slog up through steep trees to the base; 1.5 to 2 hours.

A true one-pitch wonder. Start with a 25-m, freestanding pillar that often bulks out to be quite moderate. Continue upwards on increasingly easier ice. If the bottom pillar is not formed (not visible from the road), you can scramble around on the right.

Rappel and downclimb route. Some fixed anchors and trees may be found.

Mountain Dew 20 m III, 4

Found one drainage left (west) of *A Bridge Too Far* (82 J/14 246365). Not named for a popular soft drink, this freestanding pillar is usually soaked. Rappel the route.

Tasting Fear 35 m III, 5

This climb is a short vertical pillar located 50 minutes past *A Bridge Too Far* in a small canyon of Galatea Creek (82 J/14 242362). Due to open water below the climb, the first ascent party rappelled into the canyon from above. In colder times, you may be able to approach from the creek directly.

A vertical pillar for 25 m easing slightly near the top. Walk left above the cliff to slopes which lead back to the creek. Cross it, then head up to the trail.

Kidd Falls ** 75 m IV, 4

The obvious falls above the Galatea Creek parking lot (82 J/14 274366). A dramatic Z-fold in the bedding planes creates a huge bowl above the route. Several groups have had avalanche incidents here. One pair had an avalanche launch over the leaders head and bury the belayed up to his neck. From the parking lot, cross the suspension bridge and continue to Galatea Creek. Continue to the Galatea/Terrace trail junction and head up open slopes on the ridge to the right of the drainage; 1 to 1.5 hours.

The first is a long pitch on sustained ice leading to a small ledge. A shorter, steeper pillar leads to the top. Rappel.

Saddam's Insane * 100 m IV, 5

On the east side of Mt. Kidd, left of the summit is a large broad gully with low-angle ice flows along the bottom. On the south-facing wall of the gully is an obvious ice fall with the same aspect as Kidd Falls and doesn't always form (82 J/14 277380). From the Galatea parking lot, follow the Terrace Trail to the rocky, open stream bed coming out of the gully. Continue up the gully to the ice/snow system on the right leading up to the route. Both the approach and climb have extreme avalanche potential.

Several hundred metres of steepening terrain lead to the route. An easy pitch leads to a second pitch of steep, chandeliered and technical climbing. Rappel the route.

Jeff Marshall on the first ascent of Saddam's Insane (see inset).

Sinatra Falls *** 350 m III, 2

Sinatra Falls, the undisputed Rockies champion for the title of 'Most First Ascents', was probably climbed in the late '70s. It is located in the first gully north (right) of the wide drainage containing *Saddam's Insane* but to the left of the large cliff bands below the East Face (82 J/14 285382). From the Galatea Creek parking lot follow Terrace Trail for 40 minutes until below the route; then hike another 30 minutes to the base. There are miles of avalanche terrain above the route. Most of the ice is covered in debris later in the season.

A long, easy route with ice pitches to 80°. Follow the obvious gully system (may have up to seven pitches of ice depending on the amount of snow). A great ramble! Traverse left (south) from the top of the gully through bush and trees to a broad open ridge; follow it back to the Terrace Trail.

Le Lotus Bleu ** 150 m V, 5

Le Lotus Bleu is located in the deep gully that splits the lower cliff bands on the East Face directly below the summit and straight across from the Evan-Thomas Creek pull-out (82 J/14 284393). Walk from Kananaskis Village south 3 km or from the Galatea Creek parking lot north the same distance.

Depending on the water level and your constitution, it may be possible to ford the Kananaskis River from the golf course. Take the trail until you are directly under the route or just south of it. Go up a bare shoulder until at the base of the mountain (two hours). Go up an ice gully if the conditions permit or as on the first ascent scramble up the buttress to the left, then traverse avalanche prone slopes to the base of the ice; four hours total. Several parties have used this route as an approach to reach a prominent rib on winter attempts of the face. Beware of avalanche conditions; there is over 700 m of slopes above.

Several narrow steps up to 80°. brings you to the main fall. The first 50-m pitch is vertical followed by 25 m of rolling ice. Rappel the route.

Cryogenics ** 100 m IV, 5 R

This thin climb located down and right (north) of *Le Lotus Bleu* (82 J/14 284394) would make a challenging approach to *Le Lotus Bleu*. It does not always form and should be avoided during times of high avalanche hazard. *Cryogenics* is best visible from Highway 40 at the turn-off to the RV Park.

Two short steps of WI 3 ice lead to the foot of the main fall, a narrow curtain of thin and chandelier ice, which rears to vertical in the upper half (55 m). A short walk leads to a 10-m pitch of thin ice in a narrow, water-worn groove. Rappel the route.

Wedge Smear 30 m II, 3

On the south side of the highway is a small bowl on Limestone Mountain above Wedge Pond. A short flow can be seen at approximately 82 J/14 294356. Park at the Galatea Creek parking lot and walk 500 m north along the highway and follow an old road traversing across a slope to the northeast towards the climb. It has been used as a practice area for years.

Fortress Junction

Solid Cold 25 m III, 3
Park at the small pull-out north of the Fortress Junction gas station, 30.4 km south of the Barrier Lake Visitor Centre. The route is visible in the gully above (82 J/11 304297). Climb up the north side of the gully and traverse into it at the last moment or rappel from a tree at the top of the falls. An apron leads to a wide curtain of good ice that's hardly worth the effort. To descend, walk left over the rise and walk down the north side of the gully.

Palm Sunday 45 m IV, 4
This climb is located above the Fortress Ski Resort Road in an east-facing bowl between Mts. Inflexible and Lawson. The route itself faces north (82 J/14 272268) and would be considered a desperate act with any amount of snow. This is a one-pitch pillar that doesn't always form. Rappel the route.

Moonshadow Gully ** 80 m IV, 4
This route forms early. Located in the back bowl of the Fortress Mountain Ski Area, it should be avoided later in the year with the buildup of snow and the great white wave from above.

From the base of the Ski Resort, follow the T-bar to the top of the ridge, cross to the left and descend a maintenance road into the back bowl. Cross out of the ski area to the obvious gully (82 J/14 255306).

A short moderate pitch leads to 50 m of classic WI 4 ice. Rappel the route.

Marshall Arts * 200 m IV, 5 R
Draining the bowl left of *Moonshadow Gully* numerous thin smears and variations may exist. Take your pick depending on what's formed and your own 'psycho-level'. The same avalanche warnings for *Moonshadow* apply here.

The first pitch is radically thin and marginally protected by two bolts. From there, it is a "normal ice climb" to the top. Rappel from ice and bolts.

King Creek

King Creek Seepages ** 45 m II, 2
Park in a pull-out on the east side of the road at the tight canyon near the junction of the Kananaskis Lakes Road and the Highway 40 road closure at the Provincial Park boundary. Hike up the canyon ; 30 to 40 minutes (82 J/11 346200).

Three seeps on the right-hand wall give good ice bouldering and top roping with an occasional dead log to clamber up. Good fun. Rappel from trees.

Opal Creek

Drive 54 km south on Highway 40 to the Kananaskis Lakes Trail junction. After December 1, Highway 40 is closed beyond here. Drive, ski, or mountain bike from the provincial park boundary for 5 km to its junction with Valleyview Road. If climbing before December 1, park here. Pass a gate and follow this road left for 200 m to the creek. Continue upstream past two small WI 3 steps to the base (30 minutes from Highway 40). Be careful in the tight canyon as you approach the route—it is a terrain trap for sluffs off the sidewalls. The top pitch of *Whiteman* is visible from the Opal Creek Bridge on Highway 40 (82 J/11 359152).

Whiteman Falls *** 95 m IV, 6

A brilliant line with an incredible ambiance. This route speaks a lot for the psychology of grading. In 1980 *Whiteman* was given a Grade 5, thus it received many ascents when few people were climbing Grade 6. Even today, it is feared much less than other modern WI 6 routes. In fact, the last pitch can be one of the hardest pitches anywhere. 30 m of overhanging (yes! 93°) ice has been seen on this route. Fortunately, it is not always so hard and should not be missed.

A deceptively hard and technical first pitch (WI 4) takes you to a comfortable cave on the left. Step out onto the pillar and find the easiest line to the top and a fixed anchor. It is often a clear straw near the top, and may have small overhangs to exit through. Wild mushrooms, the spectacular hanging tube and steeply tilted bedding planes create an exposure that you wouldn't expect on such a short route. Rappel the route.

Red Man Soars ** 55 m IV, 5.9 A1 WI 4+

Red Man Soars is found in the deep corner a few metres right of *Whiteman Falls*. It is a fun challenging mixed climb with excellent protection; 4-6 pitons to 3/4" angle, 1/2 set of wires and a few friends to #3 plus ice screws.

Climb a mixed right-facing corner just as you enter the gash. A thin ice smear may exist to the right of the corner. At the top of the corner climb very steep rock onto the arête between the gash and the slab leading across to *Whiteman*.

Make four aid moves up the groove (seconded free at 5.10+) to gain steep ice pouring out of a cave. A short, exciting second pitch stems out of the cave between an ice smear on the left and a rock fin and continues up ice into a second cave. Rappel the route (50-m ropes adequate).

Barry Blanchard soloing on Whiteman Falls; Red Man Soars in the cave/corner to the right.
Photo Patrick Morrow

Smith-Dorrien Spray Trail

This gravel road leads south from Canmore past the Nordic Centre to Kananaskis Lakes and Highway 40 (64 km). Because it is one valley west and closer to the Divide than Highway 40 it receives much more snow, thus the avalanche potential is correspondingly higher. If you run into too much snow, the area offers some top-notch cross country ski trails and popular ski touring in the Burstall Pass and Black Prince areas. A warming hut is maintained at Pocaterra at the junction on the Smith-Dorrien and Kananaskis Lakes Roads. Mostly used by skiers, it has a wood stove and is a cozy place to warm up and dry out. The Kananaskis Lakes Visitor Centre 3.5 km south towards Kananaskis Lakes is open all winter for limited hours. The ranger station and park administration office can be found on the Kananaskis Lakes Trail, 500 metres west of Highway 40. The routes are described from north to south.

Spray Lakes Area

Trick or Treat 70 m IV, 4

Easily visible high in the cirque between peaks 1 and 2 of Mt. Lougheed, *Trick or Treat* is a good route to do early in the year when you don't know what else to climb. Hike up the creek then steep scree for three to four hours to the base (82 J/14 212471). Some more WI 3 ice is found farther left, high up in the bowl. Have a nice walk.

Climb one short pitch of steep lacy ice followed by easy terrain. Rappel the route.

Tool Time 55 m IV, 4

Bryant Creek is the classic approach to the famous Mt. Assiniboine. *Tool Time* and an second parallel smear (WI 5) lie about halfway along this tour above the Bryant Creek Shelter. These north-facing routes drain a huge avalanche bowl near the bottom of a large cliff called Gibraltar Rock. It seems likely that both where climbed as early as the late '70s but only the one described here is known to be climbed for sure. In the past, the nearby Bryant Creek Shelter operated by Parks Canada, made for a pleasant base camp but due to government budget cuts the shelter will no longer be open as of 1994. The trail up Bryant Creek starts from a large parking lot at the Shark Mountain Cross-Country Ski Trail. Follow the Smith-Dorrien Trail south from Canmore for 38 km to Engadine Lodge. Turn right and drive past the Lodge and continue down for 5 km to the parking lot. Follow the ski trail down and across the Spray River and continue up Bryant Creek for about 13 km to a park warden cabin. The climbs are obvious to the northwest, a short ways up the valley.

Burstall Pass

Parallel Falls ** 150 m IV, 4

Two obvious smears on the east-facing ridge above Mud Lake. Park at a gate 1 km north of the Burstall Pass parking lot. Ski west across the flats to Hogarth Lake and connect old logging roads and gullies to the base of the slope below the climbs. Continue up very avalanche-prone slopes to the base; two hours (82 J/14 176280).

Both lines offer three long pitches of varied climbing. They start to form early, thus many parties have had an epic time with thin ice as they push the season. The left-hand line is a little harder with a steep 10 m wall to finish. The right-hand is hardest at the bottom. Rappel the routes.

The Drip at the Centre of the Universe
*** 600 m VI, A2 WI 5+ R

On the East Face of Mt. Birdwood is an obvious line (visible from the road) that runs to the summit ridge (approximately 82 J/14 157263). *The Drip* had been looked at for years and it took several efforts till it succumbed. It is mostly a thin ice route with short sections of mixed climbing, a full-on alpine endeavour with 400 m of very technical climbing. It is recommended mid- to late-season when the days are longer. From the Burstall Pass parking lot, 45 km from Canmore, ski up the popular trail past Burstall Lakes to a steeper section called 'the headwall'. Turn right up a drainage gully. After 200 m turn right again up the obvious avalanche path to the base of the couloir; 2.5 to 3 hours. A less obvious snow couloir is found to the left. Be wary of avalanche conditions on the long approach slope.

Start up 95 m of snow and ice up to 90°. From a snow ledge continue up steep and narrow decaying ice for 12 m to better ice and a small alcove. A difficult 35 m double smear ahead leads to a ledge. Climb an ice ramp to the right, then pendulum left to the top of some icicles and continue up very thin 90°. ice (50 m). This pitch may go free depending upon the amount of ice. Very narrow (30 cm) and thin ice leads to more moderate ground and the snow gully in 50 metres. 200 metres of snow and easy mixed climbing leads to the summit ridge. It is possible to continue to the top (30 to 40 minutes) but most

parties find that it is getting dark at this point. Take 8 to 10 pitons (many kbs), half a set of wires, 8 to 10 ice screws. Rappel the route.

The east face of Mt. Birdwood. The Drip at the Centre of the Universe takes the right hand couloir directly to the summit.   Photo Larry Stanier.

Auto De Feu * 300 m V, A2 WI 5+

A difficult and unique futuristic route, the name describes the act of setting oneself on fire. From the Burstall Pass parking lot, ski across the flats and up the first hill. Near the top of the hill, the road forks with the right side going toward Burstall Pass. Take the left-hand fork and follow it up French Creek for 1.5 hours. *Auto de Feu* is on the right just past a large avalanche path on the second set of cliffs. A discontinuous WI 4ish route is found to the left.

The first pitch climbs up short, nasty pillars plastered to the cliff. Several pitches of easy terrain and snow wallowing lead to a seemingly impassable rock wall with a snow patch in the middle of the wall. Start tunnelling through a snow-choked hole in the rock wall–be careful, it is large and steep enough to fall out of. This bizarre feature puts you below an unconnected smear for the last pitch. Climb up splattered mushrooms and make three aid moves (pitons) to reach an anaemic hanging curtain. Snag the ice and stem to the maximum to reach the top of the climb. Rappel the route; some rock gear required.

Ranger Creek

R & D *** 90 m III, 4

A great one-pitch wonder. *R & D* is one of the first routes to form and thus sees a lot of traffic early in the season, before the snow flies. It is located in the first drainage south of Burstall Pass trailhead and easily seen on the left-hand wall of Ranger Creek (82 J/14 208248). Park at the pull-out 2.5 km south of Burstall Pass parking. Bushwhack through alders into the drainage and across avalanche-prone slopes to the base in 45 minutes.

This is a classic WI 4 pitch on usually good ice. Very easy ice continues above for 40 m. Rappel the route.

Lone Ranger ** 120 m IV, 3

At the back of the cirque, past *R & D,* is a short steep wall. At various times, up to three routes can form. Pick your way up the drainage, past wind-loaded pockets to the wall in 60-90 minutes. Also called **Ranger Creek Falls**, it is the left-most route (82 J/14 205247).

Two pitches of technical, bulgy ice lead onto easy ice and the snow slope. Walk off right and traverse back to the base. The route has the potential for extreme avalanche hazard.

The Chalice and The Blade * 100 m IV, 5 X

This route is in the middle of the cliff, 30 m right of *Lone Ranger* (82 J/14 206247). The first 10 m ascends thin, technical ice and moss to a steep WI 4 pillar to a ledge where two lines diverge to the top. The above route takes the 30 centimetre-wide, free-hanging cigar on the right. Climb next to the rock for 15 m. Traverse around the pillar to thin ice and easier angled ice leading to the top. The easier, left-hand line route is called ***The Chalice and The Spoon*** *IV, 4+*. Descend as for *Lone Ranger*.

Bored for November 55 m IV, 3

On the far right side of the cliff, 70 m from *The Chalice and the Blade* is a short pillar followed by easy ice and snow (82 J/14 208247). Combine it with other routes in the bowl.

South to Kananaskis Lakes

First Blood * 135 m V, 5

A striking pillar can sometimes be seen high on the East Face of Mt. Murray (82 J/11 211232). *First Blood* has been known to form as early as September and is recommended to be climbed early in the year before any snow accumulation. This makes the approach easier on the legs and on the mind as it traverses along a avalanche bowl.

The first ascentionists named this climb *First Blood* because it was their first climb of the season and they got pretty beat up on this long demanding route. Stop 6 km south of Burstall Pass parking lot, the climb is visible far above. Cross the creek and bushwhack into the large bowl left of the route; two hours. On the right side of the bowl climb a gully to a snow ramp. Follow this up and right.

Climb easy slabs and a 15 m ice pillar to a ledge, 50 m. Traverse right 40 m to the base of a 70-m pillar. Climb 30 m of steep technical ice to a single bolt belay on the right. Another slightly easier 40-m pitch brings you to the top (single bolt on the right). Rappel the route. The first ascent team rappelled off a long piton driven into the scree at the top. A party in 1993 added several single bolt anchors.

The Hoser 90 m III, 3

This climb is found in the southern bowl of Mt. Warspite on the left side of the drainage (82 J/11 273158 unconfirmed, another route can be seen at 282148). Park 7 km north of the Smith-Dorrien and Kananaskis Lakes Road junction and hike up the drainage for about 1.5 hours. Beware of avalanche.

The climb consists of two rolling pitches with steep steps. Rappel the route on bolts.

Kananaskis Lakes

Winter Solstice 25 m II, 3

Winter Solstice is located on a cliff band on the East Face of Mt. Indefatigable. Potential avalanche hazard is encountered crossing to the base and from above. Follow the Kananaskis Lakes Trail 15.3 km to the North Interlake parking lot and ski the Mt. Indefatigable trail for about 1 km. The climb is visible on the west side of the drainage (82 J/11 308115).

You'll find one pitch of moderate ice leading to the base of a 12-m pillar of 70- 85° ice. Belay and rappel on trees.

Elk Lakes

Located south of Kananaskis Lakes, Elk Lakes is rarely visited by ice climbers. Remember it is west of the Divide in the 'snow zone' and the routes are situated in large avalanche bowls. From Highway 40 drive the Kananaskis Lakes Trail for 12 km to Elk Pass parking. Ski south up Fox Creek on the wide cross country ski trail to Elk Pass. Follow the power line south to the junction with the summer hiking trail where there is the remains of a burned-out hut (82 J/11 368015). Take the trail to the Upper Elk Lake. Generally this is an overnight trip. Usually the climbing is excellent with potential for big new routes.

Dunlap ** 100 m IV, 5+

This is the largest climb in the area. Directly across the Upper Lake on the south wall of Mt. Fox are a number of obvious flows. *Dunlap* takes the distinctive pillar on the right. Look for two full pitches of 'love'; strenuous, steep, and chandelier ice with a hanging belay in the middle. Rappel the route.

Elk Tear * 140 m IV, 5

Elk Tear is the flow left (south) of *Dunlap*. Easy ice leads to the crux second pitch; beautiful climbing on vertical, bulgy ice. More easy ice leads to the top. Rappel the route, or go some distance back from the lip and traverse right through trees to the top of *Dunlap*.

Walking Softly 120 m IV, 3

At the southwest end of the Upper Lake beneath a huge avalanche bowl 82 J/11 330008) is a large flow which can be seen from the northern end of the lake. Two pitches of rambling ice leads to a 10-m pillar. Rappel the route.

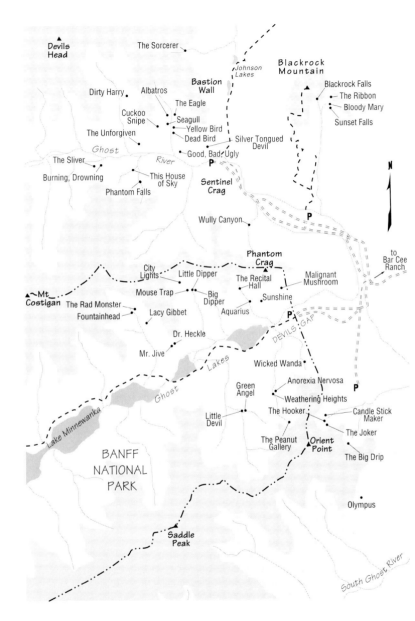

THE GHOST RIVER AREA

The Ghost River is a name that conjures up images of adventure. That's exactly what climbing in The Ghost is all about–high quality adventure. This area contains a high concentration of some of the finest ice routes the Rockies has to offer. In general there is little avalanche hazard except during the worst of cycles. There are some isolated pockets of wind slab which can usually be avoided. Good campsites and firewood are found throughout the Ghost. Situated on the eastern slope, the area is plagued by high winds and subject to frequent Chinooks. As a result there is usually very little snow to deal with, but there can be car-eating drifts. A sturdy shovel is essential. A 4 x 4 vehicle adds peace of mind. However, many people get by with tire chains and a prayer. Enjoy and savour your adventures here; it is a most unique and inspiring experience.

Reference
Polar Circus, Vol. 2, pg. 24, illus., 1986.

Getting There
The area is situated along the east slope of the Rockies north of the Trans-Canada Highway. It is near the prominent landmark called The Devil's Head, a large obelisk rock peak. From Calgary, head west on the 1A Highway to the town of Cochrane. 13.4 km west of the junction (4-way stop) with Highway 22, turn north onto Secondary Route 940 (Forestry Trunk Road), also known as Highway 40. From Banff/Canmore, follow the 1A Highway to just east of the Ghost Reservoir and SR 940. Follow the 940 north for 22.7 km to a gated gravel road on your left about 100 m **beyond** Richards Road. Be sure to close the gate behind you. Follow the rough pot-holed road for 16.6 km to the infamous Big Hill (82 O/6 295832) overlooking the Ghost River Valley and Devil's Gap. Beware of the glacier-sized drift at the top of the Big Hill, a hidden track on the left bypasses it. The Big Hill itself is blown free of snow but is littered with large stones. High clearance is helpful but not absolutely necessary (Subarus, Mazda trucks and like vehicles do just fine). One and a half hours from Calgary; two hours from Canmore.

Facilities
The nearest gas or food is in Cochrane.

Emergency
You're on your own pal! The nearest phone is at the Bar Cee Ranch on SR 940 but there may no one around. The Ghost Forest Service Station, 4.3 km north of the ranch, has a phone. Cellular phones may work from The Ghost. For emergency help, contact Kananaskis Country or Banff warden offices. See page 272.

Maps
82 O/6 Lake Minnewanka
82 O/3 Canmore

Orient Point

As you enter the Ghost River Valley near the Big Hill, you can see two bowls on the East Face of Orient Point. To the south is the immense curtain of ice called *The Big Drip.* In the bowl to the north are four possible lines–*The Joker* (82 O/6 281796) on the left; on its right, *The Hooker* (82 O/6 280796), 20 m right of *The Hooker* an icicle that has never formed and on the far right side the spectacular but rarely formed *Candle Stick Maker* (82 O/6 280797). Usually, only *The Joker* is visible from the top of the Big Hill.

Turn left at the bottom of the Big Hill. Follow the road, cross the rocky stream bed and travel 200 m to an intersection. Take the first obvious left atop a small windblown dike heading south. Follow a good track for just over 1 km until below a cut line that traverses down across a steep hillside. Park here to access all the routes. Follow the cut line until it ends. Move left up through the trees toward the drainage. Stay high on the ridge above until you can easily drop into the creek bottom. Follow the creek and climb past 130 m of WI 2 ice flows to the bowl; 1.5 hours in good snow conditions. A 50-m WI 4 pitch is found at the bottom of the bowl (82 O/6 281797) and can be used to access all three routes. If not, easily turn the pitch to the left up scree and across low-angle slabs.

The Joker ** 50 m III, 2/3

Though it may be thin in places, this is an excellent, easy route which forms every year. Climb 50 m of ice up to 75° Rappel the route.

The Hooker * 200 m III, 5

Begin with 55 m of rambling ice to a sheltered belay on the left of a chandeliered pillar. The next crux pitch hooks its way through a short section of overhanging icicles to a needed rest before you gun 25 m up vertical ice to where it eases off. Another two-and-a-half pitches of rambling ice and snow leads to a pleasant 10 m, 85° step. Rappel the route. Many of the middle pitches can be traversed around on scree ledges.

Candle Stick Maker *** 140 m IV, 5

The falls are tucked into a tight canyon on the right side of the bowl and are not visible until you are directly below. *Candle Stick Maker* is a beautiful line that offers some of the finest technical climbing in The Ghost. From the top of the WI 4 pitch found in the bottom of the bowl, head up 100 m through a narrow slot of snow and ice to a huge cave behind the initial pillar.

Climb the difficult 10-m, freestanding pillar to easier ground. The final pitch offers 40 m of vertical and overhanging ice with numerous mushrooms and caves that provide very entertaining climbing. Rappel the route. Pins are in place on the east wall but may be hard to find.

Photo Opposite:
The Big Drip in its usual shape. Approach
from the top or up the indicated rock route.
Photo Frank Campbell

The Big Drip 120 m V, 5

This is the tantalizing piece of ice that everyone sees when they enter The Ghost (82 O/6 287792). It usually forms only halfway down the cliff face. *The Big Drip* formed once to the ground, but only for a few days before it fell off. Several keen climbers walked up for a look but some sort of sanity prevailed before they started up. One experienced hopeful described it as "the wildest piece of ice I've ever seen!" If it does form again, it will become one of the hardest routes in the Rockies. Nevertheless, the top half always forms up big and fat. Feeling its presence for too long, the first ascentionists rappelled from the top to the bottom of the ice and climbed back to the top.

To get to the top of *The Big Drip*, climb *The Joker* and continue up a gully into an amphitheatre of scree. Climb through a cliff band and begin a rising traverse west towards a ridge that separates the scree amphitheatre from *The Big Drip*, 800-m vertical from the car. Downclimb on the north side of the climb for 200 m to a bolt and two-pin station near the ice (may be covered). Three rappels take you to the bottom of the formed ice.

Hopefully, you can make it up two long pitches of very steep ice and some easy ice that leads to the top. Another WI 3 pitch exists far above for those who haven't got their fill of climbing. Reverse the approach back to *The Joker* to descend. Later, a two-pitch 5.8 rock route was added to the right of the climb to facilitate reaching it from the bottom. In the late winter, the rock gets sun for a few hours in the morning and a full ascent has not been completed. To reach the bottom of the route, hike up the cut line, then traverse left through the trees and continue south past *The Joker* drainage and into the next creek coming from *The Big Drip*.

Malignant Mushroom on Phantom Crag.

South Ghost

Olympus 50 m III, 5

This climb is located on the south side of Orient Point above the South Ghost River Valley (82 O/3 290777). Approach as for *The Joker* but continue along the road past *The Big Drip* and take the next right fork. The ice is visible from the valley at this point. Follow the track to where it climbs out of the valley, hike around a hill on the south side and up scree to the climb. The climb is just visible on a good day from The Ghost access road.

It is a one-pitch testpiece starting with a freestanding pillar of good ice easing off towards the top. Rappel the route or walk off to the right.

Devil's Gap

Devil's Gap is easily the most accessible area of the Ghost. Many of the routes are within easy walking distance of the Big Hill if your vehicle or conditions aren't up to snuff. From the bottom of the Big Hill turn left and follow a faint track across the rocky stream bed to the dike on the west side of the stream bed. Turn left at the inobvious road just past the dike and cross the flats into the trees which takes you to the well-marked Banff National Park boundary. Park here—it is illegal to drive farther. If the road through the trees is drifted over, continue straight (instead of turning left) past the dike and work your way onto the main stream bed, heading west and following faint track and the easiest line to the same parking spot at the park boundary. A short path leads to the first Ghost Lake which in winter is a dry, frozen mud flat.

Orient Point

Wicked Wanda ** II, 4+

Easily visible from the parking area on the north side of Orient Point (82 O/6 275812). Walk several hundred metres west of the parking area, then south through trees and past a short step of ice to the base in 30 to 40 minutes.

A 70-80° pitch leads to a ledge on the left. The next 35-m pitch can be very technical as the high winds in the area often blow the drips about, creating unique caves and overhangs. When in this condition, the route can be demanding on your technique and head space. In fatter years it is straightforward. Rappel the route.

Planter's Valley

Weathering Heights *** 100 m III, 4

This climb is found in Planter's Valley, the valley immediately west of *Wicked Wanda.* From the parking area follow the path toward the first Ghost Lake. Continue into the canyon on the left. The route is the first obvious line about halfway up the canyon on the right wall (82 O/6 266803); one hour.

The route follows two pitches of green and yellow ice that is narrow, varied, and sunny. Rappel the route.

Anorexia Nervosa * 130 m III, 4 R

Across the valley from *Weathering Heights* is a narrow slot with this climb. The route is a little run out and, as the name implies, very thin.

A moderately-hard, thin route with ice up to 85° The rock near the top goes at 5.6. A good day when combined with *Weathering Heights*. Walk off right.

The Peanut Gallery III, 4

Continue up the valley past *Weathering Heights* (82 O/6 271797). Up to four short pitches can be found including some vertical pillars with long snow slopes between. Rappel steps or walk around them on the left.

Hoodoo Hall

This is the next drainage west of Planter's Valley, its name inspired by the interesting hoodoos along the valley floor. Hike across the first Ghost Lake (dry) to the southwest end and angle into the drainage. Follow the frozen creek past the hoodoos until a narrow fork is seen to the left (82 O/6 254800), 1.5 to 2 hours. The following two routes are up this spectacular canyon.

Little Devil 20 m III, 3

Fifteen minutes from the mouth of the canyon, just where it turns south (right), *Little Devil* is found on the left wall pouring out of a frost pocket (82 O/6 258799). It doesn't always form. Thin ice leads to steeper ground near the top. Rappel the route from two pitons in place (be sure to double check them).

Green Angel *** 50 m III, 4

Green Angel is one of the nicer one-pitch routes around to the right of *Little Devil* (82 O/6 259799).

Climb up a short step to a well-protected belay behind a pillar. A full rope length on sustained beautiful green ice leads to the top, bolt belay. Two interesting flows can be explored just above. Rappel the route.

Phantom Crag

Malignant Mushroom ** 55 m II, 5

Situated on the north side below the huge walls of Phantom Crag is this popular, sunny route (82 O/6 269830). It is easily visible from the parking area. Hike up through the trees to the right of the route, 30 to 40 minutes.

Climb one long pitch of mostly vertical and excellent ice. On the first ascent it sported many large mushrooms; however, they don't seem to be an annual occurrence. A bolt belay (often covered) is on a small ledge on the left side. Rappel the route, 50-m ropes are adequate. It is possible to easily walk off to the right.

Sunshine * 45 m II, 3

This climb is a low-angled route found on the same cliff band 500 m west of *Malignant Mushroom* (82 O/6 264827). Follow the riverbed from the parking area and angle up through trees to the base. A thin, dirty, mixed step near the base can be avoided on the left.

Climb up good ice with short steps past several trees frozen into the climb. If using this climb as an approach to *Aquarius*, continue up the slope to the base of the cliff and traverse left. To descend *Sunshine*, rappel from trees.

Aquarius ** 60 m III, 4

Aquarius is located in the narrow drainage west of Phantom Crag above and left of *Sunshine*. Either climb that route and traverse left or from the first Ghost Lake hike up slopes left of the drainage to the base of a large rock wall (Spectre Crag), then traverse right into the gully (82 O/6 261827). The drainage direct occasionally forms low angle thin ice steps, not recommended to descend. The falls is not visible from Ghost Lake and forms every year.

Climb 50 m of interesting ice with good rests to a fixed belay on the left. A short groove leads to a fixed belay on the right and The Recital Hall. Rappel the route.

The Recital Hall

This spectacular bowl is reached only by climbing *Aquarius*. Perfectly oval and barely 100 m in diameter, The Recital Hall is one of the most bizarre areas in the Ghost. It offers two difficult and technical climbs that rarely form.

Fearful Symmetry ** 60 m III, 6 X

Located on the left side of The Recital Hall, *Fearful Symmetry* is a most unique climb. Visible from the first Ghost Lake, this bold lead sports two narrow, freestanding pillars separated by several 1-2 m overhangs formed by the intense winds of the area. This is not a route for the fainthearted.

Easy ground is climbed to a bolt belay behind the pillar. The next pitch is primarily overhanging with a good rest above the overhangs. On the first ascent, the bottom pillar had a 30-cm crack, creating a hanging dagger. Rappel the route. 35 metres of climbing leaves you 7 m out from the base of this incredible column.

Fearful Symmetry in The Recital Hall.
Photo Bruce Hendricks

Rainbow Serpent *** 75 m III, 6

Tucked into the far right corner of the Hall, *Rainbow Serpent* is only visible when directly below it. Is a spectacular aesthetic pillar that is climbed in two pitches. The top pitch always forms, but the bottom pillar is often broken off.

From a belay on the large ledge 15 metres up, the first pitch climbs a cracked, freestanding pillar on lacy chandelier ice to a comfortable belay on the right. The second, harder pitch works its way around overhangs and caves to a narrow pillar and a unique ice arête near the top. Rappel the route.

Rainbow Serpent.
Photo Joseph Josephson

Constellation Valley

The next four climbs lie in the drainage west of *Aquarius*. Hike across the first Ghost Lake (dry) and continue 500 metres to a point about halfway to the second Ghost Lake. Move north into the major drainage. Bypass the first canyon on slopes to the right (the chest-deep pools of water here are not fun to fall into). Some tedious walking leads to another interesting canyon. At the end of this canyon are the first three routes; two hours. One of these routes must be climbed to reach the fourth, *City Lights*. This drainage, particularly *City Lights*, has the highest avalanche potential in the Ghost Area so look out for wind-loaded slabs. Riding a mountain bike to the end of the first Ghost Lake can save up to 45 minutes travel time and can be a saviour on the inevitably wet death march back to the car.

Big Dipper ** 100 m III, 4

This is the obvious two-tiered falls located on the right side of the valley (82 O/6 246831). Despite the long walk to this climb, it is a recommended destination. Climb two excellent pitches, each with steep sections, the first being the crux. Rappel the route or rappel *Little Dipper*.

Little Dipper * 100 m III, 3

The first route visible from lower down in the canyon, *Little Dipper* starts at the same point as *Big Dipper* then goes up left. Both Dipper routes offer excellent climbing in the hard WI 3 to easy WI 4 range. Easy ice and snow is climbed to 35 m of sunny, good ice to 85° Rappel the route.

Joseph Josephson

Grant Statham on Little Dipper.

Mouse Trap 25 m III, 3

When you first see *Big Dipper* to the right, head 100 m up the left-hand fork to the falls that are tucked around at the back (82 O/6 244831). A short step leads to the route.

This route is steep for the first half and can be thin and narrow, making it a challenging climb. Rappel the route from a bolt station on the left.

City Lights ** 40 m IV, 5

The approach to this route is long, but the climbing commands an outstanding position and is recommended if you're not terribly concerned with the number of pitches. Either climb the drainage directly above *Mouse Trap* or from the top of *Little Dipper* climb left up through the trees until you eventually come into the *City Lights/Mouse Trap*

drainage. *City Lights* always forms and is an obvious curtain below a blocky peak, fittingly called Costigan's Boil (82 O/6 241833); 1.5 hours above the Dippers. Expect a very long day with a 700-m elevation gain from the car over many kilometres. The City of Calgary is visible from the climb.

A challenging pitch of mostly vertical, often brittle ice. Considered a classic "Frank 4" as the first ascentionist is infamous for calling everything "Grade 4". Rappel the route.

If avalanche conditions permit, continue straight down the drainage below the route. This gully turns into a tight canyon with several short steps of ice. These steps are easily down climbed but would be dangerous in the dark. Keep going down until at the bolt station atop *Mouse Trap*. Otherwise, head right (remember, climber's right) into the trees before you enter the canyon and traverse to the top of *Little Dipper* and rappel that route.

Second Ghost Lake

Mr. Jive * 45 m III, 3

A wide curtain of good ice in the trees west of Constellation Valley (82 O/6 239816) is visible from the parking area. Walk across the first Ghost Lake and down the stream bed to the second Ghost Lake in 45 minutes. Cross the frozen lake (don't worry; it's less than a metre deep), and beat north up a steep slope to the base.

Mr. Jive starts easily leading to 15 m of 80° ice. A second, similar route called **Dr. Heckle** (45 m III, 3) can be climbed in the trees (82 O/6 241817) to the right and is not visible until you're almost on it.

Rappel the route.

Lacy Gibbet *** 300 m IV, 5

This is an aesthetic line with good ice in a wild position with a southern exposure; well worth the 1.5 to 2 hour approach. Approach as for *Mr. Jive*, but bushwhack to the northwest into the open stream bed. The bottom pitches are visible from here, as well as a large unformed curtain to the right of *Lacy Gibbet*. Continue up the canyon, passing the second tight spot on scree to the right and taking the right fork whenever there is a choice (82 O/6 233823). *Lacy Gibbet* is the left-hand of two possible lines and forms early every year. During the first attempt, while placing a screw on the final crux pitch, the leader had his axe blow out, leaving him dangling by one tool hooked through a half driven ice screw. A gibbet is a type of gallows used for displaying the bodies of executed criminals.

The first 45 m is technical up to 80° and is followed by two and a half rope lengths of rolling terrain to another 45-m pitch of steeper ice (WI 3/4). After topping out on this pitch you'll be presented with an amazing freestanding pillar a short distance up the gully. This is a technical 30-m vertical column. Easy ice leads to the top. Rappel the route.

Fountainhead * 50 m IV, 6

Approach as for *Lacy Gibbet*, but at the final fork 300 m before that route, head left (north) for another tedious hour (82 O/6 226828). Fountainhead and the top half of *Rad Monster* are visible within the first couple hundred metres of entering the left fork; be sure to check for the routes here and save yourself the walk if they're not there. These routes are very remote (they start almost as high as the top of *Lacy Gibbet*) but are

Fountainhead on the left and The Rad Monster on the right in tough conditions.

worth it if this is your kind of climbing. *Fountainhead* is the left-hand of two freestanding pillars. Prepare yourself for one nasty pitch with very technical and strenuous ice. When it is well-formed, it can be like *Pilsner Pillar*; when it is not, be ready for something much, much harder. Several pitches of rolling steps can be climbed above.

The Rad Monster * 50 m IV, 6

This route is on the right-hand pillar, 30 m from *Fountainhead* (82 O/6 226828). This is yet another gnarly route that is usually a little easier than its neighbour. Rappel the routes.

North Ghost

This part of the Ghost is less frequented due to the slightly longer drive and the greater possibility of getting stuck before you arrive at the climbs. The North Ghost includes all the routes along the main Ghost River and *The Sorcerer* (technically in Waiparous Creek but best accessed from the Ghost). Once at the bottom of the Big Hill several options exist to reach the North Ghost. The best way is to stay on the obvious road on the east side of the riverbed. Detours into the riverbed may be needed to avoid drifts. Cross the riverbed (hopefully dry) near a cable crossing and continue along a good road past the Black Rock hiking trail to the canal diversion and a bridge. In years with deep drifts, an adventurous route is to gain the gravel dike on the west side of the river just past the cable crossing and follow this to near the bridge. From the bridge either continue through the trees (drifts) or cut out right and follow a difficult path near the river. These options converge at the end of Sentinel Crag (6.4 km from the top of the Big Hill) on a rocky plain where the river turns west. Park here. If you have a monster truck and are feeling particularly macho, you may try to cross the river to get closer to routes such as *The GBU* and the *Valley of the Birds*. But don't say I didn't warn you; I'm not the only one who has ruined a climbing rope while pulling my car (with 60 cm of water inside) out of the river!

Wully Canyon

Immediately north of the bridge walk or drive south along the west side of the canal below *Wully Wall* (the large cliff on the right, identified by a tree island in the middle of the crag). Turn into the canyon between the south end of *Wully Wall* and the north end of *North Phantom Crag* (82 O/6 262849). Several short WI 2 flows have been explored in this aesthetic canyon.

North Side

The Good, The Bad and The Ugly (The GBU) ** 45 m II, 4-5+

From the parking area, walk ten minutes along the south side of the river to a wide curtain of ice directly above the river on the north side (82 O/6 242866). Be creative to get across the river with dry feet. It is possible to drive right to the base of *The GBU* if you have a big enough vehicle.

Climb any number of lines on good ice, generally harder on the right. The central pillar offers exciting freestanding pillars and overhangs that are rarely climbed. Rappel the route.

In the small alcove just left of *The GBU* is a flow called **The Indifferent** (40 m II, 3). Another 60 m upstream, a short route called **Angel Eyes**, a WI 3 or 4 depending upon ice conditions, falls directly into the river.

Silver Tongue Devil *** 45 m II, 5 R

Directly across the river from the parking area is a steep crag with a prominent cave on the left side (82 O/6 249869). This route is a spectacular sliver pouring from the cave with shadowy overhangs leering above. Cross the river and hike up a steep slope for 30 minutes to the base. Unfortunately it's only been known to form twice and it doesn't last long with its southern exposure. Coincidentally the climb appears devilish with leering eyes and wet tongue, but the name originated when Frank Campbell was called a silver-tongued devil after he sandbagged his partner on the first ascent by rating the route "oh... about Grade 4". A very challenging and superb pitch!

Thin, narrow and unprotectable ice for 20 m leads to a brief rest before the final 25 m of thicker dead vertical ice pouring from the cave. Rappel the route from a bolt belay in cave.

Alan Kane

Frank Campbell on first ascent of Silver Tongued Devil.

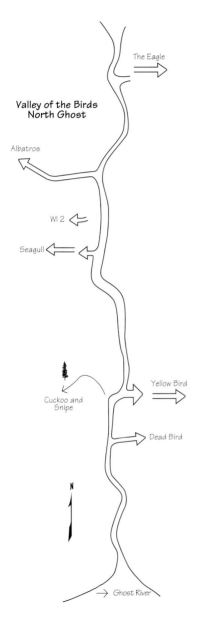

The Eagle

Valley of the Birds
North Ghost

Albatros

WI 2

Seagull

Cuckoo and
Snipe

Yellow Bird

Dead Bird

N

Ghost River

Valley of The Birds

Understandably, the *Valley of The Birds* is one of the more popular areas in the Ghost. It offers fascinating climbing up narrow ice flows reaching a number of short climbs close together that allow you to bag several routes in a day. In the next drainage to the north, five minutes past *The GBU* you will see the *Valley of the Birds* as a mysterious blue flow appearing from a narrow slot (82 O/6 240867). If your vehicle can't get across the river, tight boots and good gaiters are recommended for the river crossing; "run fast and step high!"

Dead Bird * 45 m III, 3

This classic narrow ribbon is not as bad as the name implies. It was once shunned in the search for the hollow glory of 'hard' routes. *Dead Bird* is situated on the east side (right) and does not always form and is the first falls you'll encounter in The Valley (82 O/6 240870).

One long, narrow pitch to a tree belay is a good approach to *Yellow Bird*. Rappel the route or traverse left toward *Yellow Bird*.

Yellow Bird *** 30 m, III, 4

This climb is probably the best route in The Valley. 30 minutes from the entrance to the valley and just past *Dead Bird* is a 20-m wall of ice on the right (east) wall. Climb up this wall and walk to the base of a wet pillar of green/yellowish ice (82 O/6 240873). *Yellow Bird* was previously described as being on the left side of the canyon.

Climb a beautiful, sunny pitch of 80-90° ice. A belay is possible behind the pillar part way up. Rappel the route.

Guy Lacelle on The Eagle.

Seagull ** 30 m III, 4

Located across The Valley (west wall) and 15 minutes beyond *Yellow Bird* (82 O/6 238873), *Seagull* forms early in the year. When well-formed, it is a steal at WI 4. A short step (may be thin or bad ice) leads out of the canyon to scree below the route.

A narrow pillar of excellent wet ice leads to a tree belay. Occasionally it will form up thin and technical. Rappel the route.

Albatros ** 100 m III, 3

Named for the bird that flies alone on high winds, *Albatros* starts in a small cleft on the left wall where the canyon narrows, 200 m upstream from *Seagull* (82 O/6 239874). The right fork is a narrow step leading toward *The Eagle*. This excellent, varied route makes for a fine day when combined with other Valley classics. Rappel from trees.

The Eagle ** 35 m III 5

Originally given a WI 4, this was a very underrated one-pitch route. *The Eagle* rarely gets climbed and has given even the best of climbers a serious work-out. "Harder than Pilsner" claimed one very talented climber. Climb up the creek to the right of *Seagull* and *Albatros*. This spectacular falls is found on the right wall in a small amphitheatre (82 O/6 241875) which collects the a lot of sun and accounts for much of the difficulty of the route by creating rotten ice. High winds also throw the drips about creating overhangs and the distinctive wings that branch off at mid-height. Another Frank Campbell testpiece.

Climb a strenuous freestanding pillar to the overhang below the wings. Be creative to ascend the overhang and onto easier ice above the wings. Occasionally it will form as a more 'normal', yet still difficult, freestanding pillar. Rappel the route.

Cuckoo Falls 40 m III, 2

This route is one of two short climbs, found above The Valley to the east (82 O/6 237870). It is visible from the Ghost River and has three possible approaches. You can climb directly from the Ghost River through steep trees. Another way is to head up The Valley and, just before the canyon narrows between *Dead Bird* and *Yellow Bird*, climb a gully to the left and up a steep hill. Contour left for 500 m to the falls on the cliff face above. The best approach is to climb *Albatros*, then traverse left around the ridge and slightly down to the routes. *Cuckoo Falls* is the left-hand route and is a low-angle pitch with several steep steps. Rappel from trees.

Snipe Falls 10 m III, 3

The right-hand route which forms every year as a short pillar of steep ice. Rappel the route with old bolt *in situ*.

North Ghost - North Side

The Unforgiven * 40 m III, 3

Continue west past *Valley of the Birds* for 800 m (20 minutes) to where spectacular bedding planes rise steeply above the north side of the river (location of the famous rock route, *Alberta Jam*). This seep lies on the right side of these cliffs (82 O/6 232868). The crux is getting up the 150 m of loose scree to the base (not to mention the river crossing).

This climb is best done in the early season before Chinooks turn it to mush. Rappel the route.

Dirty Harry 60 m III, 4

This is a remote, difficult climb up the large drainage to the north and just west of *The Unforgiven*. The fall is on the east cliff face before the creek forks (82 O/6 227882) and doesn't always form; 2.5 hours.

20 m of moderate ice leads to a pillar followed by an eight-metre column of overhanging mushrooms leading to easier ice. Rappel the last two pitches, then walk off left.

North Ghost -South Side

This House of Sky *** 500 m? III, 3

From the parking at Sentinel Crag, walk west following roads in the trees on the south side of the river (no river crossing, yeah!). Pass the first major drainage and hike up the second smaller drainage to the south, 1 km past the *Valley of the Birds* (*The Unforgiven* is across the river to the north). *This House of Sky* starts 300 m up the drainage in a tight canyon branching right (west) (82 O/6 231863).

How does that classic rock and roll song go? "I can see for miles and miles...". Well here, you can climb for miles and miles. It's hard to think of a realistic length for this route. Just enter the canyon and continue upwards until it's obvious you can't go any further. I won't say any more about this classic waterfall. Go explore it for yourself. Rappel and down climb route, one 50-m rope adequate.

Photo Opposite:
"Who needs hard routes? All you need are short routes with good gear, interspersed with moments of sheer terror." Barry Blanchard on Burning in Water, Drowning by Flame.

Phantom Falls * 40 m III, 4 R

A testpiece that deserves more attention; unfortunately, it seems to rarely form, depending upon your definition of 'being formed'. The first ascent found challenging mixed climbing. From the branch of *This House of Sky* continue up the left (south) fork 400 m to a large impassable rock wall and *Phantom Falls* (82 O/6 231859). The climb is visible from the main valley near the Ghost River, an easy walk from the car. Check it out; if it's not 'formed', easily retreat back to the *Valley of the Birds* or head up *This House of Sky*.

40 m of thin, narrow and intermittent ice up to 90° Rock/mixed climbing may be required. Rappel the route.

Burning in Water, Drowning by Flame * 30 m III, AO 6 X

On the south side of the river, just past *Phantom Falls*, is an impressive overhanging rockwall. On the lower reaches of this cliff, about 1 km beyond *Phantom Falls* lie two routes (82 O/6 220864); 40 minutes from the car. Walk along the river until the routes are visible. Hike up a steep slope to reach them (several river crossings may be required; a log bridge may be near the mouth of *Phantom Falls*). *Burning, Drowning* is the left-hand route.

Climb a 10-m smear underneath a 2 m overhang. The first ascentionists tied off a frozen chock stone and used it lean out and snag a tool into a free-hanging dagger. Cut loose and mantle onto the front of the icicle then continue up steep ice to the top. The key on the first ascent was a large mushroom that they were able to knee-hook up by their heads and salvage their flaming forearms. Wild! Rappel the route from tree.

The Sliver *** 40 m III, 6 R

A good early season route that often forms by early October, *The Sliver* is located 100 m right of *Burning, Drowning* and easily recognized by its slender shape. It is a choice route with varied and sustained technical climbing. A variety of Bugaboos to fat Lost Arrows and ice screws are needed for protection. The longer days and spells of warm weather that are common by mid-season, will destroy what little ice is needed for this route.

No more than one metre wide, the crux of this partially freestanding pillar is 30 m long. Rock moves, heel-hooks, lie-backing off icicles, and full body hugs are among the creative techniques used on this outstanding testpiece. Rappel the route or rappel from trees to the right or walk off 300 m right.

Johnson Creek

The famous route, *The Sorcerer*, lies north of the main Ghost valley in Johnson Creek but is best approached from the North Ghost. From the parking area near Sentinel Crag, cross the river north (sometimes a log bridge) to a small meadow. Head northeast on a narrow road along a steep hill between Black Rock Mountain and a large rock wall (Bastion Wall) on the left. Follow this for 45 to 60 minutes to the first of two Johnson Lakes. At the north end of the first lake head left up an open slope into the trees and continue up and right and over the small ridge into the creek bed draining *The Sorcerer* (82 O/6 243893); 1.5 to 2 hours. This approach is also used to reach the route *Hydrophobia*, see under Waiparous Creek.

The Sorcerer *** 185 m IV, 5

This stunning route is set in the back of steep amphitheatre with Dolomite-like walls on all sides. If you are to do just one route in the Ghost River area *The Sorcerer* would be it.

Climb a shield of ice to a sloping ledge. Continue up a short 85° pillar to where the climb narrows (two bolts). Snow and easy ice lead to the upper column which is climbed in two full pitches. The column starts on near-vertical ice, easier on the right, leading to a large cave. The final pitch makes an outrageous traverse left then up sustained technical ground. Most parties ignore the short pitch and cornice to the top. Rappel the route. Do not attempt to descend any nearby gullies.

Nearing the top on the first ascent of The Sliver.
Photo Patrick Morrow

Photo opposite: The Sorcerer.

Ghost River Area 85

Black Rock Mountain

A beautiful peak of large complex cliff bands poised on the eastern edge of the North Ghost River, Black Rock Mountain is easily visible as you drive north from the Big Hill. *Black Rock Falls* is the obvious pillar high in the south-facing cirque. Drive as for the North Ghost but turn right at the Black Rock hiking trail sign, 2.5 km past the Big Hill. Drive a short distance and park near the river. The approach for the next four climbs starts here. Find a sign and a gate on the opposite bank of the river which indicates the start of the trail and walk into the trees to an information board. Turn right into the stream and follow it 1.5 to 2 hours up to an obscured fork in the stream underneath some impressive gold and black rock walls. There are several one-pitch routes that are fun and in a spectacular setting, a place worthy of The Ghost.

Black Rock Falls ** 35 m III, 4+

Obvious from the Ghost River, this climb is not as big as it looks from the valley floor. Worthwhile and in a great location *Black Rock Falls* should be climbed before the sun and Chinooks destroy the ice. Follow the stream bed from the information board and stay left up the most obvious drainage and climb snow and scree to the base of the falls (82 O/6 278880).

Climb one pitch of technical, lacy ice. Rappel the route.

Photo opposite:
Steep and scenic climbing on Black Rock Falls.

Bloody Mary 20 m III, 4

Approach as for *Black Rock Falls* to the point where the creek divides. Follow the creek right 200 m to an impassable rock wall. Climb scree to the right and up past an unique gendarme into an obvious gap above, then contour back into the creek bed and follow it until *Bloody Mary* emerges from a deep cleft between impressive walls (82 O/6 282878).

A 15-m, freestanding pillar which doesn't always form. Rappel the route (one bolt in place).

Sunset Falls ** 70 m III, 3

Approach as for *Bloody Mary* but 300 m to the right in a shallow gully (82 O/6 283878). *Sunset Falls* forms every year and is easily combined with *Black Rock Falls* for a good long day.

Climb 20 m of easy ground to a snow ledge (one bolt). Continue for one pitch of undulating ice up to 80°. Above is a pretty miniature hanging valley with meadows and good lunch spots atop rock promontories. Here you have a good chance of seeing mountain sheep. Rappel the route. An orange bolt and piton are *in situ* at the lip of the climb on the left.

The Ribbon 50 m III, 2

Climb *Bloody Mary* and follow the drainage to the foot of the climb (82 O/6 2811881). Or traverse left across the drainage from the top of *Sunset Falls*.

This could be called The Curtain, as that is how it sometimes forms. A little more interesting are several smears to the right which are occasionally mixed, up to 5.4 rock. Rappel the route.

Accessing Waiparous Creek makes getting to the Ghost River seem easy. But spectacular limestone walls and high quality ice make it worth a journey. Choose a spell of nice Chinook weather and make a weekend of it. In three days you can climb every route in the area.

Getting There

Access requires a 4 x 4 vehicle or an ATV. Follow SR 940 past the Bar Cee Ranch into the forestry reserve. 16 km north of Bar Cee Ranch, turn west onto a dirt road signed Waiparous Valley Road. Drive 3 km past Camp Mockingbird to a junction. Turn left onto a rougher road which is passable for another 4 km. At the foot of a deeply-trenched hill, turn left into a parking area. There are several stream crossings which are generally easier after the creek has frozen over. ATV trails lead up Waiparous Creek almost as far as the route *Indian Scalp*, 11-12 km distant. For the adventurous, cut lines, the odd access road, and open meadows can be followed to within an hour of the other routes.

Facilities

Ha-Ha! You must be dreaming. The Ghost Forest Service Station is located 4.3 km north of Bar Cee Ranch and about 7 km south of Waiparous Creek. Staffing is very limited in winter but there is a pay phone.

Emergency

If and when you reach a phone, call Kananaskis Country Emergency Services for assistance. See page 272.

Map

82 O/6 Lake Minnewanka

South Fork Johnson Creek

Both *The Sorcerer* and *Hydrophobia* are located in the South Fork of Johnson Creek near the Johnson Lakes. The top of *The Sorcerer*, *Hydrophobia*, and the main Johnson Creek drainage are visible from SR 940 from a spectacular viewpoint 18 km north of the Bar Cee Ranch. *The Sorcerer* is best approached from The Ghost River and is described in that section.

Hydrophobia *** 150 m V, 5+

This spectacular and continuous waterfall is plastered at the back of a cirque amongst massive rock walls. It would be a widely sought-after and often-photographed climb if it were closer to the road. As the first attempt party neared the top, they were hit by a massive water release lasting 30 minutes. Soaked to the skin and with frozen gear, they managed to retreat, leaving most of their gear in place. Staggering back through the bush, they reached their car after dark and very wet and hypothermic. They returned and completed the route the next weekend. Such is climbing in The Ghost and Waiparous. If you have the proper vehicle the best approach is up Waiparous Creek. However, few of us have a 'monster truck' so most parties approach the climb from The Ghost River by hiking past *The Sorcerer*. Follow the trail as for *The Sorcerer* but continue on the trail to the second Johnson Lake where the trail makes a sharp bend to the east. Break left and hike across the lake. Then bushwhack northwest into the next drainage north of *The Sorcerer*. Take a compass, especially if there is no snow to leave tracks. *Hydrophobia* is obvious; allow three hours (82 O/6 232902).

Climb a 25-m apron to a cave belay behind the first pitch. The pillar out of the cave is the crux and the difficulty is dictated by how long the chandelier and technical ice lasts, most often 10 to 15-m worth. As described after the first solo ascent in 1992, "The first half of the route consists of short overhanging steps separated by long stretches of vertical. The upper half goes much better with more rests and only marginal periods of desperation". The ice is sustained WI 5 but only gets sweeter and sweeter the higher you go, finishing with a deceptively steep 'sting in the tail'. Rappel the route.

If you have time, it is highly recommended to continue up scree to the ridge line where the views of Devil's Head and the upper Ghost River are unbeatable. Once on the ridge, traverse southeast and over a small summit. From here either go east and rappel off *The Sorcerer* or continue due south and walk down the *Valley of The Birds*.

*Hydrophobia in
WI 6 shape*

Johnson Creek

The following three climbs are in the main Johnson Creek drainage just north of *Hydrophobia*. *Caroline Falls* can be seen from the mouth of the *Hydrophobia* cirque but all routes are best approached via Waiparous Creek, unless you like long bushwhacks.

Venus * 50 m III, 3

A nice, easy climb located 500 m from the valley entrance in the main drainage on the south side (82 O/6 219907), directly across from *Caroline Falls*. Several short steps of WI 2 followed by a large ice platform and then 25 m of WI 3. Rappel the route.

Caroline Falls ** 50 m III, 4

The first main waterfall on the north side of the valley (82 O/6 218912), *Caroline Falls* is a classic pitch on excellent ice. Rappel the route.

Marion Falls *** 100 m III, 5

This climb is found in the next break past *Caroline Falls* on the north side of the valley (82 O/6 211912). Climb easy ice to a beautiful, technical pillar. Overhanging mushrooms and lacy ice makes for great climbing and leads into a more featureless pillar of good ice. Belay is possible in a cave on the right above the mushrooms. Rappel the route.

Waiparous Creek

One valley north of Johnson Creek is a south fork of Waiparous Creek containing two excellent climbs, both on the north side.

Kemosabe ** 100 m III, 4

This route is located in a tight cleft immediately left of a huge rock wall that forms the end of a ridge dropping into the valley (82 O/6 218934). *Kemosabe*, the first route in the drainage, is obvious from the creek bed. 45 m of WI 3 with some steep sections leads to a long second pitch that is sustained 85-90° ice to the top. Rappel the route.

The Ice Funnel *** 150 m III, 4

Ten minutes past *Kemosabe* in the next gully (82 O/6 217930) is an aesthetic, varied climb snaking up an impressive rockwall. Start with a short vertical pillar to an undulating narrow section. A steeper section leads to the top. Rappel the route. It is recommended to traverse right on scree ledges to the top of *Kemosabe* and rappel, then climb that route.

The Indian Scalp 50 m IV, 3

This is a remote climb in the main Waiparous Creek drainage even farther north of *Kemosabe*. *Indian Scalp* is located on the right (north side) in the second major tributary after passing an impressive 300 metre-high prow of rock on the right (82 O/6 185963). More ice can likely be found further up the valley but you're going to pay for it if you want it.

A short steep pillar followed by undulating ice. Rappel the route.

to Nordegg

940

Clearwater River

James River

to Sundre

Just Enough

Sweet Dream

Ya-Ha Tinda
Ranch

Dream On

Ya-Ha Falls

P

Elk Droppings

Fjord Falls

Forget-Me-Not Falls

Trickle Falls

Last But Not Least

Ivory Falls

Warden
Hut

Eanee,Meanee
Minee,Moe

Kinda Nice

Red Deer River

Scotch On The Rocks

Lodge
(closed in winter)

940

to Cochrane

THE DRY RANGES

The Dry Ranges include all routes from Waiparous Creek north to the Saskatchewan River and the David Thompson Highway. Climbing in this area offers a typical front range experience–high winds, relatively little snow (but large drifts), and warmer temperatures. Most of the climbs are accessed off the Secondary Road 940 and the Ya-Ha-Tinda Ranch Road in the vicinity of the Red Deer River. They have relatively quick approaches, provided you find the right parking spot.

The total number of routes in the area is rising every year and most seem to form regularly, making it a close destination for climbers in the Red Deer/Sundre area. There are many unexplored river valleys which will undoubtedly yield some ice climbs if and when someone makes the journey. Beware; access to some valleys is strictly limited. Check with the Banff warden office. Much of the front range land on the eastern slopes of Banff Park lies in Forest Land Use (FLU) Zones. Administered by the Alberta Forest Service, FLU Zones prohibit the use of any vehicles including snowmobiles and ATVs. Only foot, ski, horse, and mountain bike travel is allowed in these zones.

Getting There

From Calgary drive west on Highway 1A past Cochrane. 13. 4 km past the Highway 22 junction, turn north onto SR 940 (Forestry Trunk Road) and continue 82 km to the Red Deer River. This route is faster and about half the distance of taking Highway 22 from Cochrane to Sundre. If coming from north of the Bow Valley, drive 10 km on SR 584 west from Sundre, then turn south on a secondary road (Coalcamp sign) which leads 48 km to SR 940. Turn left for 3 km to the Ya-Ha-Tinda Road which heads west from a junction 100 m north of the bridge over the Red Deer River. The road is marked with an "Alpine Outfitting" sign. In warm weather, it can have sections of heavy mud with deep ruts.

Facilities

The best place to obtain information on the surrounding area and location of FLU Zones is at the Alberta Forest Service District Office located on Main Street, in Sundre. The office is open from 8:15 am to 4:30 pm, Monday to Friday and has maps for sale of the surrounding area. The nearest gas and food is in Sundre. Primitive camping sites are abundant.

Emergency

The Mountain Aire Lodge on the south side of the Red Deer River is closed most of the winter but there is a pay phone outside the lodge. The best bet for emergency rescue assistance is from the nearest RCMP detachment in either Nordegg or Sundre. The ranchhands at the Ya-Ha-Tinda Ranch are very informative and helpful and would likely be available to assist in an emergency. The Burnt Timber Shell Field Office located 2 km east of SR 940 also has an emergency phone, open 8:00 am to 5:00 pm weekdays. See page 272.

Maps

82 O/11 Burnt Timber Creek
82 O/12 Barrier Mountain
82 O/13 Forbidden Creek

Ya-Ha-Tinda Ranch Road

The following climbs are all located west of SR 940 somewhere along the road leading to the Ya-Ha-Tinda Ranch.

Kinda-Nice 55 m III, 4

Drive west toward Ya-Ha-Tinda Ranch 7 km and park in an obvious clearing on the south side of the road near a bend in the river. *Kinda-Nice* can be seen as the first major route to the southwest (82 O/11 107224). Proceed across the Red Deer River (hip waders or running shoes would be helpful). Bushwhack in a direct line for 45 to 60 minutes.

Climb one pitch up undulating ice to the base of the upper pillar. Two lines offer themselves, a small pillar on the left side broken by a snow ledge or a sustained curtain to the right. Rappel the route or walk off to the right.

Eanee, Meanee, Minee, Moe *
20-45 m III, 2-4

Drive 12 km west on the Ya-Ha-Tinda Road. The climb or rather four distinct flows 50 m apart, is visible to the south (there is an old fire burn some 400 m above the climb). A knee-deep crossing of the Red Deer River is required to reach these climbs (hip waders or running shoes recommended). Once across the river, bushwhack for about an hour to the route.

The left-hand route (*Eanee)* is the longest but the middle two are the hardest (*Meanee* and *Minee*). These three routes are very close together, while the fourth (*Moe*) is 50 m to the right. All offer great ice with excellent views. Rappel from trees.

Forget-Me-Not Falls 20 m II, 2

Drive 14 km west along the Ya-Ha-Tinda Road and park in a small pull-out on the north side of the road and west side of Boulder Creek. Hike north up the drainage. Enter the canyon and solo up several steps. Then take the left-hand fork to the base of the climb, 30 minutes from the car.

This is an easy climb of good ice in a very scenic canyon. Rappel from tree.

Last But Not Least 25 m III, 4

This climb is described as "a steep climb on go home ice". Presumably, this means good, plastic ice. Drive 17 km west along the Ya-Ha-Tinda Road. The climb should be visible on the left (south) high up on the cliffs of the facing mountain, locally known as Goat Mountain. The base is reached in about 45 minutes from the road. This is another route that requires a fording of the Red Deer River.

There is a steep pitch ending in a small cave. Rappel the route.

James Pass

The following three routes are found in the Eagle Lake/James Pass vicinity. Drive westbound along the Ya-Ha-Tinda Ranch Road for exactly 20 km from SR 940 and turn north at the Frontier Outfitter sign. Drive another 250 m to the Eagle Lake Trailhead parking lot.

Dream On ** 90 m III, 4

Walk east along the road for 2.5 km and around Eagle Lake for another kilometre to a road which is followed for 1.5 km to the north side of James Pass. *Dream On* is easily visible to your left. Although the approach is 5 km, there is only 100 m of elevation gain.

The climb starts with a pitch of easy ice leading to ledge followed then a nice long pitch of steepening ice to a tree belay (rockfall hazard from cliffs above). Rappel and downclimb the route.

Sweet Dream * 50 m III, 3

Sweet Dream is a series of seepages with a variety of different lines and steepness found 50 m right of *Dream On* and makes an excellent combo with that route. Rappel from a large tree.

Just Enough 50 m III, 3

Approach as for *Dream On*, but walk only about two-thirds the way around Eagle Lake on the south shore. Once the climb is visible, about 250 m above the lake to the north, cross the lake and bushwhack up to the route.

A number of smears and seeps present themselves and get lots of sun. An early season ascent is recommended before they turn to mush. Rappel the route (beware of loose scree atop the climbs).

Ya-Ha-Tinda Ranch

The next six routes are all found west of the Ya-Ha-Tinda Ranch and are accessed by parking at the pole gate at the entrance to the Ranch 24 km west of SR 940. The area west of the ranch is now a FLU Zone so you cannot drive past the ranch buildings, which are about 1.5 km from the Banff National Park boundary.

Fjord Falls * 45 m III, 3

From the parking lot a large grassy meadow is visible on the south side of the river about 4 km to the west. To get to *Fjord Falls* you must reach this meadow. Head down the road to where it starts to elevate. Head south across the Red Deer River (30-60 cm deep) and continue west until you gain access to the meadow. Cross the meadow in a southwesterly direction until the first creek bed and follow the east side of the creek to a well-cut trail. Follow this for 1 km to the climb (82 O/12 958294). Below a set of hitching rails, a path will take you to the base; two to three hours. **Note:** the official name of this drainage is Hidden Creek and Hidden Falls. Signs bearing these names have been erected by the Forestry Service.

In a narrow, almost-enclosed canyon is 45 m of 65-80° ice. Rappel from a tree or walk off back to trail.

Ya-Ha Falls ** 40 m III, 4

There are two one-pitch pillars in the southeast-facing cirque on Wapiti Mountain between the Ya-Ha-Tinda Ranch and the park boundary. Walk or bike west to a bridge over the stream coming from the cirque. Follow the stream north, taking the first branch to the left. Climb easy rock on the left side to the bottom of the falls (82 O/12 885296).

There is good climbing on each pillar with the left-hand being the most difficult. Rappel or walk off.

Banff National Park

Ivory Falls * 140 m III, 5

From the ranch, continue west on the road to the Banff Park boundary. *Ivory Falls* is found about another kilometre into the park in the first drainage to the right and can be seen from the road (82 O/12 885276).

Two excellent pitches start the climb. The first is 50 m of WI 3 with a tree belay. Pitch two is a sustained curtain for 45 m on 85° ice. The final, crux pitch is a long walk up the gully (up to an hour) and is a steep 45-m pillar of good ice. Rappel the route.

Trickle Falls 80 m III, 3

This route is found in the next gully west of *Ivory Falls*. Walk or ride 1 km past that route. *Trickle Falls* is visible from the road in the smaller drainage to the north (82 O/12 879271). It can been combined with *Ya-Ha* and/or *Ivory Falls* for a good day.

Climb 50 m of undulating ice followed by a 30-m pitch with some steep sections. Rappel the route.

Elk Droppings 70 m of ice III, 3

Four kilometres west of the park boundary is a large drainage coming out of the north (Tyrrell Creek). *Elk Droppings* is located up a pretty canyon that branches east near the mouth of Tyrrell Creek. The first pitch can be seen from the road.

Enter the canyon on a pitch of excellent ice and then walk another 1.5 km upstream to a 25-m pillar of steeper ice. Rappel and downclimb route.

Scotch on the Rocks ** 90 m III, 4

This is a pretty route that is visible from the warden cabin about 10 km west of the park boundary. The route faces north so it will be good early and late into the season. If the road is clear of snow it makes a worthwhile trip by combining ice climbing with mountain biking. Just before the warden cabin, cross the Red Deer River and continue past the turn-off to the cabin to a gully on the northwest side of Mt. White. A short scramble leads up to the base.

Two moderate and enjoyable pitches lead to a large cave behind the upper curtain. Make a typically hard move out of the cave and proceed up steep ice to the top.

Scramble up from the belay until it is possible to access slopes to the right on which you walk off.

Martin Creek Falls 100 m V, 4

This remote waterfall is buried deep in the Clearwater River drainage. The first ascent team approached the route via the Icefields Parkway by skiing up Mosquito Creek and over Quartzite Col to Clearwater Pass. They followed the Clearwater River east to Martin Lake and skied west up Martin Creek and the lake at the end of the valley, a five-day trip. The route is found above the lake on the classic headwall below a hanging valley. Due to the committing nature and avalanche hazard on this ski tour, few people make the journey. I suggest that you approach from the east via the wide valley of the Clearwater River. Make it a 'mini-expedition' and look for new routes all the way up the Clearwater. Enquire in Sundre about access to the park boundary from the east. It is about 15 km from the boundary to Martin Lake and another 8 to 10 km to Martin Creek Falls. The views of the North Face of Mt. Willingdon (3373 m) are awesome.

The first 25 m of the climb ends at the entrance to a deep canyon. Walk to the head of the canyon to 70 m of steep and tricky climbing. The climb is topped by a cornice. Rappel the route from below the cornice.

Crack of Doom 75 m IV, 4

This route is accessed from SR 940 near the town of Nordegg. You can drive up SR 940 from the Red Deer River but it is 174 km of rough unmaintained road. The best access is from Highway 11 (David Thompson Highway). Just west of Nordegg turn south onto SR 940 and drive 9 km to the Saskatchewan River Bridge. Immediately south of the bridge is a parking area. Follow the Almer Trail west until the trail meets a wide beaver dam. Cross the dam to the north and pick up a trail leading west through a narrow grove of trees. Follow the trail west through a series of meadows until you reach the first creek bed. Follow the creek bed up 2 km to the climb, a total of 15 km from the bridge. Were these guys dedicated or what!

A pretty pillar located in a large amphitheatre with three or four other potential climbs ranging from WI 3-5. *Crack of Doom* takes the main falls up a fan of ice to an upper pillar which sported a 30 cm crack on the first ascent. Walk off either left or right.

THE BOW VALLEY

Being close to population centres and with a selection of over 70 routes, the Bow Valley is the core of waterfall ice climbing in the Rockies. It includes routes along the Trans-Canada (#1) and 1A Highways from the mountain front near Mt. Yamnuska to Lake Louise. A few additional routes west of Lake Louise are also included. The Bow Valley is divided into three sections–Canmore Corridor, Banff Region, and the Lake Louise Group. As it traverses such a large area, the Bow Valley has a wide variety of routes and prevailing conditions. Climbs on the eastern slopes tend to have less snow and are affected by Chinooks. The Lake Louise Group generally has more snow and winter conditions prevail throughout the season.

Getting There

Several highways converge on the Bow Valley. The Trans-Canada Highway (#1) passes through the south side of the valley from Calgary to Canmore (110 km), past Banff (20 km from Canmore) and continues 50 km to Lake Louise and beyond. A secondary road, the 1A Highway, parallels much of the Trans-Canada Highway on the north side of the valley. From the west, Highway 93 south from Radium, BC enters the Bow Valley at Castle Junction, 28 km northwest of Banff. The Icefields Parkway (Highway 93 North) from Jasper, joins the Trans-Canada Highway 2 km north of Lake Louise.

Facilities

The major Bow Valley communities of Canmore, Banff and Lake Louise have a selection of hotels, motels, bed and breakfasts, pubs and shops to suit any pocket book. In Canmore, a popular hang for climbers is at the Alpine Club of Canada Clubhouse. Banff, Castle Junction, and Lake Louise all have international hostels with electricity and running water. See the Travel Information section, page 14. As of 1994, the only 24-hour gas stations in the area are at Dead Man's Flats just east of Canmore, and in Banff. In Canmore or Lake Louise service is available from 7 am to 10 pm. Plan accordingly.

Emergency

When climbing east of the Banff Park gates (Canmore Corridor) emergency personnel can be reached through Kananaskis Country Emergency Services. Banff and Lake Louise areas fall under the respective Park Warden Service. See page 272.

Canmore Corridor

All routes in Old Fort Creek, Goat Mountain, Jura Creek, and Grotto Mountain are accessed from the 1A Highway east of Canmore. Lac Des Arcs and the Three Sisters areas are accessed via the Trans-Canada Highway. The east end of Rundle is presently reached from Canmore. As there are a variety of moderate routes with relatively little avalanche danger, expect to see lots of people tramping about, especially on weekends. Frequent Chinooks often make the climbing enjoyable. But, beware of increasing avalanche hazards and falling ice during warm weather. See map, page 99.

Map
82 O/3 Canmore

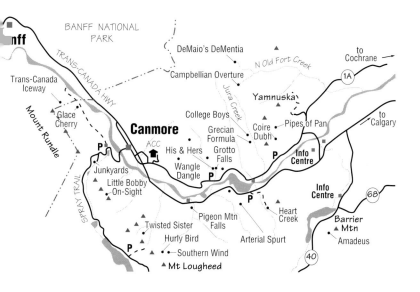

Old Fort Creek

The next three routes, located in a remote drainage north of the CMC Valley, offer a great escape from the crowds on other Bow Valley standards. Excellent camping spots abound.

From the 1A Highway, 2.2 km east of the Seebe exit (Highway 1X) turn north into the Yamnuska parking lot (no sign) and park near the quarry gate. From the top of the quarry, follow the obvious trail over the ridge to the right (east) of Yamnuska and into CMC Valley. Continue north up the other side of the valley and traverse around through trees on an obvious flat bench just below the crags. Continue north and then drop down into the flat cobblestone-strewn valley of the North Fork of Old Fort Creek.

DeMaio's DeMentia ** 200 m IV, 3

DeMaio's DeMentia can be seen from the 1A Highway while travelling west toward the mountains. Look two valleys north of Yamnuska and quite high in the back of a bowl for a narrow line snaking up the steepest part. It may be difficult to see after a snowfall. At the head of the valley are two forks; this route is easily seen in the right-hand one (82 O/3 276705). Allow five hours from the car.

Some very steep pillars can be found at the bottom of the bowl but are turned easily on the right. Continue up 200 m of easy mixed climbing to the base of the route. Three pitches of excellent ice leads to a curtain of 85° ice. This is a superb line with an unfortunate approach. Rappel and downclimb the route.

Campbellian Overture 180 m IV, 2

Approach as for *DeMaio's DeMentia*; this line is in the back of the valley at the head of the left-hand fork (82 O/3 269693). It is dedicated to Frank Campbell for his constant exploration of the front ranges year-round.

Similar to *DeMaio's DeMentia* but the 'hard' pitch is first, followed by cruiser slab ice to the top.

Descend the route. It is possible to walk off the first pitch to the right. There is a soaking wet freestanding pillar down and left of the route called **Tristan's Pillar**, 10 m III, 4.

Goat Mountain

Goat Mountain is the long and obvious peak left of Yamnuska. Three gullies split the southeast face into several distinct, large (200-500 m) rock slabs.

The two right-hand of these gullies contain routes. Park at a gated road on the north side of the 1A Highway, 1.7 km east of the Continental Lime Plant. This road accesses an old dump. Do not drive up the road even if the gate is open; you will likely get towed or have the gate closed behind you. There is plenty of room to park off the 1A.

Coire Dubh 250 m II, 3

Welcome to a long climb with little real climbing. *Coire Dubh* is recommended for beginners who want to get a feel for moving across lots of terrain. Hike past the dump and through light trees, staying parallel with Goat Mountain to your left. Continue past the first drainage to the second, larger drainage with an obvious ice flow (82 O/3 307616); one hour of nice walking.

The first flow is usually soaking wet and leads to a narrow gully of snow and low-angle ice. Turn the corner and climb a final pitch of good ice. A two-bolt belay is on a large block(s) near the right side. Rappel and downclimb route.

Coire Dubh Intégrale *** 550 m III, 5.7 WI 3

This mini-alpine route gives a great taste of mixed climbing for intermediate and experienced climbers alike. The route climbs the ice of *Coire Dubh* and continues up rock and mixed ground to the ridge line (very scenic). Be prepared for extreme winds on the ridge. This is one of the few winter mixed routes that is also climbed in the summer and is rated 5.4. But in winter, a 5.4 climber would find it pretty 'out there'. The rock is above average and the climbing is intricate with good gear. The rock was formed from a large coral reef, thus there are a large number of pockets and tri-cams work well to protect the many 'bidoigts'. The climbing can be desperate after a snowfall so wait for the winds to blow the rock clean.

Climb *Coire Dubh* into an amphitheatre where the ice ends. Above, a number of variations have been done. Pick whatever looks most enticing and enjoy (see topo). **To descend**, continue easily along the ridge to the left. Climb over the top of Loder Peak then down the main southwest ridge for another two hours to the road. Don't try and cut down off the ridge early; it's much quicker to follow it directly to the road.

Pipes of Pan * 300 m V, 5

In the large gully right of *Coire Dubh* and left of a large rock prow called Goat Buttress lies *Pipes of Pan*. The last pitch is visible from the Trans-Canada Highway, but doesn't always form. To see the final crux pillar, look on the steep cliff due left of the top of Goat Buttress and

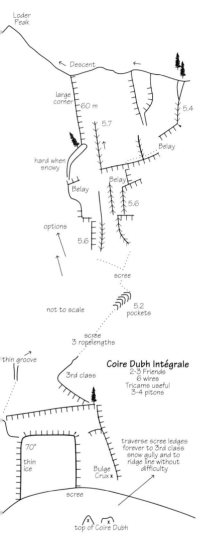

right of the main snow gully going up to the ridge. Approach past *Coire Dubh* and a large rock slab to the gully; two hours (82 O/3 307635).

Up to six pitches can be found culminating in a difficult WI 5 pillar very high up the mountain. Rappel from ice and pitons. The adventurous may continue to the ridge and follow an exposed traverse left to the road or right toward Yamnuska, either of which would make for a long day out.

Jura Creek

Jura Creek is a deep valley west of Goat Mountain. Park on the 1A Highway across from the Continental Lime Plant, 2 km northeast of Exshaw. Walk easily through trees and into the canyon. A number of other small smears, once climbed in a failed quest for bigger things, are located three to four hours up the creek.

Grecian Formula 100 m III, 3 R

Grecian Formula rarely forms, but offers some fun mixed climbing when it does. It is located one hour up Jura Creek on the left just past a narrow section (82 O/3 615287). Small to medium Friends are useful. Rappel the route.

The College Boys * 40 m III, 4+

Approach up Jura Creek for about two hours until you see an obvious pillar to the left. Hike another 45 minutes up to the base (82 O/3 635279). The pillar is visible from the top of *Coire Dubh Intégrale*. It seems to form every year.

Climb a one-pitch, near-vertical pillar. The first ascent on Boxing Day required several aid moves due to a belly full of turkey. Rappel the route.

Grotto Mountain

The following eight routes all lie somewhere on Grotto Mountain. All but two
are in Grotto Canyon, a popular summer hiking and rock climbing venue.

One Thin Line 45 m III, 3 R

This rarely-climbed route in Steve's
Canyon is in a narrow and steeply sided
drainage east of Grotto Canyon. It is not
known if the route forms regularly. Park
at Grotto Mountain near Grotto Pond,
10.8 km east of the Trans-Canada overpass or 3.5 km west of Exshaw. Follow
the summer trail west to the first creek
bed and then take the creek upstream
past a 5 to 10-m step of ice and then
another 20 minutes upstream to a steep
slab of thin ice. Rappel the route.

Wangle Dangle 40 m III, 5.7 WI 4

On the rock band way above the west
end of the Burnco strip mine on the
South Face of Grotto Mountain is wide
section of green icicles which are easily
seen from the Trans-Canada or 1A Highway. Park at a small turn-off on the
north side of 1A Highway, 2.6 km east of
the Trans-Canada overpass. March
through steep trees and scree past the
mining scar towards the route; approximately 2.5 hours (82 O/3 207595). Be
wary of trespassing on Burnco property—you could be prosecuted if caught!
Wangle Dangle climbs WI 2 ice to the
right of the largest icicle for 10 m then
traverses left on downward sloping
ledges and shattered rock for 15 m to
the ice. Traverse onto the freehanging
dagger and continue to the top. Rappel
from trees.
Wangle Dangle has been known to
touch the ground in many separate
places. Several 'complete' ice routes

have been claimed and it is uncertain
who has climbed what. The complete
pillar starts at only 30 cm in diameter
but this heavily mushroomed pillar
gradually builds into a huge curtain.
The climb offers "plenty of gymnastics
and features some classic rests enjoyed
while sitting atop huge mushrooms".

Grotto Canyon

Park at the unsigned parking lot 9.7 km
east of the Trans-Canada overpass or 4.6
km west of Exshaw. From a trail on the
west end of the lot, hike through trees
past the #2 Baymag plant into the canyon. Continue on the frozen stream bed
past pretty rock walls to where the canyon forks; 30 minutes. *His* and *Hers* are
the obvious pillars pouring out of the
rock wall (82 O/3 248588).

His * 12 m III, 4

His, the left-hand of the two pillars is a
short route, not to be underestimated. It
is vertical throughout and usually
sports poor ice. As a result, many people have hit the deck here. Early in the
season it is thin and very chandeliery.
As the season progresses, constant traffic creates large overhangs and pitted
ice. The bottom of the pillar is often
chopped away, seriously undermining
the base of support and it has been
known to collapse under the weight of
a climber. Once the rope is up it is a top
rope heaven.

Hers * 12 m II, 4

Hers is the right-hand pillar and a little
easier than its neighbour for it usually
bulks out near the bottom and provides
more rests. Try top roping (or leading, if
you're brave) the overhanging left side.
A third pillar once formed in the corner

Tom Payie

The ever-popular Grotto Falls. Ken Chambers in early season before the ice flow bulks out to fill the entire groove.

right of *Hers* and is called **Cousin It** 15 m II, 4. Freestanding near the bottom, the first piece of protection is a bolt clipped on a nearby rock climb.

Little imagination is needed on how to get off any of these pillars.

Grotto Falls ** 55 m II, 3

A classic short route. From the T-junction at *His* and *Hers*, hike 100 m up the narrow drainage to the right. It is a popular weekend route–as many as 20 people have been seen on the route at one time. Without a bunch of people, Grotto can be fun–a good warm up for *His and Hers*.

It is usually climbed in two pitches with two bolt belays on the ledge about halfway up. Another bolt belay is found on the rock step to the left a few metres back from the top of the climb. Rappel the route.

Crystal Tear 200 m III, 3

From the T-junction at *His* and *Hers*, follow the left-hand fork for about 1 km. *Crystal Tear* is on the south facing slopes opposite a high cliff called Armadillo Buttress (the first cliff past the gravel cave). This rarely-formed route is another 300 m up the hillside (approximately 82 O/3 243594).

Scramble up for 150 m to where the gully narrows. Snow and two short steps leads to a final 45 m of steeper ice. Rappel and downclimb the route.

Elle and Lui IV 3-4

These parallel climbs, located between the two highest peaks of Grotto Mountain, are reached by a very long two to three hour hike past *Crystal Tear*. There is over 600 m elevation gain from the road to the base of the routes. The climbs are situated on the left in a gully furthest to the right (approximately 82 O/3 221611). It is doubtful if they have had a second ascent.

Climb a 20-m step, then continue up the gully for another hour (say it isn't so!) to a fork. The left-hand contains an easy 30-m flow, while the right-hand contains a pillar similar to *His* and *Hers*. Rappel and downclimb.

Lac Des Arcs

Along the Trans-Canada Highway 16 km east of Canmore is a wide lake called Lac Des Arcs, formed by overflow from the Bow River. There is an interchange at the east end of the lake that leads to a signed parking lot for Heart Creek trailhead, a popular summer hiking trail. The following routes are found in Heart Creek of on nearby Mt. McGillivary, the rocky peak above the highway.

Heart Creek Falls * 40-45 m II, 2-3

About 45 minutes up Heart Creek are a series of seeps. From Heart Creek trailhead follow the trail east paralleling the highway. At the creek, continue upstream to the falls (82 O/3 297557).

Two or three smears situated close to one another are great for teaching and practice with small groups. A short way up the canyon, the creek pours over a small cliff. When formed, it offers another nice WI 3 pitch. Rappel and downclimb the routes.

Arterial Spurt ** 150 m III, 3 R

Arterial Spurt is an obvious route that vies with *Sinatra Falls* for the most 'first ascents'. Park at Heart Creek trailhead. Behind (southeast) the parking lot, follow the left side of an obvious deep canyon. Once above the canyon stay left on high ground and traverse into the large bowl on the East Face of Mount McGillivary (650 m of elevation gain). This route sometimes forms on the smooth slab in the back of the bowl (82 O/3 286552). Beware of small loaded snow pockets.

Climb up to four pitches of sometimes thin low-angle ice. Rappel the route. Pitons or wires may be useful.

The Water Hole * 45 m II, 3

Two small smears occasionally appear at the right end of McGillivary slabs above Lac Des Arcs (82 O/3 268565). Two kilometres west of the Heart Creek/Lac Des Arcs interchange, park along the Trans-Canada in the pull-out next to the lake. Scramble up the far right side of the road cut and walk easily though trees to this classic among the Bow Valley store of moderate routes.

Parallel smears of 70-85°. ice. The left-hand is longer, better and more often formed. Rappel from trees.

Irish Mist 65 m II, 3

Irish Mist, located at the west end of McGillivary Slabs (82 O/3 267565), is very obscure and rarely forms. When it does, it travels essentially up the descent gully used for summer rock routes on the slabs. Park as for *The Water Hole*, but breach the road cut at a low spot in the middle, and continue past a cabin to the cliff. Climbed in three short pitches the route may include some rock or mixed moves. Rappel the route.

Three Sisters

The land along the south side of the Trans-Canada from Dead Man's Flats to Canmore is privately owned and presently under considerable development. This will undoubtedly change the approach tactics for all routes in the area. Approaches described here are valid for the 1993/94 season. Be careful not to trespass and if in doubt, enquire with the Town of Canmore (678-5593).

Also, this same area has old hidden mining scars, so watch for mine shafts and large overgrown open pits, especially if descending in the dark. It can be very dangerous.

Pigeon Mountain Falls 10 m I, 2-3

A good site for teaching, but not for much else. This small waterfall lies on land leased by the Thunderstone Quarry. On one hand, the quarry owner says that he doesn't mind people climbing there, but has also called the RCMP to have climbers removed. Please be polite and maintain a low profile.

To reach the climb, drive south from the overpass at Dead Man's Flats toward Three Sisters Resort. Thunderstone Quarry is on your right. Park at the end of the quarry just up the hill from the entrance. Do not access the climb through the main building/working area. Walk downhill across the end of the quarry towards the creek to where the climb pours over a small cliff.

Hurly Bird * 50 m IV, 4

Two obvious routes, visible from the Trans-Canada near Dead Man's Flats sometimes form below the North Face of Mt. Lougheed. *Hurly Bird* is the right-hand route (82 J/14 208494). Three approaches are possible: the most obvious

The "Social Climbing Team" takes on Southern Wind, Troy Kirwan leading, Joe Josephson belaying.

one is to bushwhack up Wind Valley from Dead Man's Flats (Grade VI+); the most practical one is to drive down the Smith-Dorrien Spray Trail from Canmore and park at Spurling Creek 5 km south of the Spray River Ranger Station. Follow a trail (look for a cairn next to the road) along the north side of the creek to Wind Pass then, traverse right to the Wind Tower/Lougheed col, three hours; the most enjoyable way to approach is by helicopter from Canmore into the col in about six minutes. From the col scramble down a gully on the northeast side of the col into the basin. Hike down one kilometre past some anaemic smears to the routes on the right. Beware of lee-loaded slopes below the col.

Mellow ice leads to a pleasant freestanding pillar of excellent ice. Rappel the route. It may be possible to continue to the ridge as mentioned below for *Southern Wind*.

The Southern Wind *** 250 m IV, 3

Despite its long approach *The Southern Wind* is one of the best WI 3 routes around. It is the second of two smears on the North Face of Mt. Lougheed. Approach as for *Hurly Bird*, 200 m to the left (82 J/14 207494).

The first crux pitch can be rather thin and technical. The next pitch climbs a short pillar on narrow ice. Continue up easier-angled ice for 100 m to a snow gully. Either rappel the route and walk out five hours to Dead Man's Flats or continue up snow to the ridge and traverse easily right below the North Face of Mt. Lougheed back to the col.

Twisted Sister ** 300 m IV 5.7 R, WI 4

An obvious north-facing pillar, *Twisted Sister* is situated below a prominent sub-peak up Stewart Creek between the Three Sisters Mountain and Wind Ridge. It is a long early season climb. Chinooks melt it away later in the season and snow buildup makes the approach harder than it already is, and increases the avalanche danger. Park along the Trans-Canada Highway , 2 km north of Dead Man's Flats , and bushwhack into Stewart Creek. Follow old mining roads upstream until they fade out and continue on faint paths to scree below the route; three hours (82 O/3 170519). Due to unpleasant buildup and powder avalanches on the lower-angle sections, the route is not recommended during or after a snowfall.

Trudge up scree to a right-trending weakness in the rock slab below a conspicuous crescent-shaped overhang. Climb up right in a shallow groove to a steeper corner (bolt). Continue up the corner (crux) to a pin station on the right, 45-m run out (kbs, small tricams). Get onto the ice and climb four long pitches of winding WI 2 (some fixed belays). The final 50-m pitch is not nearly as steep as it looks from the road, a classic WI 4. Rappel the route.

Little Bobby On-Sight ** 150 m IV, 4+ R

Numerous variations of this climb exist. The first ascentionists finished out to the right on a narrow runnel that ended in an overhang below the top of the crag. An unclimbed left-hand version up the main gully ends at about the same height but deposits you at the top of the cliff. This surprisingly good climb provides intricate thin and mixed climbing.

It is located on the right side of the Ship's Prow, a large prominent cliff just west of the Three Sisters Mountain. Two totally different approaches are available. One is a quick flight in the helicopter (the route is visible from the heli-pad in Canmore) or else a long three to four hour slog up steep timbered slopes. If you are walking, park at the Quarry Recreation Area between the town of Canmore and the Nordic Centre and walk east along private property until below the gully running down from the wall. Then, put your head down and give 'er.

A pretty pillar pours out of the main gully and then fans into several separate smears. The right-side leads directly to the pillar and has several protection bolts placed on an earlier attempt. The left-side, dubbed **Elvis has Left the Building** variation, climbs a thin pitch and has an even thinner traverse right into the pillar. Climb the steep technical pillar for 30 m. Then climb the aesthetic runnel to the right or make mixed moves into the main gully. Continue up to the top of the cliff (looks like a short but rotten pillar). If you climb to the top of the cliff, walk off to the right (beware of avalanche slopes). Otherwise, rappel the right side.

East End of Rundle

Canmore Junkyard *** 20-60 m I, 2-3

Considered the ultimate practice area, the *Junkyards* offer wide and varied expanses. 1.1 km past the Canmore Nordic Centre turn left at the marked Grassi Lakes turn-off. Park at the end of the road in the signed parking. Hike up to the ice in several minutes.

There is lots of variation and room for many climbers. The far left side contains low-angle ice for several pitches. The middle, *Scottish Gully*, is a fun narrow pitch. The right has acres of rolling terrain with a steep curtain. Rappel from trees and/or downclimb.

Glace Cherry 50 m III, 2

On a cliff band directly across from the park gates (82 O/3 094649) is a small pillar at the base of a huge avalanche-prone gully. Approach from the Nordic Centre or, as on the first ascent, by canoe across the Bow River.

Trans-Canada Iceway *** 200 m IV, 4

High on Mt. Rundle, above the park boundary is an almost hidden gully. Look into bowl to the right of a huge buttress above the boundary cut line. *The Iceway* is on the shorter wall on the left side of the bowl.

Follow the Smith-Dorrien Spray Trail south from Canmore to the Nordic Centre. Check the Nordic Centre trail maps to locate the trail along the Bow River towards Banff. Mountain bike or hike along this trail to the boundary cut line; then hike up to the base of the buttress. Traverse right into the bowl and the base of the route, four hours (82 O/3 079648). A helpful way to find the proper basin is to count the gullies in a western direction starting from the large cliff at the east end of Mt. Rundle. This route lies in the eighth main gully towards Banff.

This is a fine climb offering four sustained pitches of narrow, Scottish style ice. A second ascent and later a solo ascent, has confirmed it as an excellent route and well worth the long approach. The best descent is to walk off into the huge bowl to the right. This route would be certain death in high avalanche conditions and is best done early in the season.

Photo Opposite:
Don Chandler climbs Cascade in the dark ages.
The future can be seen far away in the
distance on Mt. Rundle.

Patrick Morrow

Banff Region

The Banff Region includes Cascade Mountain, Mt. Rundle, routes above Lake Minnewanka and those west toward Castle Mountain. Mt. Rundle is the massive peak that dominates the skyline for 20 km between Canmore and Banff. On its brooding Northeast Face are a concentration of some of the most challenging ice climbs in the world. Cascade Mountain is the peak above the airfield at the east exit into Banff.

The climbs on Cascade are moderate in nature and very popular due to the short approach. However, they have a sunny exposure and lee snow-loaded bowls above the routes leave them open to high avalanche potential. In terms of the number of accidents, *Cascade* is undoubtedly the most dangerous waterfall in the Rockies. On one telling day in 1993, 18 persons were involved in a single avalanche! Lake Minnewanka and west to Castle Mountain have a smaller concentration of routes but they are high quality. Check with the warden service and the weather office for updated avalanche conditions. See map page 111.

Maps
82 O/3 Canmore
82 O/4 Banff
82 O/6 Lake Minnewanka
82 O/5 Castle Mountain

Cascade Mountain

Four avalanche-prone gullies are found along the South Face of Cascade Mountain. *Cascade Waterfall* is the obvious line above the airfield east of Banff. *Rogan's* and *Cascade* always form but often melt away during warm spells, then reform several times throughout the season.

From the Banff east exit on the Trans-Canada, turn north and drive along the Lake Minnewanka Road and park in a small pull-out on the left, 200 m past the cattle guard. Walk through light trees to the base of either route in 15-20 minutes. *The Tube* and *The Urs Hole* are approached from farther along the Lake Minnewanka Road.

Rogan's Gully * 300 m II, 2

In the deep gully right of *Cascade Waterfall* is a moderate snow and ice climb. An 18-m step leads into *The Narrows*. Continue past small steps to a fork, both which have ice. The left is easier. Rappel and downclimb route. Beware of manky fixed stations. Another common descent is to downclimb on the rock to the right of Rogan's Gully. This is the descent used for summer rock climbs and requires one rappel off a tree near the bottom.

Cascade Waterfall *** 300 m III, 3

The obvious waterfall, 50 m right of *Rogan's Gully*, is a climbing classic. The bowl above is very avalanche-prone especially on warm sunny days. Falling ice and rock, both natural and man-made, can be a serious problem as well. If conditions are doubtful or with parties above you, an alternative route is recommended.

It is a long route but only the final 75 m are steep. The bottom pitches are commonly soloed or avoided to the right. The final two pitches offer occasionally thin ice to 80° Bolt belays can be found on the right. Rappel the route for two pitches then downclimb or bypass the rest. Alternatively, climb another pitch at the back of the bowl and traverse left to the top of *Rogan's Gully*.

The Tube 30 m II, 2

Immediately right of *Cascade Waterfall* is a deep gash, *The Tube*, that doesn't always form. Continue along the Lake Minnewanka Road for 300 m and park at the far end of the Cadet Camp.

Some exposed rock scrambling to the right may be required to bypass the initial rock step. Higher, are two short tubes of ice formed behind large chockstones. Another WI 4 pitch can be found a short walk up canyon. Descend the route.

The Urs Hole * 95 m II, 2, 5

The right-most Cascade climb is below a bowl that drains a majority of the South Face. Don't even look at this route after the first significant snowfall of the year. Drive along the Lake Minnewanka Road for 1.3 km and park at an open stream bed near the landfill. Walk easily to the climb.

Climb a series of short steps up to 8 m long to where the gully narrows. Several more widely-spaced steps lead to a pocket glacier of avalanche debris that has turned into ice. This requires some squeezing, tunnelling, spelunking-type manoeuvres to negotiate. Descend the route.

A short way beyond the pocket glacier is **The Urs Hole Direct Finish** ** (45 m III, 5), a series of beautiful icicles and chandeliers that form a corner of ice in a smooth water chute. It makes a good early season testpiece as it becomes 'lost' under avalanche debris as the season progresses. Rappel the pitch or walk left (west) to gain the top of another fork of *The Urs Hole*.

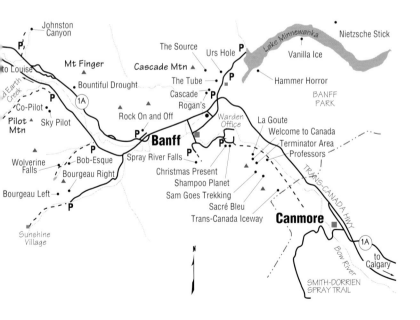

The Source 100 m IV, 5.7 WI 5

Located way above *The Urs Hole* almost halfway up Cascade Mountain is *The Source*. Climb *The Urs Hole* to its end. At the junction above the pocket glacier, take the left fork and climb one pitch of WI 3. Continue up the gully until you reach open slopes. *The Source* is now in view. Climb a gully or the ridge below to reach the climb; three to four hours. A definite early season route!

Climb 25 m of 5.7 rock to belay. Traverse right and up snow slopes to the base. Climb steep ice to a final 50-m chandelier pillar. To descend, rappel 50 m from a large boulder. Use a tree to rappel the lower rock buttress, then retrace the rest of route.

Lake Minnewanka

From the Banff east exit, turn north. Drive past Cascade Mountain 5 km to the end of Lake Minnewanka Road to a large parking lot. The following routes lie to the east along Lake Minnewanka. Ice skates have been used to access the routes in early season when the ice is relatively smooth. As the season progresses, the ice gets rougher and makes for good mountain biking.

Hammer Horror ** 30 m II, 4+

Park at the south end of the dam and travel 2 km east across the lake to a small out-wash fan below the gully. Ascend the left side through the trees and bypass a lower cliff for about 150 m. The climb is visible from just off shore or from the picnic area on the north side of the lake (82 O/3 071773).

Climb a narrow pillar that is free-standing for half its length. For an easier ascent try stemming off the rock. Rappel the route.

Vanilla Ice ** 70 m III, 2

From the parking lot, ice skate for 40 minutes or mountain bike for 20 minutes to the major turn in the lake. The climb is on the south side only minutes from shore (82 O/6 109805).

This climb is a wide flow of ice with no avalanche hazard that gives good climbing away from the maddening crowds in the Bow Valley. To descend, walk off.

Nietzsche Stick 80 m III, 3

The first ascensionists, finding the lake in exceptionally smooth condition, used hockey skates and a sail to reach this climb–an innovative approach in 45 minutes! It is located 360 m above the lake on the north side just east of the warden cabin. Climb up through the trees, avoiding small rock bands, to the base (approximately 82 O/6 080819).

Climb two pitches of sunny, moderate ice. Descend the route and skate 1.5 hours (three hours with a strong head-wind) back to Banff.

Ghost Lake

A number of other ice flows have been explored around Lake Minnewanka as far east as the inlet near Ghost Lakes. Many side canyons and cliff bands along the lake await exploration and I leave them for your own discovery.

Mount Rundle

The following routes are approached from the Banff townsite. Drive to the Bow Falls parking lot near Banff Springs Hotel and Golf Course. Continue across Goat Creek Bridge and along the golf course. Park 2.9 km from the bridge where the road splits. The routes are accessed via the right-hand fork. 100 m past the fork is a blockade. DO NOT drive past this point even if the gate is open. This section of road has been reserved for dog sledding teams—please don't jeopardize relations.

Christmas Present *** 200 m III, 3 R

This underrated route doesn't often form. Walk 400 m past the blockade to a sharp double bend to the left and look on the cliff bands above in a shallow gully. Hike up through the trees for 30 minutes to the base (82 O/4 032693).

Rarely is the initial slab frozen so either sketch directly up the rocks or traverse around from the left via exposed treed ledges into a small scree bowl. Low-angle ice and rock leads to a short right-facing corner. Either climb the corner and continue up slabs to a large ledge or traverse left across rock ledges for 25 metres to a long right-facing corner. Climb up the corner, about 5.5, to where it arches severely to the right. You can escape into the trees and down to the left at this point. To continue up the route, make a difficult step right across a very smooth slab or jump to a small tree on the end of the large ledge. Continue up generally thin but low-angle ice for another two pitches nearing 80° at the top.

To descend, walk off right, however, some diligence is required to weave through the steep trees amongst scattered rock slabs. If you pass the next open avalanche path (scree) right of the route, you have gone too far. If in doubt, several short rappels should suffice.

Shampoo Planet ** 190 m III, 5.10, WI 3 R

This devious route is found in the next gully left of *Christmas Present*. Walk 200 m past the double bend in the road and look up an avalanche path to the route. *Shampoo Planet* can be seen as a low-angle smear of ice that ends over a steep wall 20 m off the ground (82 O/4 035692). Hike up to the route past some tricky slabs in about an hour. It is best done early in the year before much snow accumulates and while temperatures are conducive to rock climbing.

Start up a corner of thin ice and through mushrooms to a right-trending corner. The next 30 m may have little or no ice requiring hard rock climbing and dry tooling (5.10 or A2). Some frozen moss adds welcome purchase to the baby-smooth slab. Take lots of gear including Friends, wires and 10-12 pitons. Belay on a small stance where the corner arches to the right. Step left under a loose block and sketch up a groove to the right end of a horizontal moss seam. Handrail across the seam using ice tools and slinging moss horns for protection to the ice smear. Cruise happily up thinnish but easy ice for three pitches with a fun 0.5 m wide seam and a WI 3 pitch near the top. Walk off as for *Christmas Present*.

Touch Me if You Can 95 m III, 4

This climb formed once about 300 metres past the Nordic Centre Trailhead to the left of the above routes. It has never formed again. There are two pitches of thin ice in a left-facing corner steeping to 90° with a small pillar. A rack of wires and Friends required. Rappel.

Joe Josephson thankfully nearing a belay on the first ascent of the Replicant.

Nordic Centre Trail

The following Mt. Rundle climbs are approached from the trail that follows the Bow River to the Canmore Nordic Centre. Park as for Christmas Present. Walk or mountain bike along the road 3 km. To the right is a large wooden sign and the start of the trail to the Canmore Nordic Centre (82 O/4 039695).

Welcome to Canada IV, 4

Welcome to Canada splits the large headwall to the right of The Terminator with a deep gully. About 2 km past the trailhead look up the first large open gully with The Terminator hanging high above to the left. Continue up the gully to the first rock band (82 O/3 049689). On the right side of the gully, a short dirty corner places you above the cliff.

Continue straight up the drainage where you will encounter a number of thin runnels and short pillars up to WI 4 in difficulty. If unformed you can usually traverse past the steps on exposed ledges. Alternatively, bypass the entire bottom section by slogging through the trees on the right and drop into the drainage below the upper headwall. Climb the deep gash in the headwall on moderate ice for a 650-m training adventure.

Rappel and downclimb the route. Some rock anchors may be in place but be prepared to leave your own. It is possible to traverse off to the right on down sloping ledges all the way back to the Golf Course near Christmas Present.

Mt. Rundle from the Trans-Canada.
The routes: A) Sacré Bleu B) Professors,
C)Sam Goes Trekking D) The Terminator Area
From Left to Right: The Terminator, The Replicant,
(unformed), Postscriptum, Sea of Vapors),
E) Welcome to Canada F) La Goute (Hidden).
The approaches: 1) Terminator (hiking) 2)
Terminator (climbing), 3) Welcome to Canada
(climbing) 4) Welcome to Canada (hiking).

Jeff Everett

La Goute * 50 m IV, 6+

Follow Welcome to Canada until below the main gash in the upper headwall. *La Goute* is found to the right pouring out of a shallow gully. It is one of the hardest one-pitch routes in the range.

This awesome testpiece rarely forms completely and has a very long approach for one pitch. Nevertheless, it will give your biceps a run for the money. Rappel the route.

The Terminator Approach

A line to the left of Welcome to Canada has been described as an approach to *The Terminator* area. When formed, the climbing is worthwhile, offering good views with a magnificent ambiance. It is not as desperate as its ephemeral cousins. A variety of approaches will reach the ice (see photo page 115). Pitch one begins at 80° then eases off to a snow slope. Another pitch offering a sustained section of vertical ice (WI 4+) is found above. 50 m of WI 3 ice puts you on the ledge below *The Terminator*.

Most parties attempting routes near *The Terminator* bypass the approach ice. To do so, leave the main trail and continue up the gully below the route *Welcome to Canada* for 200 m to the first rock band (82 O/3 049689). On the right side of the gully, a short dirty corner puts you above the cliff. This cliff can also be avoided by traversing up through the trees from the right. Above the cliff, gain high ground left of the gully and continue through trees, past a short rock slab (avalanche hazard here).

Continue up through the forest until you reach a scree slope below a large rock buttress. Traverse to the left side of the buttress and climb up short rock steps into the right margin of the *Profes-*

sor Falls drainage. Slog up through deep snow to a rib just left of *The Terminator*. Traverse down and across an avalanche prone slope into a small east-facing Cul-de-Sac in the rock band. In the back of the Cul-de-Sac at its lowest point, make a few moves of rock climbing and finally you'll arrive at the 50 m WI 3 pitch below *The Terminator*, a minimum of three hours. Beware of isolated pockets of bad snow. All descents from *The Terminator* area should reverse this route, or if avalanche hazard permits, you may continue down *Professor Falls*.

Sam Goes Trekking * 40 m IV, 4

High on Mt. Rundle about 500 m left of *The Terminator* is one pitch that almost always forms. Approach as for *The Terminator* up to the prominent rib above the *Professor Falls* drainage. Rather than drop over the rib toward *The Terminator*, cross left until below a hidden gully. Easily climb the gully and a snow slope to the base; four hours (approximately 82 O/3 051684).

Climb an enjoyable 80° pitch. The first ascentionists were accompanied to the base by Sam the dog. Rappel off a rock anchor on the left, then off a boulder right of the gully to come off the lower rock band.

The Terminator *** 150 m V, 6+

Undoubtedly the most watched chunk of ice in the Rockies. Having formed completely only once, *The Terminator* is an awesome, pure line. After the first ascent, which took two days, the route was given a controversial Grade 7. After three additional one-day ascents that same winter, it was downgraded even though the few people that did manage to climb it called it "the hardest thing (they'd) ever done". Regardless, this

The Terminator (centre) and Sea Vapors (right) in 1992/93.
Only the very top of The Replicant is visible right of Terminator.

offers one of the most outrageous climbs you could ever imagine. See The Terminator Approach on page 116.

The route consists of three vertical, sustained, and very full pitches. Pitch one is the crux, as it freehangs for over 30 m and runs a full pitch to a cave on the right. A second pitch of featureless ice leads to a second, shorter freehanging curtain. A final pitch on improving ice hits the top. In the winter of 1992-93 the pillar came within 10 m of touching the ground. Several parties were able to gain the freehanging dagger from behind to create a exceedingly difficult and dangerous pitch (A2 WI 7 X) known as *T2*. Bolt belay/rappel stations were added in 1993 but will probably be covered in ice.

References

Polar Circus. Vol 1, pg. 11, illus, 1986; *Canadian Alpine Journal*, Vol 76, pg. 2, 106 illus., 1993; *Vertical*, Numero 60, pg 95. illus., Juillet 1993.

The Replicant ** 145 m V, 6+

The Replicant is a great route immediately right (10 m) of The Terminator. Sometimes the two routes join together in places. It was named after the genetic clones in the science fiction film, *Blade Runner*. The clones are reported to have lived their lives so intensely that they burned out after only a short while.

The first crux pitch climbs an apron of thin ice to a technical, vertical pillar capped by a fierce overhanging section; 50-m belay on 87° ice. The second slightly easier (WI 6) 50-m pitch traverses right and then up a detached curtain pouring off a roof, followed by vertical ice to a stance. Finish with a 45 m WI 5 pitch on excellent ice pouring from a large crack. Rappel the route.

Postscriptum 45 m III, 5

Two parallel pillars seeping from the rock are often found 25 m right of *The Terminator*. *Postscriptum* is the right-hand column. It is a great but often cold location that is a good alternative to its nasty neighbours. Add *Postscriptum* to the Terminator Approach Ice to create a long and challenging route (Grade IV, 5). A single rappel bolt in place; a backup is recommended.

Sea of Vapors * 165 m V, 7+, R

During a tropical Chinook in February 1993 this amazing line called *Sea of Vapors* appeared, streaming down a broad corner 30 m right of The Terminator. Climb *Postscriptum* to a hanging belay. The second pitch traverses right on spotty ice and up incredibly sustained and very thin technical ice. Find a hanging belay on the left (wires and #3 Friend) after 40 m. A third 50-m pitch (WI 6+) of slightly thicker ice leads to a hanging belay below an overhang.

The final 30 m goes over a mushroomed overhang and vertical ice to end in the corner/overlap from which the route emanates. Adequate protection is very scarce throughout, yet the belays are solid. Take a half set of Friends up to #3, half set of wires, tricams are useful, six pins kbs to one inch and ice screws for *Postscriptum*. No bolts were used. The name comes from a landmark on the moon. The route was likened to "climbing frozen mist up an alien landscape". Rappel the route.

References

Canadian Alpine Journal, Vol 76, pp. 104, 105 illus., 1993 ; *Vertical*, Numero 60, pg. 94, illus. Juillet 1993 .

Bruce Hendricks stepping out in more ways than one on the first attempt of Sea of Vapors.

Professor Falls *** 280 m III, 4

Professor Falls ranks with *Cascade* as one of the most popular waterfalls in the Rockies. It was named after the eccentric Eckhard Grassman. Buried under the deep shadow of Mt. Rundle with a constant water supply, *Professors* is one of the first routes to form and the last to melt. Its tiered nature and usually good ice make it an introduction for many people to steeper multi-pitched ice climbs. A Rockies classic! Despite popular conviction this route DOES have some avalanche hazard. At least one party has been three-quarters buried at the base of the last pitch. Other avalanches have been seen to clear the Bow River. Beware.

To approach *Professors,* walk or mountain bike along the road 3 km beyond the parking area. To the right is a sign and start of the trail to the Canmore Nordic Centre (82 O/4 039695). Follow this trail for about 3 km until you see the obvious blue pillars of the *Professors* gully about 400 m up a relatively clear stream bed; 45-60 minutes from parking (82 O/3 056688). Usually there is a well-defined donkey trail to the base. The previous guide listed *Professors* west of *The Terminator*. Subsequently, many visiting parties headed up slope toward *Welcome to Canada*, only to encounter ugly bushwhacking.

Three steep tiers of ice offer usually wet but good steep climbing. A number of unnecessary bolt/chain anchors have been added to the first three pitches although you can walk off any pitch. Several shorter steps and 150 metres of snow lead to the final, crux pitch. A full 40 m in excess of 85° which is sometimes quite thin and technical. Get there early; slow crowds and falling ice are a real drag in this narrow gully.

Several descent options exist. From the top of the route traverse out left and descend through steep trees avoiding any rock slabs. It is possible to traverse back to the gully below the final pitch and downclimb the intermediate steps to the top of the third pitch. Otherwise, continue down steeper terrain just left of the gully with two half rope rappels or a full rope rappel to near the top of the third pitch. Be suspect of loose rappel trees. If you traverse too far left before rappelling, it gets quite ugly and steep with numerous 10-m rappels. Once atop the third pitch you can either rappel from a bolt anchor on the right or from below the large rock in the gully, traverse left 20 m and lower from branches down a 3-m slabby corner then traverse easily right on a ledge to the base of the pitch. From here traverse out of the gully and follow easy ledges down, using several lengths of fixed rope to lower off the steeper sections.

Sacré Bleu ** 100 m IV, 5+

Unaware of a previous ascent, a party climbed the route and called it *Under the Volcano*; thus, many locals refer to it by that name. This fine route is situated below one of the largest avalanche bowls imaginable; most ascents occur early in the season before any amount of snow accumulates. *Sacré Bleu* is located in the bowl left (east) of Professor Falls. Continue along the trail past that route for 15 minutes until directly under the volcano (82-0/3 058679). Bushwhack right of the gully. Traverse snow slopes below the upper headwall into the gully proper. Continue up 150 m of easy ice and snow to the base. Allow up to four hours and be patient, the climbing is worth it. The best but longest approach is to climb *Professors* and traverse left from the top.

Grant Statham enjoying a typical pitch on Professor Falls.

A classic 50-m pitch up to 80° leads to a fixed belay on a ledge to the left. The second pitch continues up 10 m to the base of a long, steep 40-m pillar. Grunt your way up to a bolt belay in a small gash that makes the climb look unformed from the road. Rappel the route and reverse the approach march.

Sulphur Mountain

Spray River Falls ** 170 m IV, 5

Known since the mid '70s as *Spray River Falls*, this climb has also been called **Selenium Falls**. Located on the east side of Sulphur Mountain, it is good in early season. The approach gets very difficult in deep snow. Late season may also find good travelling as the snow pack sets up. From Banff townsite follow signs to the Upper Hot Springs. From the east end of the parking lot, follow the summer trail past a small switchback to a large gully. *Spray River Falls* can be seen in the second main drainage with a striking pillar halfway up the climb (82 O/4 654006). The slope from the trail to the base is longer than it looks—300 m, and is desperate in bad snow conditions; 1.5 to 2.5 hours.

Start with a 5-m steep step followed by 60-70 m of snow and ice. A full rope of WI 3 ice leads to the crux pillar. Continue up for 30 m of consistently vertical ice to a ledge. Another more moderate pitch leads to a large snow bowl. Descent to the right is possible but it is recommended to rappel the route.

Spray River Falls near Banff.

Trans-Canada Highway

The following routes are on the south side of the Bow Valley and are reached from the Trans-Canada Highway between the Sunshine Ski Resort turn-off, 9 km west of Banff, and the Highway 93 South (Radium Highway) intersection at Castle Junction.

Bourgeau Right-Hand *** 310 m IV, 4 R

A classic route, 500 m right of the *Left-Hand* route, *Bourgeau Right-Hand* is many people's favourite WI4 route. First climbed in 1973, *Right-Hand* represented a huge leap in local standards. Aid techniques were not developed until the following season and the route was climbed free. It is often very thin on the first two pitches and difficult to protect. The route and descent are subject to high avalanche hazard. Check with the warden service for updated conditions. From the east side of the Sunshine Village parking lot hike up through the trees to the right side of the avalanche gully below the route; 60-90 minutes to the base.

Climb 30 m of sustained climbing up to 90° leading to the crux second pitch. Climb a short steep pillar which is often thin with poor ice. More broken terrain with several short steps on good ice leads to a final 45-m wall of 75° ice.

To descend, some fixed rappel anchors may be found; otherwise, walk off across scree to the right. DO NOT traverse straight across the shallow lee-loaded gullies which can usually be avoided by walking several hundred metres above. If in doubt, belay across them. The run out below is uncompromising as it drops 500 m to the parking

Tim Auger breaking new ground on the first ascent of Bourgeau Right-Hand, 1973.

Bourgeau Right-Hand in more modern times. Sharon Wood leading on first pitch.

lot. Continue across the scree to a ridge separating a large back bowl. Pick your way down to the base of the bowl/ridge, then turn right back to the trees and the parking lot.

No Breaks * 45 m III, 4+

Pouring from a crack/chimney 100 m right of *Bourgeau Left* is a fun technical pillar that is very narrow in places. A worthwhile climb if you're in the area and have the time. Rappel the route.

Bourgeau Left-Hand *** 185 m IV, 5

One of the finer climbs in the Rockies, it was the first climb to be given a Grade 6 rating in 1974. Modern grades put it at a solid WI 5. Unfortunately it does not always form and is threatened by large avalanche slopes from above and below. It is regularly bombed for avalanche control, and it is imperative to contact the Banff Warden Service for the latest conditions. Nine kilometres west of Banff on the Trans-Canada Highway follow signs and the morning ski crowds to the Sunshine Village parking lot. Walk past the gondola and from the far end of the parking lot follow the creek a short ways to some orange flagging tape. Continue up steep slopes to the right and either climb WI 3 steps in the gully direct or work up through ledges around rock slabs to the right. Allow about an hour.

The first two pitches are rather legendary as they are often very thin overlying smooth slabs. Occasionally they detach from the rock and give off an eerie 'bonging' noise when climbed. Protection can be difficult. From a large snow ledge, a short third pitch leads to the final crux. A curtain with a long vertical section to the top. From a cave on the right ten metres above the snow ledge, a 55-m pitch will reach the top anchor. Rappel the route. On the bottom tier, two fixed stations are found on the left and the upper tier has two fixed stations on the right.

Bourgeau Left-Hand with fixed belays indicated. Barry Blanchard can be seen nearing the top.
Photo Patrick Morrow

Faux Pas 60 m IV, 4

This remote climb is located in a high drainage on the right side as you ski toward Healy Pass from the Sunshine parking lot (82 O/4 825619). Park as for Bourgeau-Left and ski up Healy Creek for about 3 km and the route is found 300 m above the creek; 1.5 hours. See Chic Scott's *Ski Trails in the Canadian Rockies,* page 63 for detailed information. The route is in large avalanche country and an early season ascent is recommended.

Climb WI 2 approach ice until it steepens. Continue up 80° ice to a WI 4 pillar and the top. Rappel the route.

Wolverine Falls 200 m IV, 3

From the Trans-Canada Highway, park at the Bourgeau Lake trailhead, 2.9 km west of the Sunshine overpass. Walk or ski to Bourgeau Lake. Cross the outlet stream coming from the lake to the first switchback in the trail. Ten minutes of bushwhacking above the switchback leads to the climb (82 O/4 850668). The falls does not always form and has major avalanche hazard. It is recommended this be an early-season climb, before any snow accumulates.

The first ascent team found a rambling, broken climb of short steps with great views of neighbouring Mounts Bourgeau and Brett. Walk off to the left.

Bob-Esque 10 m III, 3

This is a short pillar found on the right side of an avalanche chute on the left as you walk towards *Wolverine Falls* (82 O/4 854665). It makes a good consolation prize if there are no other formed routes around.

Sky Pilot * 100 m IV, 6

This is a stellar route on the northeast side of Pilot Mountain that has fully formed only once. It is seen easily from the Trans-Canada Highway at a point 8 km west of the Sunshine Village overpass (82 O/4 824721). Park at Red Earth Creek Trailhead 11.3 km west of the overpass. Ski up the trail (a popular ski tour) for just over 2 km. Traverse southeast through dense trees then up steep slopes to the base; three to four hours.

Climb three pitches with a very steep and serious freestanding pillar for starters. Rappel the route.

Co-Pilot 100 m IV, 5

Co-Pilot is a steep route located about 300 m around the large rock buttress right of *Sky Pilot* (82 O/4 819727). It had two difficult pitches that have never been seen after the first ascent. Rappel the route.

By Hook or By Crook 150 m II, 2

This climb is located in a shallow gully on the left side of a treed, cliffy section 17 km west of the Sunshine Village overpass (82 O/4 778771) above the Trans-Canada Highway. Approach the climb on a small wooded ridge for 230 m. The only reason it is included here is because it has a good name.

Climb small steps of ice in the gully to a 30 m pitch of WI 2 ice which exits through a V-notch. Another curtain called **Two Minutes for Hooking** is found 100 m to the right.

Rappel from trees to the right.

1A Highway

The 1A Highway joins the Trans-Canada 5.5 km west of Banff, and travels along the north side of the valley to Lake Louise.

Rock On and Off * 50 m III, 5.8 WI 3

4.5 km west of Banff on the Trans-Canada Highway is a scrappy cliff above the road on the north side. *Rock On and Off* lies near the middle of this cliff. 1 km farther west turn right onto the 1A Highway. Park at the Fireside Road 400 m from the Trans-Canada Highway. Walk along the road to the Edith/Cory Pass trailhead. Continue along the trail until below the route. Ascend through trees to the climb; one hour (approximately 82 O/4 945703).

Climb low-angle ice to rock. Move right and ascend a chimney to a treed ledge. Climb 15 m of ice above. Rappel the route. Another nice WI 3 pitch is located 50 m right of this route and was found to have a bolt on its top.

Bountiful Drought ** 70 m II, 3 R

A fun climb and a good introduction to thinner ice climbing at a moderate angle, *Bountiful Drought* is visible from the 1A Highway but may be best visible from the Trans-Canada. The climb lies in the lower reaches of the major drainage below *The Finger*. Follow the 1A Highway west for 10 km to a roadside pull-out. Hike up through the trees staying left of the climb; 30-60 minutes depending on snow conditions (82 O/4 883744).

The first 20 m consists of three short WI 2 steps. The final section provides delicate but not strenuous climbing on thin ice for a full 50 m to a tree belay. The angle varies between 70-75°. Walk off to the left.

Johnston Canyon *** 10-40 m II, 2-5

Although a crowded summer tourist location, few people journey into this area in winter. At the Upper Falls a wall of ice 60 m wide is dissected into spectacular freestanding pillars easing off to low-angle slabs to the right.

Prism Falls is the largest pillar on the left. Park at Johnston Canyon Bungalows Camp (closed in winter) 3 km east of Castle Junction. Hike up the developed walkway 2.5 km to the end. Turn right at Paint Pots junction.

Rappel the route or walk off and downclimb to the right. The Lower Falls consisting of technical hollow ice above open water, has also been climbed.

Silverton Falls 95 m II, 2

This climb is often blocked by stretches of open water and is thus recommended during spells of cold weather. It may not exist during warm spells. Park near Castle Junction at the plowed pull-out for Rockbound Lake/Castle Mountain. Walk north up the ski trail and turn right at the *Silverton Falls* junction. The upper section offers six steps of ice up to 12 m in length. Walk off.

Mon Ami * 150 m IV, 4+

Located between Protection Mountain and the west face of Castle Mountain is a large bowl requiring a four-to-five hour approach up the drainage from the 1A Highway. Park at a pull-out on the east side of the road 8.4 km north of Castle Junction. Hike or ski up through trees past several small cliff bands into the drainage. *Mon Ami* is hidden on the right side of the bowl (82 O/5 717880).

Traverse into the route from the left past a 5.6 chockstone. The climb consists of three pillars trending up to the right. Rappel the route.

Johnston Canyon Lower Falls.

Lake Louise Group

World famous for its stunning mountain scenery, the Lake Louise Group offers an idyllic setting for waterfall climbing. More importantly, all approaches begin in The Village at Laggan's Mountain Bakery and Deli which offers delicious bread, pastries, pies and sandwiches. Apart from a few routes around the lake, most climbs require a ski approach to the base.

Recent snow stability and weather forecasts and park information is available at the Visitor Centre, located at the north end of the main shopping centre (Samson Mall). Here, you can also register for climbs. See map page 132.

Map
82 N/8 Lake Louise

Climbing near the cave on Louise Falls.
Photo Patrick Morrow

Lake Louise

From the townsite of Lake Louise, drive west through the 4-way stop and continue up the hill for 3 km to the Château Lake Louise and a large parking lot. The following four routes are found near the far end of the lake or beyond, in the Plain of Six Glaciers.

Louise Falls *** 110 m II, 4+/5

With close access and little avalanche hazard, this is guaranteed to be one of the most popular routes in the range. Get there early. Despite it being a fairly wide climb, it is hard to hide from exploding ice fragments pouring down from climbers above you. *Louise Falls* was originally climbed free in 1974 due to the determined efforts of Jack Firth. The intimidating crux pillar looming over the route is many climbers first hard pitch and it still turns back many parties. Follow the path in front of the Château and along the northwest side of the lake. *Louise Falls* is the first and obvious climb above the trail at the end of the lake.

Two varied pitches lead to a big cave behind the pillar. On these pitches it is possible to sneak an easy gully on the right, climb a steeper curtain on the right of centre, or ramble up bulges on the left side of the climb. Most parties seek the security of the cave, but it is an intimidating (and often wet) step out onto the pillar. Alternatively, try climbing directly from the left side (this way, two pitches will take you to the top of the pillar). Quite often a spectacular freestanding pillar forms on the **right side** (WI 5). A nice rest ledge exists before the final 15 m of steep ice to the top. From the cave you can make it to the top in one pitch. Thin ice and some moss/tree moves make exit manoeuvres exciting.

From the top, a walk off to the right is possible. Beware of a couple of small avalanche-prone gullies and make sure you go far enough right to avoid the cliff bands. If you don't make it up the pillar, traverse right to the treed rock rib just below the cave from where a 50-m rappel will take you to the ground. There are also several rappel trees on the left side of the waterfall, but they are awkward to reach.

Cable Gullies 15 m III, 2

Opposite the valley from *Louise Falls* lies a large cliff band topped by even larger avalanche slopes. *Cable Gullies* lie in deep clefts along the right side of the cliff. These short pillars are reached by walking past *Louise Falls* and crossing the creek near the head of the lake. Because these routes usually last well into June this is not a bad time to climb them when you don't have to worry about avalanche hazard (usually!). Combine it with some cragging at the back of the lake for a full, sports action day.

Linda Ice Nine * 310 m III, 4

Somehow, locals have thought the real name for this route was *Linda Nice Ice* but the first ascentionist has assured me the name is correct. This is a long gully climb that only gets good near the top. Continue past *Louise Falls* along the Plain of Six Glaciers trail (the track is not set past the lake, but it is often broken) for 1.6 km. *Linda Ice Nine* is above the trail at this point and a plod up the slope is required to reach it. This is in severe avalanche terrain so be sure to check with the Lake Louise wardens

for the conditions in the area.

Some short steps lead to a long snow gully which leads to two or three more pitches of undulating ice. This route is not recommended after a snowfall. Not only will the avalanche hazard go up, but this section gets covered in snow making for poor (and wet) climbing. A steeper pitch at the top of this section leads to another snow slope and then the final crux curtain of vertical ice. Right of the second-to-last pitch a difficult freestanding pillar may sometimes form. Descend either side of the route. A single rope is sufficient for rappels.

Oasis 50 m III, 3

Located 800 m beyond *Linda Ice Nine* to the right of the toe of the Victoria Glacier is a wall of ice up to 60-m wide. As with *Linda Ice Nine*, this route is located among tremendous avalanche terrain. Be certain of prevailing snow conditions before considering an attempt.

This climb offers a variety of different lines ranging from 75° to sections in excess of 85° Overall, it's an enjoyable climb in an impressive alpine setting. Rappel from trees.

Paradise Valley

Moraine Lake Road is located 1 km before you reach the Château Lake Louise. Park in the large parking lot on the left. Ski up the road (track set) 2 km to Paradise Creek. Turn right onto the Paradise Valley Trail. Follow the Paradise Valley signs— it is easy to get lost on the many trails leading north toward Lake Louise and Fairview Mountain. Refer to Chic Scott's *Ski Trails in the Canadian Rockies,* page 103 for more detailed information.

Jeff Everett approaching The Tease on the first ascent.

The Tease ** 85 m III, WI 5

Continue up Paradise Valley and turn right (north) into the first drainage coming down between Sheol and Saddle Mountains. *The Tease* is located on a quartzite cliff on the Northeast Face of Mt. Sheol, about two hours from the car (82 N/8 546928). The top is visible from the 1A Highway as you drive north towards Lake Louise. It is called *The Tease*, because you'll get to the top of this short route and yell "I want more!" The first ascentionists climbed up difficult rock from the left (5.9, tied-off blocks for protection) to an unformed icicle then continued up steep ice for another pitch. In good years the pillar forms completely. Expect awesome views of the North Face of Mount Temple. Rappel the route.

The Friendly Giant * 85 m III, 4

Approach as for *The Tease*, but ski southwest up Paradise Valley for another 4 km to the Giant Steps. The route is located left of the large gully on the South Face of Mt. Aberdeen; allow up to three hours. (82 N/8 526900). There is only a small avalanche slope above the route but the ski approach has exceptionally large mountain sides rearing above it. Save this route for a clear day; you'll thank yourself for the views. Climb the short initial pillar and continue up for 50 m to a nice cave below the upper pillar. This short pitch leads to a snow slope and a tree on the right. Rappel from belay tree (sling) for 35 m to another tree (sling) and then another 45 m to the ground.

An easier one-pitch route called ***The Friendlier Giant*** (WI 3) is located 50 m to the right of this route.

Mount Temple

Begin the approach as for Paradise Valley but continue up Moraine Lake Road (track set) for 8 km to the viewpoint overlooking Moraine Lake and Consolation Valley. It is another 3 km downhill to Moraine Lake. **Note:** the road crosses under avalanche paths towards the lake. Just before the lake on the right (south side) are some picnic shelters if you want to camp out. In an emergency, there is a pay phone at the lodge (closed in winter) next to the lake. The phone was working in the winter of 92/93.

Striving for the Moon ** 1000+ m VI, AO 5+

Striving for the Moon makes a significant alpine addition to the East Face of Mt. Temple. Found between the Big Step on the East Ridge and the Aemmer Couloir, this route 'strives' up the largest gully system to the base of the Black Towers. Think about climbing this route only in times of reasonable avalanche hazard. Ski to the viewpoint where the road turns right and goes down to Moraine Lake. About 2 km towards Moraine Lake from the viewpoint, move right up through trees past a small lake to the gully (82 N/8 570895). The route is clearly shown on page 22 of *Selected Alpine Climbs in the Canadian Rockies* (photo).

Several pitches of moderately hard ice lead to a very steep and strenuous pillar about halfway up the gully. Several pitches higher, take a right-hand fork in the gully and up some thin ice. Take the obvious traverse line around the buttress back into the left-hand gully. Bivi sites can be found by traversing along quartzite ledges to the left. Continue up deep and usually horrible snow conditions to the East Ridge.

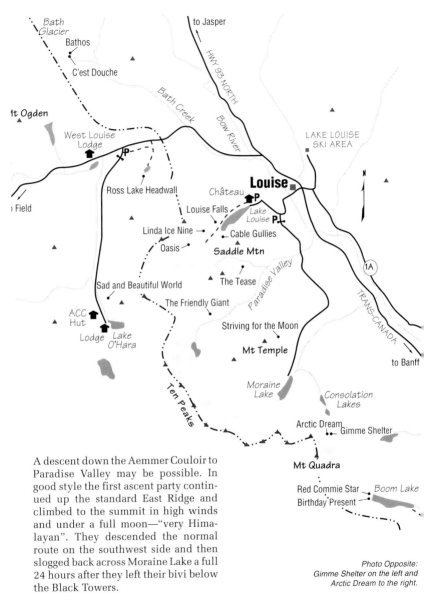

A descent down the Aemmer Couloir to Paradise Valley may be possible. In good style the first ascent party continued up the standard East Ridge and climbed to the summit in high winds and under a full moon—"very Himalayan". They descended the normal route on the southwest side and then slogged back across Moraine Lake a full 24 hours after they left their bivi below the Black Towers.

Photo Opposite: Gimme Shelter on the left and Arctic Dream to the right.

Joseph Josephson

Mount Quadra

Gimme Shelter ** 300 m VI, 7 R

Climbed far ahead of its time in April 1983, this is a beautiful but desperate route which may still be the hardest route in the range. *Gimme Shelter* was originally attempted by Alex and Jeff Lowe, but they backed off, claiming it was too thin, only days before the 'local' first ascent. It has formed only once since and has yet to be repeated. Ski to Moraine Lake and then continue south on to Consolation Valley. If formed, the route is obvious in the centre of the Northeast Face of Mt. Quadra, right of the snow couloir and left of a large buttress; allow five to six hours for the approach (82 N/8 597826). On a clear day, the climb is visible from the upper (#3) parking lot of the Lake Louise Ski Area, 2.5 km northeast of the townsite. Remember, it is found on the main section in the centre of the wall and not in the recessed section on the right. Some smears are commonly seen in the recess and are often mistaken for *Gimme Shelter*. *Gimme Shelter* could be climbed in as few as five pitches but will undoubtedly be done in more (the first ascentionists climbed seven) because you'll need to stop and belay wherever you may be lucky to find enough ice. A cramped bivouac was improvised on the prominent ledge about two-thirds of the way up the route.

Quotes Kevin Doyle after the first ascent, "Not really very reassuring climbing, this one-half to one-inch business, but fortunately, I could breathe a little easier when it gave way to some really thick two-inch ice after 60 or 70 feet, which was also rotten and accepted a perfectly useless ice screw. Some worrying moments later, I reached one of the plates of ice, three to ten inches thick and usually a couple of feet square, which presented themselves every 160 feet along the route on these thin pitches. The ice had steepened considerably." The first ascentionists rappelled from conduit and used no bolts.

Reference
Polar Circus, No. 1, Pg. 21 illus., 1986.

Arctic Dream *** 300 m VI, 6

The winter of 1991/92 was the only time this route has been known to form. In fact, it was the first time *Gimme Shelter* even remotely came close to forming since its bold first ascent. Located 20 m to the right of *Gimme Shelter* but considerably thicker, *Arctic Dream* offers incredible climbing in an audacious alpine position. Hopefully, in the future these routes will be more consistent.

Climb two pitches of moderate ice to the base of a long sustained pillar. Climb technical ice up the pillar for three full ropelengths. Another 55 m of WI 4 ice leads to a snow gully below the seracs. Rappel the route. (This could also offer a reasonably quick and safer descent for *Gimme Shelter).*

On the third ascent of *Arctic Dream,* the team continued on past the serac barrier to reach the glacier above. This added four difficult pitches on some very poor glacier ice. Total length of the climb including the **Direct Finish** is 500 m. To descend, walk down the obvious snow couloir to the left with one short rappel (also an alternative descent for *Gimme Shelter).*

Bath Creek

The two following climbs are located up Bath Creek in an alpine setting with an alpine approach.

Park on the right (north) side of the Trans-Canada Highway, 9 km west of Lake Louise. Park in the first of two plowed lots, just before the highway crosses the bridge over Bath Creek. From the parking lot, head north to the railroad tracks, cross the tracks and continue up Bath Creek 8 km to the routes; two to three hours. See Chic Scott's *Ski Trails in the Canadian Rockies*, page 110. Visible from the Trans-Canada as you drive north past Lake Louise, *Bathos* and *C'est Douche* are the two most prominent parallel smears. A number of other routes may be possible in this area.

C'est Douche * 90 m III, 3

Spindrifts and thin ice on the first pitch give this route an alpine feeling and is easily done the same day as *Bathos*. This is a beautiful setting that few climbers ever explore. Traverse to the top of *Bathos* and rappel that route.

Bathos ** 100 m III, 4

A pretty route in the gully right of *C'est Douche, Bathos* is defined in Webster's Dictionary as "dramatic contrast or humour in the midst of drama; a ludicrous descent from the elevated to the mean". The route climbs up good ice for 50 m, then rambles to the top. Rappel the route.

The rarely-visited Bath Creek.
C'est Douche (left)
Bathos (right).
Photo Frank Campbell

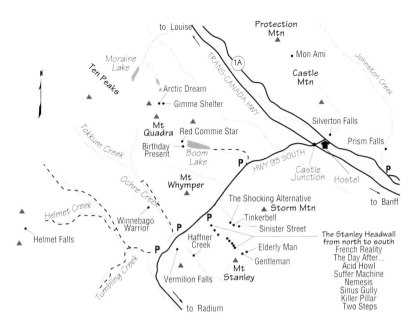

to Louise

Protection Mtn ▲

1A

• Mon Ami

TRANS-CANADA HWY

Moraine Lake

Ten Peaks ▲

Castle Mtn ▲

Johnston Creek

Arctic Dream ▲

• • Gimme Shelter

Silverton Falls

Prism Falls

Tokkum Creek

Mt Quadra ▲

Red Commie Star ▲

Birthday Present

Boom Lake

HWY 93 SOUTH

Castle Junction

P

Hostel

Ochre Creek

Mt Whymper ▲

to Banff

Helmet Creek

Helmet Falls ▲

▲

The Shocking Alternative

Storm Mtn ▲

Winnebago Warrior

P

P

Tinkerbell

Sinister Street

The Stanley Headwall
from north to south
French Reality
The Day After...
Acid Howl
Suffer Machine
Nemesis
Sinus Gully
Killer Pillar
Two Steps

Haffner Creek

Elderly Man

Gentleman

Tumbling Creek

P

Vermilion Falls ▲

Mt Stanley ▲

to Radium

A   B   C

Philippe Pibarot

136 Radium Highway

Also known as the Banff-Radium Parkway, this road runs from Castle Junction on the Trans-Canada Highway to Radium, British Columbia. What this area lacks in quantity of ice climbs, it makes up for in quality and difficulty. Large cliffs which loom over cold, fog-infested valleys add a certain oppressiveness that is unique to the region. Except for Boom Lake, all the routes lie west of the Continental Divide (Vermilion Pass). The area is subject to deep snow conditions. Routes are best approached on skis and have varying degrees of avalanche hazard. A newer area around Boom Lake has a number of moderate routes with little avalanche hazard.

Getting There

The Radium Highway begins at the Trans-Canada and 1A Highways at Castle Junction 28 km northwest of Banff or 22 km southeast of Lake Louise. The Radium Highway travels 105 km east and south to intersect with Highway 95 at Radium in The Columbia Valley. All the routes are concentrated closer to Vermilion Pass on the Continental Divide, only 10.2 km from the Trans-Canada. Vermilion Pass is easy to miss, therefore the mileage markers given are measured from the Trans-Canada overpass.

Facilities

Castle Mountain Hostel, located on the east side of the Trans-Canada Highway at the junction of the 1A and Radium Highways, is a comfortable spot with running water and showers. Gas and basic foods at inflated prices are sold at Castle Mountain Village Store near the hostel. Native land claims around Castle Junction may change access and facilities. Marble Canyon warden station is closed in winter.

Emergency

Contact the Kootenay or the Banff Warden offices. Pay phones are located at Storm Mountain Lodge (closed in winter) 8.2 km west of the Trans-Canada Highway, and at the Marble Canyon Warden Station (17.3 km from the Trans-Canada). See page 272.

Maps

82 N/8 Lake Louise
82 N/1 Mt. Goodsir

Photo opposite: Stanley Headwall with belays indicated.
(A) Acid Howl (unformed).
(B) The Day After les Vacances de Monsieur Hulot.
(C) French Reality.

Boom Lake

Park at Boom Lake Trailhead east of Vermilion Pass, 6.4 km west of the overpass. The trail is usually packed or broken as it is a common ski tour. The routes are easily seen close together on the left side at the far end of the lake, 1.5-2.5 hours depending on snow conditions (82 N/8 791625).

Some unclimbed smears may be found farther to the right. The 50 m snow slope to reach the routes (and a gully feeding into it from the left) is avalanche-prone; however, there is little hazard from above while on the routes themselves.

Birthday Present * 150 m III, 4

This two-tiered climb with a pitch of snow in the middle is the most obvious route on the left side of the lake. It starts on the right side of the avalanche cone coming out of a snow gully to the left.

Climb two pitches of ice with the top being the crux. An easier variation called *Waterworks* (WI 3) banks out left from the snow band. Rappel from trees on the right.

Red Commie Star * 50 m III, 4

Look in the gully just right of *Birthday Present*. *Red Commie Star* can be identified by a broken, hanging pillar above.

This is a narrow climb with two steep steps with a break in the middle. The unclimbed pillar above would make a great route if it formed. Rappel the route.

Reference

Canadian Alpine Journal, Dr. Risk, Vol. 74, pg. 46 illus., 1991.

Storm Creek

Several climbs are found in this valley parallel (northeast) of the Stanley Glacier Trail. Park 11.5 km west of the overpass. Do not park in the avalanche zone threatening the road. Be sure to park east of the "No Stopping" sign. Some smears and pillars are just visible at the top of a cliff on the right side of the drainage. The described routes lie farther along and are not visible until quite far up the valley. They are good routes, but the approach may leave you singing the blues. When leaving the road, pick just about any line leading into the valley. Copious amounts of deadfall created as a result of the Vermilion Fire in 1968, combined with no established trail can make it a rough go. It is probably best to wait until February when the snowpack is sufficient to cover the deadfall. These parallel climbs are on a steep wall on the right (southwest) side of the valley; two to three hours. The potential for avalanche hazard is your normal Rockies mix—nothing outrageous but all dependent on conditions.

The Shocking Alternative ** 100 m IV, 4

About 3 km up the ravine is the first substantial and continuous of three parallel drips (82 N/1 677718). Begin with a 10-m step to a steep snow ledge. Climb more WI 3 to a cone of ice beneath an overhanging block under which you can get a good sheltered hanging belay. Climb the 30 cm wide cone above to gain steep ice for 20 m after which the ice eases off. Climbed in three pitches. Two rappels down the route.

Tinkerbell ** 150 m IV, 4

Look for a climb similar in character to *The Shocking Alternative* about 250 m to the right (82 N/1 675719). *Tinkerbell* offers some interesting thin ice problems on brittle ice. Pitons may be useful for the first belay. The second hanging belay is off a natural rock thread and the third belay off ice. Rappel the route or traverse left and descend *Sinister Street*.

Sinister Street *** 50 m IV, 4

This left-hand smear, 50 m right of *Tinkerbell* (82 N/1 676719) was the scene of a bold solo first ascent.

This fine, sustained climb begins with an 8-m, freestanding pillar and ends around beautiful, overhanging scoops that form near the top due to wind. Rappel the route; a single bolt anchor is on the left.

Dave Thomson

Sinister Street.

Stanley Glacier Trail

This popular summer hiking trail to the base of the North Face of Mt. Stanley is one of the main attractions on the east side of Kootenay Park. Winter creates an ice box that has a surprisingly large amount of frozen water. All the routes face northeast so don't expect to be tanning at the belays. From the Trans-Canada, drive 13.5 km west on Highway 93 South to the Stanley Glacier trailhead. A steep, switchbacked ski trail carries you to the valley above. The trail emerges from the trees underneath a huge, menacing cliff band (600 m) looming on the right. Three ice smears can be seen from the highway at the mouth of the valley on this massive 'Headwall'. At various times the trail is threatened by avalanche slopes from both sides. The avalanche cones (200 m or so) leading to the base of the climbs can be terribly wind-loaded with bottomless depth hoar, requiring circuitous route-finding up seemingly straightforward slopes to reach the base of the routes. Routes are described from right to left as you ski up the valley.

French Reality *** 145 m V, 6+

This wild route is the first obvious pillar that spills out of the hole at the mouth of the valley. *French Reality* does form regularly, although not every year. Ski up the switchbacks, then continue through the forest far right of the route. Stay near an area of burned trees because the forest to the left has several cliff bands. Once below the Headwall, traverse left for 300-400 m on a large avalanche prone ledge to the base of the route.

The first short pitch traverses a narrow and thin vein to a fixed belay on pitons. The next pitch up a steep narrow corner is often very thin with vertical sections (rock gear useful) to the base of some large splattered mushrooms. Find your way past the mushrooms on vertical and often brittle ice. The final spectacular tongue (crux) takes 90°+ ice to an aesthetic cave just below the prominent ledge that runs across the entire face. Rappel the route on fixed bolts and pitons as follows (as described in 1991); first at the top, second right, third at the bottom of the pillar (may be covered with ice), fourth at the bottom of the gully.

The Day After les Vacances de Monsieur Hulot ** 270 m V, 5.9 A2 WI 6

The outrageous nature of this climb is reflected in its title. Named after a series of famous French movies about a particular Monsieur Hulot, it was first climbed by an Anglophone and a Francophone, thus the bilingual title.

This dripping of ice, about 150 m past *French Reality,* has never formed ice completely to the ground. It begins in a wide series of spectacular pillars and amazing mushrooms onto a ledge halfway up the route and then pours into a single narrow icicle that fails 30 m short of the ground. Either approach from a large ledge below *French Reality* or ski directly below the route to a large cave at the bottom of the cliff band. Although the line is not a pure one, there is fantastic mixed climbing with excellent rock and beautiful ice features. *French Reality* and *Acid Howl* are pure ice climbs that do not always form, but as a mixed line this route will be climbable most seasons. A rock rack of 10 pitons, 3 Friends and 6 wires is adequate. No bolts are used.

Climb a rock corner 5 m left of the cave (5.8) to gain the large ledge. Start-

ing left of the black headwall containing the hanging icicle (piton), free climb a left-facing corner on good hard rock to a ledge on the left (piton). Climb a short pitch up a steep groove (A2) to a two piton belay. Continue aid climbing up the groove on overhanging rock to ice. Climb 10 m of ice to a ledge and traverse right to a fixed wire. Continue right to a hidden chimney with a thin smear of ice. This exciting and difficult section leads to a snow ledge and an apron of bad ice below the upper pillars. Continue up the apron to a belay in a small cave. Trend right through crazy mushrooms and icicles to a ledge below the final pillar. 25 m of very steep and lacy ice leads to the top and a ledge below a large overhang. Rappel the route. Two rappels on ice, then three rappels (fixed) down rock.

Acid Howl * 320 m V, 6+ X

400 m past *French Reality,* a third ice vein called Acid Howl originates with two to three separate lines halfway up the Headwall. These smears pour onto the prominent ledge and then fall into two huge parallel freestanding pillars. Another freestanding column is found near the bottom and is not visible from the highway unless you hike up the road cuts on the north side of the road. This very physically demanding route was first climbed in minus 30°C

Climb a short step of bad ice and snow to the base of the first pencil. The first ascent found unconsolidated overhanging ice for 30 m that required major amounts of cleaning to find hook placements and psychological protection. Another two pitches of WI 3 and snow arrive at two parallel pillars. The left-hand pillar will form more regularly but both have been climbed. Either one offers tremendous sustained and tech-

Jeff Everett

Frontal view of The Suffer Machine.

nical climbing for a full 50 m to a belay. Continue up a short step of steep ice to a ledge below a WI 5 pitch on the right that leads to the prominent ledge. Another WI 6 section could be found straight up the left pillar. From a short bowl, a choice of three steep smears lead to the top. Rappel the route.

California Dreamin

No concise information has been revealed about this route. Debates range from which smear it really is to xenophobic arguments over whether or not the Americans who climbed the route did in fact climb anything. Not being able to decipher all the competing ideas, I have quashed them all by using the names given above. They adequately describe all the climbing in the area and it doesn't really matter what they are called. They offer excellent and difficult climbing that is highly recommended.

Reference

Rock and Ice, Vol. 11, pg. 46-7, Jan/Feb 1986.

Suffer Machine 200 m V, A2 WI 5

Farther up the valley the headwall becomes slightly lower with large avalanche slopes above. Two major and obvious routes are found 250 m apart, *Suffer Machine* on the right and *Nemesis* on the left. Neither are visible from lower down in the valley and require several hours of skiing to the base. Beware of avalanche hazard on the large slope below the routes.

The first attempt of this route, which has never completely formed, was with an aluminum extension ladder to reach the broken-off pillar. Not quite able to make it, the first ascent team finally aid climbed up the rock on the right and

Nemesis in usual conditions.

pendulummed onto the ice to continue up three pitches of steep climbing on good ice. If it ever forms completely it will be an outstanding, pure ice climb.

Reference
Canadian Alpine Journal, Vol 75, pp. 62-4, photos, 1992.

Nemesis *** 160 m VI, 6

This Rockies classics represented a major jump in standards on the first ascent in 1974, again in 1980 after the first free ascent, and in 1991 when it was first soloed. Today *Nemesis* remains a tremendous challenge to even the best climbers and is one of the few early climbs that has not been downgraded or lost its reputation. It is usually climbed in a day but start early and expect to come home in the dark. Approach as for *Suffer Machine*; however, there is a slight rib below the route that makes the approach slope less threatening. Beware of avalanche slopes above.

The route forms every year but with varying quality. Rarely are climbs as continuously steep as this one, averaging 85° throughout. It is usually climbed in four pitches but has been done in three. Guy Lacelle, with an extra long rope, once did the route in one and a quarter pitches, the first 'pitch' taking four hours. Expect the ice to be thin and occasionally rotten on the first two pitches leading to a sloping ledge. The crux is usually the third pitch off the ledge which gradually improves near the top. A short pitch is needed to finish. Some fixed stations exist on the rock to the right but be prepared to leave up to four rappel anchors.

Reference
Polar Circus, Vol 2, pg. 58, illus., 1987.

Sinus Gully * 75 m IV, 5.6 WI 3

Despite the long approach, this is a nice route about 200 m left of *Nemesis*.

A long crux pitch leads to a cave below a huge overhang. Climb easy rock on the left-hand wall to a traverse line widening onto the snow ledge above *Killer Pillar*. Continue left for 60 m to a short exit pitch of ice. Traverse left across avalanche slopes to turn the cliff and post hole back to the base or rappel *Killer Pillar*.

Killer Pillar * 50 m IV, 5+

This steep testpiece pours off the front of the buttress between *Two Steps* and *Sinus Gully*. Look for the obvious pillar to the right as you approach *Nemesis* that doesn't always form.

Work your way up one pitch of difficult climbing past technical mushrooms and featureless ice. Rappel the route.

Two Steps 45 m III, 2

The left-most gully before the Headwall flattens out into a large avalanche slope.

Good ice with several steeper sections. Rappel the route or walk off left across avalanche slopes.

Jeff Marshall gunning for the top on the first ascent of Killer Pillar.

Mount Stanley

The following two routes on Mt. Stanley were done after a freak autumn season Arctic front. They are chimney climbs in true Scottish fashion with fun mixed climbing. Their inclusion in a waterfall ice guide is specious at best, as they are alpine routes with long approaches. They are included here for two reasons. First, they are cold weather climbs (i.e. late fall to spring) that need a certain amount of water ice to be enjoyable or recommended. Secondly, they are indicative of the vast amount of (and largely untouched) quality climbing, both alpine and water ice that is to be found in this valley. Check it out!

A Gentleman's Day Out IV, 5.8 mixed

As you ski up the valley, look above the obvious tree covered rock bench just past Killer Pillar. The route is found hidden in a tight gully on the front of the buttress above the bench on the lower left side of the North Face of Mt. Stanley. It begins at reference 82 N/1 666692 and runs up and left for four or five pitches. The first ascent party traversed into the *Y-couloir* and continued across the summit of Mt. Stanley and descended the standard North Ridge.

An Elderly Man's Day Out IV, 5.7 mixed

Around the buttress to the left of Gentleman's Route at 82 N/1 669692 and after four to five pitches, this route ends on the same slope as A Gentleman's Day Out. Another alpine route, *The Outlander Couloir*, begins about 400 m left of here at 82 N/1 672692 and goes to the summit of an unnamed peak between Stanley and Mt. Ball. On the first ascent of Elderly Man's Route, the team traversed over this summit and descended to the east.

Haffner Creek

Haffner Creek Ice Flows ** 20-25 m II, 3-4+

This exciting canyon is loaded with numerous flows over steep, narrow walls. Park at the large parking lot and warden station at Marble Canyon. Cross the Highway and ski across the parks campground and into Haffner Creek. Continue upstream for 30 minutes. The flows are obvious.

Climb on any number of steep flows and pillars (some freestanding). There must be over 20 to chose from. Possibilities for playing around and testing techniques are unlimited. Most pillars have tree anchors.

Marble Canyon

A number of seepages flow off the canyon walls along this popular summer hiking trail. A few people have climbed on them over the years. However, this practice is not recommended. Most of the seeps do not rise to the very top of the canyon walls. This can make it difficult to top out on any route, especially if you choose to lead them. You must climb to the top of your chosen route for it is impossible to walk out of the canyon. Rappelling into this very tight canyon can be tricky due to large amounts of snow around the rim with fragile overhangs of vegetation and rotten rock. This makes approaching the rim dangerous for your health and can destroy the plant life in the area. Please, there are better areas to find short pillars of bad snow-covered ice.

Winnebago Warrior ** 375 m IV, 4

Park at the large parking lot and warden station at Marble Canyon. Ski past the canyon and up Tokkum Creek for one hour. The climb is visible on the left (82 N/1 581748). This long, early-season climb should not be attempted when there is any sort of avalanche hazard. Seeps funnel down from over 1000 metres above. Oh yah, you must cross Tokkum Creek without getting your feet wet.

Look for the route identified by a short pillar in a gully at the start. Continue up lots of WI 3 ice with a crux curtain higher up. Named in honour of a friend who chose graduate school over ice climbing. Imagine! Rappel and downclimb route.

Vermilion Falls * 200 m III, 4+

The first pitch is visible on the south side of the road several hundred metres west of the Marble Canyon Warden Station. It is located in the middle of a large avalanche path, (82 N/1 616692). Park 1.0 km west of the warden station. Cross the river and then walk through the runout zone to the base; two hours.

The first 40-m pitch climbs a steep curtain to a pillar. The 150 m of rolling WI 2 above is often covered in snow. Rappel the pillar or from the top of the climb, descend through trees to the left.

Helmet Creek

Helmet Falls *** 300 m V, 4

"How to go to jail in one easy step". This is what two Calgary climbers learned after breaking into the Park Service Cabin near the base of this remote waterfall. Although they got by with community service, they still haven't lived down this notorious incident. After you ski 16 km into this waterfall, you'll understand why they looked for more comfortable lodging. The trail is rarely broken and you can expect a long day to reach the falls. On a more inspiring note, *Helmet Falls* has been climbed in a day car-to-car! Park at the Paint Pots trailhead, 20 km from the Trans-Canada overpass at Castle Junction. Ski up Ochre Creek. Several kilometres along, the Tumbling Glacier Trail comes down from the left. Keep going straight and turn left at the Helmet Creek Trail. This leads to near the base of the climb (82 N/1 475707); five hours total.

The climb is a spectacular, massive wall of ice. The first two pitches are the crux, then continue up for three or four more pitches. Rappel the route.

The massive Helmet Falls.

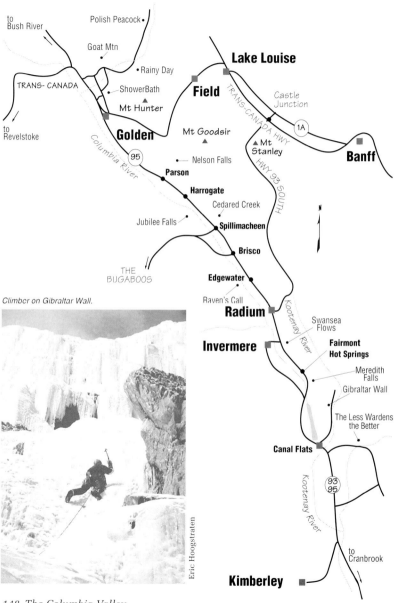

to Bush River

Polish Peacock •

Goat Mtn

• Rainy Day

Lake Louise

TRANS- CANADA

ShowerBath

Field

Castle Junction

▲ Mt Hunter

TRANS-CANADA HWY

(1A)

to Revelstoke

Golden

Mt Goodsir ▲

▲ Mt Stanley

Banff

(95)

Columbia River

HWY 93 SOUTH

• Nelson Falls

Parson

Harrogate

Cedared Creek

Jubilee Falls •

Spillimacheen

Brisco

THE BUGABOOS

Edgewater •

Kootenay River

Raven's Call

Radium

Swansea Flows

Invermere

Fairmont Hot Springs

• Meredith Falls

Gibraltar Wall

The Less Wardens the Better

Canal Flats

(93) (95)

Kootenay River

to Cranbrook

Kimberley

Climber on Gibraltar Wall.

Eric Hoogstraten

148 The Columbia Valley

THE COLUMBIA VALLEY

This broad valley otherwise known as the Rocky Mountain Trench forms the western boundary of the range and parallels the west slope for hundreds of kilometres. Life in the Columbia Valley is a slow-paced, relaxed affair, symptomatic of the mild winter weather experienced here. As a result of these warmer temperatures, the climbs don't form until late December and fall apart by early March. There is a lot of private property along the main highway (#93/95). Permission may be required to get to some climbs but most are serviced by open logging roads. Access is often a matter of finding the right road that leads to the route(s). This wide expansive valley doesn't have tons of water ice, but the selection offers some good easy to moderate routes and a couple of difficult testpieces. Most routes have absolutely no avalanche hazard which is a huge bonus when compared to the rest of the Rockies.

Getting There

From the Trans-Canada Highway at Castle Junction take Highway 93 South (Radium Highway) to Radium Hot Springs. In Radium, at the 4-way stop (Radium Crossroads), turn north on Highway 95 to pass through the small communities of Edgewater, Brisco (Bugaboos turnoff), Spillimacheen, Harrogate and Parson to Golden to re-intersect the Trans-Canada. From the Radium Crossroads south, follow Highway 93/95 past Invermere, Fairmont Hot Springs, Canal Flats and Cranbrook, and, if you wish, clear to Coeur d'Alene, Idaho (Highway 95) or Kalispell, Montana (Highway 93).

Facilities

Along Highway 93/95 between Radium and Fairmont are numerous resorts, motels and other tourist attractions. There are no hostels or other official winter camping areas but primitive camping can be accomplished off logging roads scattered along the west side of the valley. The mild weather makes this a real option in winter but make sure you find a private location off the beaten track. Commercial hot springs at Radium and Fairmont provide a relaxing diversion, but save your money and check out the Lussier Hot Springs on the White Swan Lake Road south of Canal Flats. Refer to the Less Wardens the Better route description for details. There are no 24-hour gas stations or convenience stores in the south end of the valley so be prepared.

Emergency

A logging camp or a private residence may be tucked away in some areas but you will usually have to reach the main highway to find a phone. Contact the Invermere or Radium RCMP detachment for assistance. See page 272.

Maps

82 J/4   Canal Flats
82 J/15 Fairmont Hot Springs
82 K/16 Radium Hot Springs
82 N/2   McMurdo

Gibraltar Wall.

150 The Columbia Valley

Highway 93/95

The following routes are found in the Upper Columbia Valley and Kootenay River Valley south of Radium Hot Springs. The routes are described from north to south and are accessed from the east side of Highway 93/95.

Swansea Flows * 30 m I, 2

Swansea Flows is located almost directly east of Invermere. From the turnoff into Invermere (13 km south of Radium) head south on Highway 93/95 another 500 m. Turn left (east) on Cooper Road and follow that road for 1 km to the Westroc Mining Road and turn right (south). Drive approximately 2 km and park at an old farming road that leads toward the climb. Walk 15 minutes to the base to an easy practice seep low down on a cliff band.

Meredith Falls 25 m II, 3

A straightforward climb, located in a small wooded gully approximately 1 km south of Fairmont Ski Area, *Meredith* is best located from near the Hoodoo Resort, 3.5 km south of Fairmont. Take the main turnoff into Fairmont Hot Springs Resort (36 km south of Radium) and head south from the Mountain Side Golf Course until you are below the waterfall which is not obvious from the road. Hike uphill and then into the stream bed near the base of the climb.

Climb directly up the flow coming over a steep rock band. Rappel from trees.

Gibraltar Wall *** 145 m II, 4

The western Rockies equivalent of the Weeping Wall, *Gibraltar Wall* forms every year and is a sunny route with three distinct lines of equal difficulty. From Highway 93/95 about 60 km south of Radium, turn into Canal Flats. Paralleling the main drag to the east is a dirt road that heads north. Follow this road as it turns east and continues up the Kootenay River. Drive for 27.2 km from Canal Flats to where Gibraltar is visible on the west side, five to ten minutes away.

The route is a wide expanse of ice in three steep tiers separated by good belay ledges. Rappel the route or walk left until you can easily descend.

The Less Wardens the Better 45 m I, 3/4

The Less Wardens the Better makes a nice south-facing climb but it doesn't always form. Drive south from the Radium Crossroads 65.7 km (4.6 km south of the Kootenay River Bridge) to White Swan Lake Provincial Park Road. Turn left and drive the good gravel road for about 17 km to the hot springs (look for an outhouse and a small brown building on the right side). Continue 1 km further along the road until the falls are visible on the left (north) side only five minutes from the road. The climb is a seep of 80-85° ice that is rated three stars because of the added bonus of free natural hot springs to recover in. Rappel off trees.

Highway 95

The following routes are found on both sides of Highway 95 between Radium Hot Springs and Golden. They are described from south to north.

Raven's Call *** 45 m II, 5

Clearly visible from Highway 95 just north of Edgewater above the west side of the Columbia River, *Raven's Call* is an excellent challenging climb in a pleasant setting with a nice approach. It usually doesn't form until late December but seems to come in regularly. From the 4-way stop at the Radium Crossroads, drive 4 km west on Horsethief Road and turn right (north) onto Steamboat Mountain Forest Service Road/Red Rock Road. Drive north paralleling the Columbia River and stay left on the main road. At the 14 km marker, Steamboat Mountain Road heads left, but you stay right for another 1 km (road may not be maintained at this point) until you see a livestock pen on your right. Park and walk due east toward the river valley and intersect a small stream. Follow it down on the north side to the top of the falls, ten minutes from car. Rappel the route or walk down on steep rock and snow to the north to reach the base.

This beautiful pillar forms in two parts. The bottom part is a mushrooming pedestal which is usually climbed on either side to avoid the mushrooms. The climb finishes up a round freestanding pillar which usually cracks near the top. Belay off trees at the top.

The classic Raven's Call.

Cedared Creek Seeps * 30 m II, 3

This climb features north-facing ice which stays formed later into the season than do most climbs in the valley. From Radium, drive 4.5 km north from Spillimacheen on Highway 95 or 6 km south of Harrogate General Store. Park where small logging roads head east through an area of recent logging (1994) and ski or snowmobile up the road. After approximately 2 km, head right (south) into Cedared Creek and follow a deteriorating road to where the drainage narrows. The climb is found on the south wall of the canyon.

This moderate climb can be climbed on various lines. Rappel off ice or an incipient bush. Five minutes further upstream on the south side is another route called **The Tumor** ** 70 m II, 3.

Jubilee Falls 35-70 m III, 2-4

This is a group of climbs which form on the East Face of Jubilee Mountain and are visible west across the Columbia River 8.5 km north of Spillimacheen or 2 km south of the Harrogate General Store. Park on Highway 95 across from the climbs. Cross the Columbia River and then hike up through dense forest to the gully draining the climbs; two hours. The river is quite shallow and may be frozen but if not, you can cross the river on a bridge (Westside Road) that heads west out of Spillimacheen. After 2 km turn right (north) onto Giant Mascot Mine Road for about 1 km, then turn right (north) onto Jubilee Mountain Forest Service Road. Drive as far as possible, then ski or mountain bike down the road until it turns uphill and then traverse into the base of the climbs. A long approach. All descents are rappels from trees.

Up to four separate climbs are possible. The **left-hand line** (35 m) is the most obvious and has the largest open slope leading to it. It gives good ice with a variety of lines (WI 3/4). The two smears to the right are 60-70 m high of WI 2. A final 60-m WI 4 route forms as a pillar 20 m right (north) of the above smears.

Nelson Creek Falls ** 300 m IV, 5

Nelson Creek Falls is a spectacular climb visible high above Highway 95 and is subject to avalanche. 5 km north of the Parson General Store on Highway 95 or 32 km south of Golden, turn east on Madden Road and intersect Campbell Road after 3 km. Follow Campbell Road north and turn east on Allen Road which leads to a private residence bordering the small drainage (Nelson Creek) coming from the climb. Walk or ski up the drainage for up to two hours to the base.

The climb starts with rolling ice (often snow covered) up to a WI 3 pitch in an open book. Climb a steep pillar to a curtain of ice and into the upper basin. Finish up 100 m of steep and sustained ice. Rappel the route.

Note: It is important to obtain permission from landowners before crossing private property.

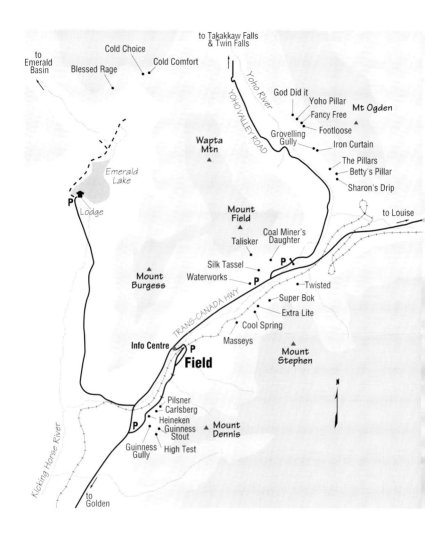

to Takakkaw Falls
& Twin Falls

to Emerald Basin

Cold Choice

Blessed Rage   Cold Comfort

Yoho River

YOHO VALLEY ROAD

God Did it
Yoho Pillar
Fancy Free   Mt Ogden
Footloose

Grovelling
Gully   Iron Curtain

Wapta
Mtn

The Pillars
Betty's Pillar

Sharon's Drip

Emerald Lake

P Lodge

to Louise

Mount
Field

Talisker   Coal Miner's
Daughter

Silk Tassel   P X

Mount
Burgess   Waterworks   P

Twisted

Super Bok

Extra Lite

Cool Spring

Masseys

Mount
Stephen

Info Centre   P
Field

Pilsner
Carlsberg
Heineken   Mount
Guinness   Dennis
Stout

Guinness   High Test
Gully

Kicking Horse River

to Golden

Roadside waterfalls abound, making Yoho National Park one of the main ice climbing venues in the Rockies. Many climbs face north, but they usually don't offer good climbing until late December. Seepages take longer to form in this region as it is located deep in the mountains at a lower elevation than Banff. The flip side is that consistently cold temperatures clear into March create a longer season that is not affected by Chinooks. Being in a region of heavy snowfall, there can be severe avalanche hazard throughout the valley. Avalanche accidents are common, especially on *Silk Tassel* and *Extra Light*. Field author, Graeme Pole, has written an excellent log book with photos and descriptions of most routes. It is kept at the Parks Information Centre located next to the Trans-Canada Highway in Field along with an ice climbing conditions report. Routes along Mount Ogden are assigned numbers and I recommend you check the log book for additional reference. The Centre is open 9 am to 4 pm daily (in 1994) but this could change due to government funding cuts. Weather and avalanche reports are posted outside the front door in case the offices aren't open when you come by.

Getting There

The Trans-Canada Highway is the only access into or out of Yoho Park. The town of Field is located 20 km west of Lake Louise just off the Trans-Canada. Golden is 55 km further west.

Facilities

The area offers some fine accommodations that tend to be slightly cheaper, less crowded and more relaxed than the extravagant lodgings that attract the big tourist crowds in Banff and Lake Louise. These include Kicking Horse Lodge located in Field on the west end of town, West Louise Lodge about halfway between Field and Lake Louise, and the luxurious Emerald Lake Lodge on the beautiful shores of Emerald Lake. The Alpine Club of Canada (ACC) has two backcountry huts that can be used as a base for some of the more remote climbs, the Elizabeth Parker Hut at Lake O'Hara and the Stanley Mitchell Hut in the Yoho Valley. Both require a day ski tour to reach them. There is also a very comfortable (and expensive) lodge at Lake O'Hara.

Emergency

Yoho Park wardens and the Field RCMP detachment have 24-hour emergency numbers. Pay phones are available at Field Visitor Centre or Emerald Lake Lodge. Lake O'Hara Lodge has access to a radio phone. There are no phones in the Yoho Valley. See Page 272.

Maps

82 N/8 Lake Louise
82 N/7 Golden

1A Highway

Ross Lake Headwall 50 m III, 3

Just west of the Continental Divide (Kicking Horse Pass) look south on a headwall of rock below a long hanging valley underneath the North Face of Popes Peak. Often there is a smear of ice just right of centre on the headwall. Continue west on the Highway to the Lake O'Hara parking lot 12.6 km west of Lake Louise. From the parking lot, ski east on the 1A Highway 2 km to the Ross Lake trailhead, then follow the trail south to Ross Lake. The climb is on the cliff band across the lake and up a slope, 1-1.5 hours (82 N/8 483978).

One pitch of occasionally thin ice ends in a snow patch. Rappel the route or traverse left and climb up to the hanging valley. From here it is possible to walk off across a flat bench to the right (west), then down through the trees back to the lake.

Lake O'Hara

This beautiful area has a magical ambiance in winter. You are in for a treat while visiting this seldom-visited winter area. Only one route has been done, but undoubtedly there are many more, especially near Odaray Mountain. From Lake Louise, drive west 12.6 km on the Trans-Canada to the Lake O'Hara parking lot. Follow the fire road southwest for 11 km to the lake. Accommodation is available at the ACC Elizabeth Parker Hut; call the Alpine Club in Canmore for reservations. Lake O'Hara Lodge offers more upscale service and has a radio phone that may be used in case of an emergency.

Sad and Beautiful World ** 160 m IV, 4

This fine climb is located on Wiwaxy Peak left of the popular rock route *Grassi Ridge*. As you near Lake O'Hara, the route is plainly visible from the road up to the left (east). Climb up through the trees to the left or right of a 150-m, avalanche-prone slope to the base, three hours (82 N/8 461905).

Start up 60-70 m of easy ice to the base of a major curtain of steep ice. A varied 50 m pitch of WI 3/4 leads to the base of a snow slope. Climb the snow slope to the best feature on the route, a 75 m narrow ice stream up to 80° in an iron-hard quartzite gully. Climb the gully, then walk a long ways up and right to a 15 m steep pillar. A light rock rack including pitons is recommended.

Rappel the route. Some rock anchors exist but may be covered.

Note: Several of the rappel stations were placed on the descent and therefore may be difficult to reach while climbing up the route. Near the bottom of the climb, some trees may be used out to the left but then it will require some downclimbing through tricky ledges to reach the base.

Mount Ogden

The Yoho Valley Road offers the most concentrated area of water ice in Yoho Park. The log book at the Info Centre in Field outlines 27 different smears (numbered Ogden 1-27) up to 10.5 km from the parking lot. In the past this area has been neglected because of confusion over route names, lengths and difficulties. Recent exploration has rediscovered a number of routes and created some excellent new climbs that are easily accessed. This all adds up to yet another Rockies mini-Mecca of ice climbing.

All routes have varying degrees of avalanche hazard, either from the huge slopes above or in isolated pockets near the climbs. Most routes in this guide are detailed from left to right but here they are described from right to left. This is the order in which you will encounter them as you ski up the road. It also is consistent with the order they are given in the Field log book. Park at the Yoho Valley Road parking lot 3.5 km east of Field. Ski along the road and find the route(s) that interest you, then cross the Yoho River to the base. Skis are recommended to approach all routes.

Sharon's Drip (Ogden 6) * 45 m III, 3

The former route description for this climb has caused much of the confusion regarding this area. It called for a "single pitch of moderate V-shaped ice in a gully right of *The Pillars*." There is a prominent V-shaped route, but it is by no means "moderate" (see *Betty's Pillar*). As a result, it is unsure exactly where this route lies. Either the first ascentionists grossly underestimated their abilities or *Sharon's Drip* is one of the easier flows farther right. As you ski up the road you'll come to the Meeting of the Waters

Viewpoint. Just past here the road makes a sharp turn to the northeast. Just before the corner, a moderate flow can be seen on the left side of a cliffband that hides a huge avalanche path above it. (82-N/8 406994). This may be *Sharon's Drip*. Another similar flow exists farther to the right out of sight.

Betty's Pillar (Ogden 8) ** 45 m III, 5

200 m left of *Sharon's Drip* is a deep gully. On the steep cliff face just left of this gully and above a small avalanche slope is a prominent V-shaped climb (82-N/8 399998). *Betty's Pillar* goes straight up. A second easier line follows the groove to the left which may be *Sharon's Drip*. *Betty's Pillar* was a bold solo first ascent, named in memory of a friend who died of cancer.

Climb steep ice to a small ledge followed by a 30-m vertical pillar. Rappel the route (beware of dubious trees near the top).

The Pillars (Ogden 7) 25-70 m III, 4-5

These are the most obvious pillars seen from the Trans-Canada as you come down the hill into Field. They lie around the corner left of *Betty's Pillar* (82-N/8 398997). Ski up the road until directly across from the routes. Cross the river, through some trees and climb up a short avalanche slope to the base where several varied pillars pour from the rock wall. Depending on the nature of the ice and the exact line, this route can be a good arm-pumping top rope. Rappel the route.

Iron Curtain (Ogden 14) ** 85 m IV, 6

Iron Curtain presents a stunning section of ice that deserves much more attention. Past *The Pillars* is a prominent avalanche path with a blue flow of ice at its narrowest part. Don't worry, this deathly route is not *Iron Curtain*. It is the obvious wall of ice to the left (82-N/8 394005). This challenging route was soloed in 1990. From the Yoho Valley Road, ski through the trees to the left of the large avalanche path for 30-40 minutes. The first 50 m is on sustained technical ice. It is followed by more reasonable 70° ice. Rappel from trees to the right of the route.

Grovelling Gully (Ogden 15) * 95 m III, 3

This climb was named after the grovelling creatures who whimpered up the hidden gully bordering the left side of the *Iron Curtain*. At least one of these creatures redeemed himself by returning and climbing the challenge to the right. Anyway, it's still a nice WI 3 route.

The gully is climbed in two stepped pitches. Rappel as for *Iron Curtain*.

God Did It (Ogden 16) 60 m III, 3
Yoho Pillar (Ogden 17) 30 m III, 3
Fancy Free (Ogden 18) 60 m III, 2
Footloose (Ogden 19) 60 m III, 2

These four routes are nothing spectacular by themselves; however, they are situated very close to each other and offer an opportunity to bag all four in an easy day (82-N/8 392006). They are located in an open area (avalanche-prone) left of the *Iron Curtain* and all start with sections of wide easy climbing leading to nice blue ice near the top. Check the excellent photo in the Field log book. Approach up the Yoho Valley Road past *Iron Curtain* to where the road starts to climb up the switchbacks. Turn off the road and ski along the banks of the river for several hundred metres to the base of the large open area below the routes.

Footloose and *Fancy Free* are the left and right variations of a wide band of ice on the left side of the open area. These are usually climbed first. Find a convenient rappel tree to the right that you can use after each route to put you in good position to head up *Yoho Pillar* and *God Did It. Yoho Pillar* is the blue pillar in the centre of the open area. *God Did It* heads out right from below *Yoho Pillar* with a number of variations that round out a good day with lots of moving over ice.

Yoho River Valley

Takakkaw Falls **
250 m V, 4 (X 2nd pitch)

Historically, *Takakkaw* is THE classic waterfall of the range. It was the second big waterfall to be climbed (in minus 30°C temperatures) after the ascent of *Bourgeau Left-Hand*. During the mid '70s it was the testing ground as abilities improved. *Takakkaw* is the second highest waterfall in all of Canada and a major summer tourist attraction. In winter, it is a remote undertaking and thus has dropped in popularity in recent years. Nevertheless, it is requisite for all dedicated Rockies ice climbers.

Park at the Yoho Valley Road. Ski up the road 14 km (beware of several large avalanche slopes). The climb is obvious on the east side of the valley. Another half kilometre past the summer parking lot there is a picnic shelter with a supplied wood stove. This makes for a good bivi site, although the route is commonly done in a long day from the road. Cross the Yoho River on a bridge at the south end of the parking lot and work up the slopes to the base. Approach time is dependent on the quality of the ski track along the road, and can take up to four hours if you are breaking trail. See map on page 184.

The first pitch may have a large hole of open water and the crux second pitch is usually quite thin, due to the high volume of water flowing underneath. This shield can be very fragile requiring careful technique; if it collapsed, there would be little chance for survival. The first pitch usually belays on the right side, then the second pitch traverses across the shield to steeper, more solid ice on the left and continues to a broad snow ledge (avalanche-prone). The remainder of the climb is more straightforward on good ice with an interesting exit behind a large rock at the top. Rappel the route. A fixed station may be found at the top, but be prepared to leave up to five anchors.

Twin Falls 100 m V, 4/5

Twin Falls is a very remote pair of waterfalls with a 22 km (one-way) ski approach. Continue past *Takakkaw Falls* to the end of the road and follow the Yoho Valley Trunk Trail to Laughing Falls Campground. Continue up the trail to Twin Falls Campground; then to the Twin Falls Chalet (closed) below the routes. Few people have actually made the journey into these climbs which was once combined with an ascent of *Takakkaw Falls* round trip from the car in a single day! My feet hurt just thinking about it. The climb is best combined with a ski touring trip based out of the ACC Stanley Mitchell Hut. See map page 184.

Climb either or both of the two parallel falls, each in two pitches. The right-hand is a full grade harder than the left. Rappel the routes.

Mount Field

The following routes are on the north side of the Trans-Canada on Mt. Field. *Silk Tassel* and *Talisker* have miles of avalanche chutes feeding into them. Be sure of conditions and avoid these climbs after a snowfall or on warm, sunny days. Check the avalanche report for an update on conditions. Park at the Yoho Valley Road, 3.5 km east of Field. Be sure to park in the east end of the parking lot to avoid the large avalanche run out zone threatening the road.

Silk Tassel ** 55 m III, 4

This classic is the obvious tiered curtain above the junction of the Trans-Canada and the Yoho Valley Road and forms regularly but not always. Head up the steep avalanche-prone slope through alders to the base. The walk is gentler on the legs and the mind if it has already avalanched and you can walk up on debris.

Climb up an ice apron and find a sheltered belay as high as possible on the left. The rest of the climb can be done as one long, challenging pitch. Rappel the route.

Talisker 350 m IV, 3

This climb takes the route on the ice found far above *Silk Tassel*. The quantity and quality of the climbing hardly justifies heading up this dangerous gully.

Climb *Silk Tassel* and continue up lots of snow. As many as three significant steps of ice can be found with the last being the hardest. Rappel and downclimb as quickly as possible.

Coal Miner's Daughter 50 m III, 4

Labelled incorrectly in the Field log book, *Coal Miner's Daughter* lies farther right of the indicated line. It sometimes forms out of an abandoned mine shaft some 300 m right of *Silk Tassel*. Take precautions with unstable mine rails and shafts. Rappel the route.

Waterworks 10-20 m II, 3

1.2 km east of Field is an unmarked service road on the north side of the Trans-Canada. Pull in and park out of the way near a sand pile. Walk along the left-hand road until you see a pipe coming out from a creek. Turn right up the creek to the falls, 15-45 minutes depending upon the amount of snow.

This is a wide section of rolling ice that offers a number of lines with some steeper sections. The top of the ice is easily reached making a good top roping and practice area with zero avalanche hazard.

Mount Stephen

The following six routes are found on Mt. Stephen on the south side of the Trans-Canada east of Field. They can be approached by parking as for Takakkaw Falls on the Yoho Valley Road, then walking across the river and beating up steep slopes to the railroad tracks. But most people make a long walk along the tracks from Field. From the bridge at Field cross the railroad tracks and take the main road left and drive to a parking area on the south side of the tracks at the outskirts of town. Walk down the tracks to the routes and stay out of the large grease and creosote deposits along the tracks—it makes a nasty mess of your footwear. All the routes here are threat-ened by large avalanche slopes. The routes are described from east to west as you may see them as you drive from Louise to Field.

Twisted 150 m III, 4 R

This route formed once in the winter of 1985-86 in a very nondescript location. It lies on the prominent North Ridge of Mt. Stephen. Apparently it is visible as you drive down the big hill from the east on Highway #1 toward Field. It lies below or may even come out of the mine shafts slightly left of the crest of the buttress. If you happen to see ice in this area, this is probably it. Climb three or four pitches of thin mixed climbing. Rappel the route, pitons are probably needed.

The unique first pitch of Super Bock, Grant Statham climbing.

Super Bock *** 300 m III, 5

This is an excellent route with a lot of character. Getting to the route is a 3 km walk from Field along the tracks. You can also approach directly from the parking lot at the Yoho Valley Road. If the river is open, walk along the Trans-Canada to the east side of the Kicking Horse River Bridge then walk west along the tracks through a tunnel to the route. Climb up an open snow gully to the base. It seems to form every year.

The first pitch climbs under a rock arch (making it look unformed from the road). Continue up a snow ramp to a long WI 3 pitch leading to the final pillar. Climb two steep pitches to the top, with the second being a little harder. Another short step can be found above. There is a hanging icicle high on the cliff band to the left of the route. Rappel the route. Depending on conditions, it is possible to traverse right from atop the pillar and make a long rappel into the trees; then, continue down into a steep snow gully and downclimb to the top of the snow ramp. Pitons are on the left just above the arch.

Extra Lite * 245 m III, 3

Extra Lite is an understandably popular climb that offers easy ice for a long way. However, the sizeable chunk of real estate found above the gully makes it one of the more avalanche-prone routes in the area. Check with the wardens and be sure of the conditions before venturing onto this route. Approach as for *Super Bock*; it is found 2.8 km east of Field. The route lies above a weakly defined stream bed that is barely visible from the tracks. The start of the approach up from the tracks is about 150 m west of a small line shack. Hike up through trees to a rock buttress that divides two deep clefts. *Extra Lite* is the left-hand gully.

Climb a series of short ice steps separated by snow slopes. A 50 m WI 4 pitch is located 150 m further up the gully– that makes for a long day. Rappel and downclimb the route. Some trees are available.

Cool Spring ** 35 m III, 5+

The approach is as for *Extra Lite* but is found in the deep right-hand cleft.

Expect a steep ice pillar that can be very demanding. A climber who was going to climb Aconcogua shortly after doing this testpiece was heard saying "I thought I'd never live to see Argentina!" Indeed, it can sport very technical and chandeliered ice and is not often climbed. Rappel the route from a station on the left.

Massey's * 140 m III, 4

This is probably the most commonly climbed route in Yoho. It's a one-pitch wonder with a nice first pitch followed by several pitches of rolling steps. Walk along the tracks 1.6 km east of Field to the gully found just beyond a large boulder at the tracks.

Climb 20-25 m of steep ice, often chandeliered, to where it eases off. Easy ice continues to the top. Walk off left through the trees. No rappels should be needed.

Mount Dennis

The famous beer climbs west of Field on Mt. Dennis are reached by the back road out of town. Cross on the bridge past the Info Centre and follow streets to the west end of town to the water tower and the Kicking Horse Lodge (Field is really small, so don't worry about getting lost).

On the south side of the Lodge follow the one-way, westbound road. Do not try to approach from the Trans-Canada. Parking is allowed at a pull-out with an information board, 2 km west of the power station. All routes can be accessed from here so don't try parking anywhere else. The routes are described from left to right.

If you want to check the routes out beforehand, stop at the Emerald Lake turnoff 2.5 km west of Field on the Trans-Canada. From here all the routes are easily visible. The back road is occasionally closed when the avalanche hazard is high. Avalanche warning signs are clearly posted at the road entrance and it is illegal to enter when closed. Under such circumstances you probably shouldn't be climbing anyway.

Mt. Dennis.
(A) Pilsner Pillar (B) Carlsberg Column
(C) Cascade Kronenbourg (D) Heineken Hall
(E) Labatt's Lane (F) Wild Cougar (G) Top pitch of
Guiness Gully (H) Guinness Stout (I) High Test

Photo opposite: François Damilano on Pilsner Pillar.

Pilsner Pillar *** 215 m III, 6

One of the routes the Rockies is famous for! *Pilsner* is the epitome of a free-standing icicle. Unfortunately it doesn't always form. You can bypass the pillar with some difficulty to reach the ice above but it's hardly recommended. The pillar is what you'll come here for, and a pillar is what you'll find. On the first free ascent in 1978 it was the hardest lead accomplished in Canada to that time and one of the hardest anywhere. Still a much-feared route, it can be very chandeliery with technical and scary hooking. Once in a blue moon it will get big and fat and drop down a notch in difficulty; consider it a steal in these conditions. It constantly forms differently; either on the left or the right, sometimes on both sides and rarely as one huge curtain. The route is visible from the road 0.8 km west of the parking, and hike up an avalanche path to the base in 40-60 minutes depending on conditions.

From the ledge behind the pillar launch up 40 m of dead vertical ice. Try to pick a dry line; it can truly rain down this route. Belay on good ice at the lip or continue 10 m through snow to a rock belay on the right. Up to four pitches of moderate ice can be found above. Rappel the route.

Juste Pour Rire 20 m II, 4 R

15 m right of *Pilsner Pillar* is a thin 80° smear that ends in a cave chimney. A second pitch on rotten rock above is not worth doing. There is an old piton up high on that pitch. Rappel off your own anchor.

Carlsberg Column *** 90 m III, 5

The classic WI 5 route in the range! *Carlsberg* forms without fail every year in the next gully right of *Pilsner*. Hike up through the trees 0.6 km east of the parking. A short steep section can sometimes be climbed below the main falls but it doesn't always form and the ice is usually bad. Most people head up right and climb snow and ice smears to a steep headwall and make an exposed traverse left into the base of the falls; about an hour.

This beautiful line offers several variations depending on what's dry, how 'hard' you're feeling and if anyone else is there. It is possible to accommodate two parties on the route depending upon where people are willing to climb. There is usually an easier line with other variations that are noticeably harder. The first 50-m pitch is usually the crux and ends on a ledge to the right with a fixed belay. A cave belay may be possible on the left. A second shorter pitch, easier on the left, leads to the top. Don't bother with the little steps above, they pale in comparison to what you've just done.

Traverse left and make a short rappel off a tree. Make a second, memorable rappel from another tree (two 50-m ropes required).

Photo opposite: Cascade Kronenbourg.
Inset: The first ascent of Kronenbourg.
Photos: Godefroy Perroux collection

Cascade Kronenbourg ** 80 m IV, 6 R

A series of steep icicles that rarely form entirely to the ground are found on the wall to the right of *Carlsberg. Kronenbourg* spills over the headwall directly above the approach traverse and is an excellent modern route. A thin climb by thin Frenchmen; named after a thin French beer.

The first pitch is on thin and unprotectable steep ice for a few metres followed by a freestanding pillar of brittle ice. A second pitch with a short vertical section leads to the top. Rappel the route from trees.

Heineken Hall ** 100 m III, 3

300 m right of *Carlsberg Column*, is a large avalanche gully. *Heineken* is in this gully on the left of a small rib. It is often difficult to see as the ice can be very thin and/or covered in snow. If you find *Heineken* in relatively fat shape, it is an interesting, worthwhile climb. If it is thin with bad looking ice, go climb *Guinness*.

The route is climbed in two pitches, the first one starts low angle and steepens slightly to the main falls. This pitch can be thin and technical with a covering of snow. When in good shape, the second pitch gives good challenging climbing. Rappel the route or traverse into the next gully right (*Labatt's Lane*). Descend that route and near the bottom, move right again into the next larger avalanche gully.

Labatt's Lane 185 m III, 3

Some confusion exists in which gully this climb lies. There are two major avalanche tracks right of *Heineken Hall*. The left-hand one which is narrower with more ice, is probably *Labatt's Lane*. The Field log book describes the larger gully to the right as the route. It doesn't really matter; both are mostly snow with little if any ice over small rock steps. Furthermore, they both lie in huge avalanche paths.

Wild Cougar 15 m II, 4 X

Named after a short-lived but stout beer once brewed in Calgary, this route, visible from the Emerald Lake turnoff, is located at the bottom of a small, indistinct gully between *Guinness Gully* and *Labatt's Lane*. When formed, it offers an exciting diversion to the crowds on *Guinness*. Cougar tracks in the snow and the climb were found while traversing through the trees from *Guinness* to *Carlsberg*.

The climb is freehanging for 10 m and extremely thin. Only 10-15 cm wide at the bottom, it can be quite a pump requiring heel hooks behind the pillar. Walk off to the right.

Guinness Gully ** 245 m III, 4

This popular route is approached directly from the parking area. Climb up through the trees heading slightly left to this good route, although it is broken by sections of snow.

A short step leads to the first pitch. This is the crux and varies year to year from a wide green curtain to a thin unprotectable veneer. It is fun under either condition depending on which kind of climbing you prefer. A second pitch offers a short steep pillar. This is followed by a snow walk to a two-pitch tier of undulating ice with a short steep section. Tree rappels are possible down the route. A more popular descent is to traverse right into the next snow gully and descend that (a great otter slide) back to the car.

Guinness Stout ** 80 m IV, 4+

There are two obvious falls found 150 vertical metres above the main *Guinness* climb. These offer the best sections of ice in the whole gully and are worth the long trek to reach them.

From the top of *Guinness* continue up the gully until you reach the climbs. It may be easier to go up through the trees to the left. Expect about 45-60 minutes from the top of *Guinness*. Later in the season you can expect someone else to have already made the journey and there will be a trail. The sun hits the route starting in mid-February– nice, but it can also lead to a higher avalanche hazard.

Stout is the left-hand of the two falls, and always forms. A shield of ice leads to a long steep pitch on usually beautiful ice. Rappel the route or traverse right and make one rappel from trees to the left of *High Test*.

High Test ** 60 m IV, 4+

High Test, a little easier than *Stout*, is the right-hand of the two falls above *Guinness Gully* and always forms. Belay a short ways up on a small ledge, then run one long pitch to the top. Rappel from ice or off trees to the left.

Emerald Lake

Several high quality routes are found in this very scenic area. They are, however, rated as high avalanche potential. 2.5 km west of Field turn right (north) onto the Emerald Lake Road. Follow this 8 km to the lake. All routes are approached by following the set ski trail from the parking lot around the north side of the lake. The Emerald Lake Lodge is open in winter and tradition has it to stop for a drink of scotch after a good day of climbing.

Blessed Rage ** 230 m V, 5.7, WI 6

Easily visible from Emerald Lake is a huge curtain pouring over the impressive cliff bands right of the Emerald Basin drainage. Ski around the lake and continue on ski trails through the trees until below the route. Thrash through steep cedar trees and then up large avalanche-prone slopes to the base, three hours. Skis, avalanche beacons, and shovels are highly recommended. This was an extremely bold solo first ascent in a very big and very stunning location.

Start with 55 m of WI 3 leading into a snow couloir. At the top of the couloir climb a right-facing corner with sustained mixed terrain. At the top of the corner, cut out left across snow covered slabs (beware of rockfall during warmer temperatures) to a fixed belay. Rotten ice-covered snow leads to a narrow pillar (bolt on the left side). Continue up tremendously sustained but usually good ice 55 m. Rappel straight down the route (double ropes recommended).

Cold Choice *** 110 m IV, 5

Formerly misspelled as **Cold Choose**, this is one of the best routes in Yoho. It forms every year and is visible from Emerald Lake, about 500 m right of *Blessed Rage*.

Continue along the ski trail cut line below *Blessed Rage* until near the end of the valley where it is possible to head up the very large avalanche slope to the left and traverse right to the climb. But think about the alternative approach; pick up the summer hiking ty rail in the trees to the right of a treed buttress. This takes you to a flat bench above the buttress directly below the route. By following a protected rib up the slope directly to the climb you minimize the avalanche hazard, but there are still dangerous slopes above the route.

Climb two steep pitches. The second one is a little harder. Rappel the route. You can walk off to the left but is not recommended due to large avalanche slopes.

Cold Comfort * 110 m IV, 5

This bold solo first ascent, located 10 m right of *Cold Choice*, doesn't form every year. *Cold Choice* was named for one of the first ascentionists who had to decide between two girls in Banff. Along a similar vein, the first ascentionist of **Cold Comfort** was having bad women problems. *Cold Comfort* is similar to its neighbour but a little easier. Descend as for *Cold Choice*.

Emerald Basin

Follow the ski trail past the end of the lake to the first big drainage to the north called Emerald Basin. The following two routes are found at the back of this basin somewhere left of the seracs near Emerald Pass below The President and The Vice President Mountains, two hours from Emerald Lake. The first ascentionists warn to "ski fast", as the area is predominantly avalanche-prone.

Mr. Misty 50 m IV, 4

One pitch of steep ice which can be quite rotten late in the year. Walk off.

The Royal Treat 250 m V, 5

Right of *Mr. Misty*, start with a curtain of steep ice followed by a short snow pitch. Continue up a pitch and a half of steep ice to the top. To descend, make two rappels and then walk off.

There is a large bowl between *Blessed Rage* and *Cold Choice* that contains volumes of ice at all grades of difficulty. It is unknown whether any of it has been climbed. Unfortunately all of it is severely threatened by huge avalanches slopes.

GOLDEN AREA

The west side of the Rockies northeast of Golden exemplifies what ice climbing was on the Icefields Parkway nearly twenty years ago. It is one of the new frontiers for waterfall ice in Canada. Technically part of the Rockies, but situated west of the Continental Divide, this area experiences entirely different weather patterns. Deeper but sometimes more stable snow conditions are found on the west slope of the Rockies. With lots of water running over big cliffs, the potential for an ice climbing mecca is created. Only a few routes in the Blaeberry and Valenciennes River valleys have been explored. This leaves many significant drainages open for discovery including Lyell Creek, Rice Brook, Bryce Creek, Bush River and the Sullivan River to name a few. See maps on pages 148, 170, 180, 184 and 199.

Some valleys can be reached via logging roads. As winter logging is carried out in many areas, 4WD access is a possibility. Check with the Golden Forestry Office for information and updated logging road maps. Logging trucks assume they are the only ones on the roads so do not blindly head up an active logging road without notifying the forestry office. Helicopter access is the most time-efficient means of approach as the entire area lies outside of the national parks but for those with a more modest budget, snow machines are the best compromise. Snow machine rentals may be available through outfitters in Golden.

Getting There

The town of Golden, 75 km west of Lake Louise, is situated next to the Trans-Canada Highway and is the hub of the Columbia Valley. To the west of Golden, the Trans-Canada passes over Roger's Pass and on to Revelstoke. To the east it passes through the tight and winding Kicking Horse Canyon. As a result of these geographical features, the highway is occasionally closed on either side of town due to avalanche or weather conditions. Highway 95 which joins Highway 93 at Radium, heads up the Columbia Valley south of Golden.

Facilities

Along the Trans-Canada Highway near Golden is a shopping strip with a variety of gas stations, restaurants, fast food, and motels. Most of your needs can be met here without having to go into the town itself. Pubs, groceries, more restaurants and full tourist and medical services are available in town.

Emergency

Your best bet in an emergency is the Golden RCMP detachment who can contact the appropriate emergency personnel. When exploring the remote drainages northeast of Golden you will likely be very isolated. Logging trucks or even a logging camp may be in the vicinity but don't count on it. See page 272.

Maps

82 N/7   Golden
82 N/14 Rostrum Peak
82 N/11 Bluewater Creek
82 N/10 Blaeberry River

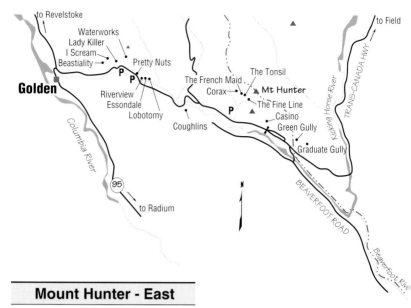

Mount Hunter - East

This area was previously described as "West of the Yoho Park Gates". However, the gates at the park boundary no longer exist. The park boundary is actually located approximately 30 km west of Field. Driving distances are marked from a gate located on the highway at the west turnoff to "Wapta Road", 2.5 km west of the Yoho Park sign where the gates used to be. All the following routes lie somewhere above on the south slopes of Mt. Hunter. The routes are among the best in the range but can be difficult to find and are subject to tremendous avalanche hazard.

Graduate Gully ** 200 m III, 3

Graduate Gully and *Green Gully* lie just inside the park boundary which is marked by a cut line. It is recommended to drive south down Beaverfoot Road (700 m east of the Wapta Road gate) to a bridge for a look. The cut line runs up and left while *Green Gully* snakes up just to the right. The first pitch of *Graduate Gully* is seen as a blue flow in the third faint gully to the right of *Green*. Park along the highway at a likely place near the park boundary. Walk up 500 m to where the first ice flow crosses a rock band.

This is a four pitch route with the second being hardest. Rappel the route.

Green Gully *** 350 m III, 4

Finding lots of running water and inspired by the name of a rock climb in the USA called "Harder than Your Husband", one of the first ascentionists named this climb "Wetter Than Your Wife" when he found so much running water. However his partner, the late Bill March, felt the need to be respectable and changed it to the present name.

Drive down Beaverfoot Road to the Kicking Horse River to where you can view Mt. Hunter. The park boundary cut line is obvious. *Green Gully* begins just right of the cut line and snakes up back left across the cut line and then back right. It is a beautiful narrow gully sporting excellent ice. Park along the highway and walk about 1 km to the route. There is avalanche hazard in the upper part.

The climb is seven pitches long on varied, entertaining ice. A long steep pitch leads to a series of shorter steps. The third pitch is lower-angled with a bolt belay. Another short seep is followed by a snow gully which leads to a tight gully, "reminiscent of classic Scottish gullies at their best". Rappel the route.

Casino Waterfall 310 m IV, 5

The description for this route sounds mega. Despite many efforts over the years few, if any, climbers have ever found this route. 1.3 km west of the Wapta Road Gate is an obvious huge curtain of ice that never forms completely and some believe this to be *Casino*. But getting onto this curtain would be an exciting exercise in classic Rockies frigging around involving loose rock and aid climbing, so it is doubtful that this is the route.

From the bridge on Beaverfoot Road look left of *Graduate* and *Green Gullies*. Between these two routes and the huge curtain (not visible from here) are several gullies and steep rock bands containing smears of ice. *Casino* lies among these and is probably the one that looks a little like *Carlsberg*. To access this area, park about 500 m east of the Wapta Road gate.

Casino is the longest and most direct line on the cliff. Park about 2 km west of the "Yoho Park Gates" and walk 20 minutes through low brush and forest to the base. Traverse in from the right side to gain the ice. A steep narrow ribbon leads to a bowl. A third pitch gives 40 m of good steep ice followed by 45 m of more moderate ice. Finish with three easier pitches with occasional steep sections. Scramble down the left side with one short rappel.

Mount Hunter - West

The following four routes lie in a complex gully system. Park 2.8 km past the Wapta Road Gate where a narrow drainage crosses the road. Several hundred metres above the road, this single drainage branches into four or five separate gullies that snake up separately. The routes all lie 650 vertical metres above the highway and there is at least twice that amount of open avalanche terrain above. If in doubt about the snow conditions, don't bother with any of these routes. Don't be fooled into thinking there are good conditions just because there is not much snow near the road. It often rains on the road, but several hundred metres above it can be snowing copiously. Two tactics are available to approach the climbs. You can travel directly up the drainage to where the gullies split; otherwise, you can hike up the rib on the left to where it turns into a side hill and continue along the treed slope into the upper gullies near *The Tonsil*. This line minimizes the hazard but you must still traverse into your proposed climb. People have walked to the climbs, but snowshoes would probably be an asset; allow two hours.

The Fine Line * 180 m IV, 4

On the right side of the drainage in the largest gully is a good varied route, best reached by following the main drainage all the way from the road. From the main gully, several hundred metres of steep snow reaches the base of the ice (82 N/7 197805). From the approach gully, only parts of *The Fine Line* are visible at any given time and it is rumoured that it doesn't always form.

Climb steep ice to a snow bay below a huge chockstone (piton belay). Climb the chimney, surmount the chockstone and continue up the snow to a open gully. Climb a screen of ice to gain a huge avalanche-prone upper bay. A large cascade to the right is climbed in two pitches. An unclimbed WI 5 finish is possible to the left. Rappel the route.

Corax ** 100 m IV, 4+

Left of *The Fine Line* is a small bowl below a steep headwall on which there are two routes, *Corax* and *The French Maid* (82 N/7 192808). They can be approached directly up the drainage past *The Fine Line* or by traversing over the rib that separates these climbs from *The Tonsil* gully. *Corax* is a tantalizing group of smears 50 m right of the obvious *Maid*, and does not often link up.

The first ascent party found one pitch of mixed climbing to the right in order to pass an unformed pillar, then climbed up two pitches of moderate ice to a cave followed by a short steep pillar to the top. This route is similar in character to *Louise Falls*. Rappel the route.

The French Maid *** 100 m IV, 6+

A wild climb which is one of the finest additions to Rockies ice routes in recent years, *The French Maid* seems to form every year but in varying quantity. It is visible from one small spot on the highway exactly where the stream crosses the road (and even a few metres to the east). You should be able to pick out the route through a narrow spot in the trees. It had been looked at for years, but was considered too 'bad' by most. This outstanding feature is one of the plums of the range and has been climbed only twice as of 1994. Approach as for *Corax*.

Climb two long, full ropelengths; 55 m ropes are nice but not required. The first pitch sports chandelier, technical (free hanging) climbing up an incredible collection of icicles and pillars to finish on a ledge with a bolt belay on the left behind the upper pillar. The upper pillar starts 10 m out from the wall and runs on relentlessly vertical but often superb ice to the top–a beautiful climb with similar ambience to *Whiteman Falls* or *Ice Nine*. Rappel the route.

Reference

Canadian Alpine Journal, Vol. 74, pg. 47, photo, 1991.

The Tonsil 90 m III, 3

Around the corner to the left of *The French Maid* (82 N/7 191812)) is *The Tonsil*. The best approach is up the rib to the left of the main drainage and then traverse through the trees to the upper gully. Head up the farthest gully on the left and look for an "obvious big fat climb with big fat avalanche hazard". A second, bigger avalanche gully feeds into this one 2-300 m below the route.

Climb the moderate wide flow that can have a mantle of snow over parts of it. Rappel the route.

Jeff Everett stretching the rope out to the half-way ledge on the French Maid during the first ascent.
Inset: The French Maid in 1992-93.

Kicking Horse Canyon

As the Trans-Canada heads west from Yoho Park and descends into Golden, it cuts through a deep spectacular canyon named for the river that rages through it. There are a number of classic moderate lines very close to the road with southern exposures. Except for *Lady Killer* and *I Scream*, they have absolutely no avalanche hazard. There are two main bridges over the river; the westernmost bridge is dubbed the Five Mile Bridge and the eastern bridge, the Ten Mile Bridge, indicating their approximate distance from Golden. The downside to climbing in the canyon is the industrial noise emanating from the highway and railroad.

Coughlins 100 m III, 3

Just west of the Ten Mile Bridge on the south side of the highway is *Coughlins*. It is high up in the trees and visible when approaching the bridge from the east heading west and characterized by a pillar of ice 300 m above the road. Park on the west side of the Ten Mile Bridge and start up a gully on the south side of the Highway about 100 m west of the bridge. Some WI 2 and hiking leads to the base and on the approach, make sure you don't trend left into another gully.

Start the climb with a 25 m step of WI 3 that leads to more snow plodding and a final 30 m pitch. Rappel off trees and downclimb.

Riverview ** 100 m II, 3/4+

Riverview is the first of a number of climbs that form on the north side of the highway east of the Five Mile Bridge, 8 km east of Golden. Plentiful low to moderate angle ice makes *Riverview* a popular beginner/practice area. Park at the west end of the Five Mile Bridge and drop down under the bridge to the train tracks and continue east for 200 m. *Riverview* is on the left about 50 m up the slope (82 N/7 106824).

The climb is in three tiers with a variety of lines. The first long pitch of steppy ice to a snow ledge is followed by more moderate ice to a smaller ledge. Finish with a 15 m steeper section to the top. Rappel off trees on the left or walk off right.

Essondale Left * 140 m III, 3

Look for the next climb east of *Riverview*. It shares a common start with *Essondale Right* but the upper pitches don't always form. Continue along the tracks past Riverview and up a gully for 200 m to a steep curtain of ice.

Climb the 10-m curtain to a basin then head into the left-hand gully following WI 3 to the top. Rappel off trees.

Essondale Right *** 120 m III, 4+

A canyon classic! It is an obvious climb with a steep crux pillar and an aesthetic finish. Start the route as for *Essondale Left* but head right from the basin to the base of a pillar.

Climb the initial pillar to a belay and finish on a pitch of good ice in a great position. The climb ends in the forest. Rappel off trees and downclimb the right side.

Lobotomy * 12 m II, 4

About 600 m right (east) of *Essondale* is a freehanging fang of ice, *Lobotomy*, that slowly forms at the far east end of the cliff. Approach along the tracks until below the climb and hike up to the base; 40 minutes. Belay and rappel off trees.

Jeff Palumbo

Jim Dodich climbing good ice with good gear on Essondale Right.

Pretty Nuts ** 180 m II, 4

This popular climb has the quickest approach of all the canyon climbs. Park as for *Riverview* and cross to the north side of the highway. Walk west 50 m and look up (82 N/7 102826).

The initial 60-m curtain gives a choice of lines and makes for a convenient practice area. Above the curtain, go straight up a shallow corner for 45 m. Alternatively, go into a left gully with a short vertical pillar (crux) followed by easy ice, then traverse up and right over a treed rib back into the right gully. After either alternative, traverse east 50 m into another gully which hides a steep 60-m line. Rappel and retrace steps down the route, all rappels are off trees.

Waterworks ** 90 m III, 3

Well away from the brutal noise of the main canyon *Waterworks* offers some classic climbing between rock walls. The approach is tricky, however (approximately 82 N/7 093833). *Waterworks* is partially visible while heading east on the highway before you get to the route *I Scream*. Continue east along the highway and park approximately 500 m past a very sharp bend where the road negotiates a deep gravel gully. The climb is located above a steep band of trees and rock and is not visible from below. Scramble through the band of trees staying to the right. Then angle left into the gully and the base of the climb.

The climb offers two straightforward pitches with a belay stance separating the two. Rappel the route.

Lady Killer *** 80 m III, 3

The top of *Lady Killer* is visible from the road. Park as for *Waterworks* in a plowed pull-out. Hike up the drainage (subject to avalanche) past a couple of ice steps to the base; 15 minutes. This good quality climb always forms and has comfortable belay ledges.

The first pitch of 75-85° ice leads to a small basin with fixed rock anchors, but climb past them and belay on the ice. The crux second pitch ascends 40 m of ice to snow slopes and a small tree to the right. The gully above offers a few hundred metres of snow and ice. Rappel and downclimb the route.

I Scream ** 70 m III, 4+

Park as for *Lady Killer* and hike up toward that route (avalanche hazard) and take a left-forking gully to the prominent pillar. The climb is visible about 1 km west of the pull-out.

Start with a 15-m slab of thin ice to a snow ramp which leads to a 15-m vertical pillar that is rarely there. If this pitch is gone, start directly below the pillar and follow a gully up and left until even with the upper pillar. From here, a ledge system on easy 5th class rock is the ticket to reach the ice. The final crux pillar is 25 m of spectacular ice. A short step above leads to the forest. The rappel route lies just left of a huge right-facing corner in the rock wall 60 m left of the climb itself. One short rappel takes you to a lone big pine on a ledge. From the lone pine rappel 40 m to another tree and make a short rappel to the base. With a 55-m rope, the last rappel is not needed.

Beastiality 40 m II, 3

This obscure route, said to be located on the right side of the second gully west of *I Scream*, does not always form.

A Kicking Horse classic. Kirt Sellers on Lady Killer.

Blaeberry River

The Blaeberry is the first major river valley north of Golden. With considerable logging and increasing housing development in the region, easier access has been created and people are now more aware of and knowledgeable about the area. Undoubtedly more routes will be discovered in this valley for years to come. Access to the Blaeberry Road is via the public back road system that accesses the residences in the area. Turn right (north) on a number of roads from the Trans-Canada Highway, 10-15 km west of Golden. The best road into the main river valley is via the Blaeberry School Road 15 km west of Golden. See maps pages 148 & 184.

Shower Bath Falls ** 60 m III, 4+

Drive west on the Trans-Canada Highway for approximately 6 km to Hartley Road. Turn right (north) and drive 2 km past the Moberly Pub and park at the intersection with the Golden Upper Donald Road. The climb is visible directly ahead in a cleft of the mountain. The approach and the climb are threatened by large avalanche slopes. Nigel Helliwell, one of the Rockies climbing pioneers of the '70s, was fatally buried here.

Note: Obtain permission from the landowner and cross into the drainage below the climb; one hour. The climb is two steep pitches. Rappel the route.

Goat Mountain Falls 25 m III, 2/4

Approximately 10 km from the Trans-Canada up the Blaeberry School Road is the Goat Mountain Lodge. Two parallel climbs of uncertain character are found directly above the lodge. They are about half a pitch high and are said to be a WI 2 and a WI 4.

Rainy Day * 110 m III, 3

Continue up the Blaeberry River and park at the 28 km marker. Look for the route on the mountainside to the right (south) high above the river in a shale gully. The climbing is good but it requires a two-hour pound up the avalanche-prone gully to the base.

Climb 50 m of easy ice to reach two lines. Left is up a thin, slightly longer pitch or the right on a shorter but steeper line. Walk off to the right and back around into the approach gully.

Polish Peacock * 80 m III, 4

Located on the toe of Mt. Poland, this is a pretty climb. Drive up the Blaeberry as for Rainy Day and park at the 50 km marker. Look to the left (north). The climb is several hundred metres above the road (on the left). About 150 m further up the road from the 50 km marker, an old logging trail takes you up to the slopes below the climb. Beware of avalanche hazard around and above the route.

Climb 30 m of moderate ice to a snow ledge which leads to a cave behind a pillar. A 80-90° pillar for 20 m leads to the trees. A small seep finishes the route. Rappel the route.

Jim Dodich

Jeff Palumbo on the first ascent of Polish Peacock.

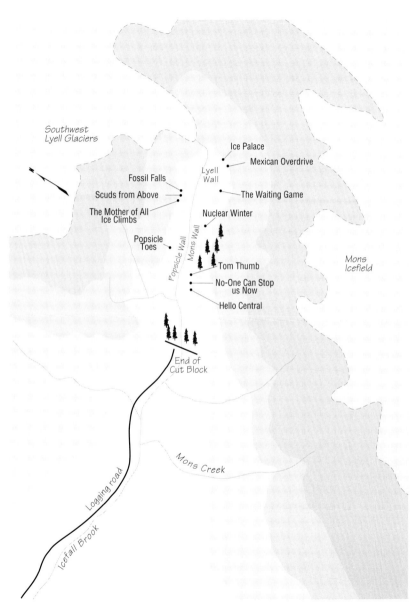

Southwest
Lyell Glaciers

Ice Palace
Mexican Overdrive

Lyell
Wall

Fossil Falls

Scuds from Above

The Waiting Game

The Mother of All
Ice Climbs

Nuclear Winter

Popsicle
Toes

Mons
Icefield

Tom Thumb

No-One Can Stop
us Now

Hello Central

End of
Cut Block

Mons Creek

Logging road

Icefall Brook

Icefall Brook

Icefall Brook is a horseshoe-shaped valley that drains the southwest side of the Lyell and the west side of the Mons Icefields into the Valenciennes and then the Bush Rivers.

This is one of the most exciting areas to be discovered in recent years and the concentration of routes is staggering. Over 100 potential routes are found within two square kilometres ranging from 10 m steps to 300 m+ giants. However, don't expect to go in and start pillaging routes at your leisure. The area is very remote and best reached by an expensive helicopter ride out of Golden. Logging roads extend quite far up Icefall Brook allowing approach on snow machine, followed by several kilometres of skiing.

To reach Bush River logging roads, take the Trans-Canada west of Golden 23.5 km to Donald Station where a right (north) turn puts you on the Big Bend Highway which eventually merges into the Bush River logging road. This is followed past Bush Landing and Bush Arm where the Valenciennes River enters the Bush near kilometre marker 96. The road up the Valenciennes is on the north side of the river and marked with "V" kilometre markers while the Bush River has "B" markers.

None of the routes in Icefall Brook are given quality ratings because they are so new and only the very top of the barrel has been skimmed. Nevertheless, *Popsicle Toes*, *Mexican Overdrive* and *Nuclear Winter* are undoubtedly excellent climbs. Only a few dedicated people have been known to explore this valley in winter and the biggest (and hardest) plums still await attempts.

Beware, the avalanche hazard in the area can be extreme. All the climbs in this remote area are rated a Grade IV commitment or higher. See maps pages 180 & 199.

Reluctant to leak out information, the main activists in the area sadly reported that Icefall Brook "sees rainfall every day of the year, especially in winter, has year-round grizzlies and winter mosquitoes six feet tall".

Map
82 N/14 Rostrum Peak.
The logging road ends at grid reference 950465. Grid references for routes are approximate.

Popsicle Wall

Popsicle Wall is the first main wall on the left side of the valley past the cut block and has one completed route.

Popsicle Toes 190 m V, 5
Found near the middle of the Popsicle Wall is a prominent climb resembling a tuning fork near the top (82 N/14 949476). Climb 75 m on rolling WI 3 ice past an obvious boulder and across a snow ledge to the main pillar. The next pitch climbs 40 m of WI 5 ice followed by 35 m of WI 4 to a bolt belay below the fork. The first ascent took the left-hand for 40 m up a steep pillar (crux) to end in a tiny flat pedestal. Rappel the route. The obvious boulder conceals bare ice that can be used to thread a sling. From the boulder, 50 m just reaches the bottom.

Mons Wall

On the east side of the canyon directly opposite the Popsicle Wall is another major cliff with a large clump of trees above.

Nuclear Winter 140 m IV, 5

A difficult, attractive climb in the middle of the Mons Wall (82 N/14 954480), *Nuclear Winter* begins in a gully beneath a series of sword-like chandeliers. It is climbed in three or four pitches. Start up a ramp with a short column and climb 75 m of moderate terrain to the upper pillar. An intimidating pitch up steep ice leads to a cave on the right, 25 m. The final pitch starts up 20 m of vertical chandelier ice easing to a gentle gully. A two bolt station is on the cliff face at the top. Rappel the route.

Tom Thumb 10 m IV, 3

The route that started it all! This short pillar coming from a small gully is significant only in the fact that it was the first route done in the canyon (82 N/14 951474).

No-One Can Stop Us Now 25 m IV, 3

On the south end of Mons Wall (82 N/14 951475) are several possibilities on short tiered cliffs. This route takes a wide expanse of ice on a steep cliff face above *Tom Thumb*. Rappel the route.

Hello Central 25 m IV, 3-4

Found on the south end of Mons Wall (82 N/14 951473). Climb the small gully or the steeper wall to the left. Rappel the route.

Icefall Wall

Separated from Popsicle Wall by a steep gully, this is the next wall upstream. The next three climbs lie on the bottom cliff band. A much larger and more serious cliff with a few waterfalls seeping from seracs is found above.

The Mother of All Ice Climbs 60 m IV, 3

A massive curtain with three tiers (82 N/14 951481) this climb is done in two pitches. Rappel the route.

Scuds From Above 60 m IV, 4

Located 100 m right (north) of *The Mother* (82 N/14 951482). Climb a short shield to 20 m of steep ice, followed by another 30 m of easier ice. To descend, rappel 50 m to the top of the shield, then easily downclimb.

Fossil Falls 80 m IV, 4

100 m right of *Scuds* (82 N/14 951483). Pitch one climbs a 15 m column then goes up and left to a small rock face; pitons for belay. Pitch two continues up easy ice to a large snow and ice ledge and a bolt belay (may be covered). Rappel the route.

Lyell Wall

Lyell Wall is a main wall on the back right-hand side (northeast corner) of the valley containing some of the bigger routes in the area.

The Ice Palace 50 m IV, 4

On the north end of the Lyell Wall and 50 m immediately left of *Mexican Overdrive* is a climb ending halfway up the crag (82 N/14 957489). Climb up easy snow and ice slopes to a steep curtain pouring from a huge horizontal roof. Rappel the route. Large and long pillars may form off to the left.

Mexican Overdrive 200 m V, 5

This narrow climb is the left-hand of three prominent, parallel smears that are 20 m apart on the right side of Lyell Wall (82 N/14 958488). Climb rolling ice to a ledge. From the ledge, a crux pitch or two leads into a shallow gully and the top. Rappel the route or traverse south then scramble down through trees to a short rappel at the south end of Mons Wall.

The Waiting Game 110 m IV, 3

The Waiting Game is directly across the canyon from *Fossil Falls* on the south end of Lyell Wall (82 N/14 957483). This wide, gentle climb has short steeper sections that can easily be avoided. Climb two full pitches followed by a final short tier. Rappel the route.

Icefall Brook, the Lyell Wall. A) The Ice Palace B) Mexican Overdrive. All other lines remain unattempted as of the 1993-94 season.

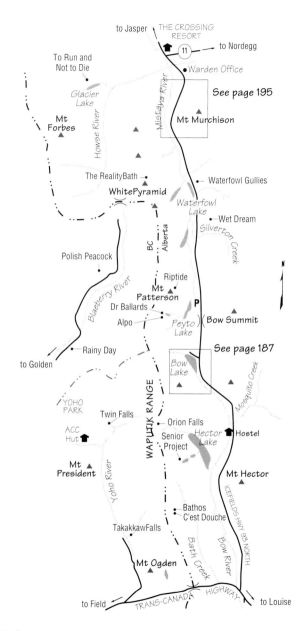

to Jasper

THE CROSSING RESORT

11 → to Nordegg

• Warden Office

See page 195

Mt Murchison ▲

To Run and Not to Die

Glacier Lake

Mt Forbes ▲

Howse River

Mistaya River

• Waterfowl Gullies

The RealityBath •

WhitePyramid

Waterfowl Lake

• Wet Dream

Silverton Creek

BC
Alberta

Polish Peacock •

Blaeberry River

• Riptide

Mt Patterson ▲

P

Bow Summit

Dr Ballards •

Alpo •

Peyto Lake

▲

to Golden

• Rainy Day

See page 187

WAPUTIK RANGE

Bow Lake

▲

Mosquito Creek

YOHO PARK

Twin Falls •

ACC Hut 🏠

• Orion Falls

Senior Project

Hector Lake

🏠 Hostel

Mt President ▲

Yoho River

• Mt Hector ▲

ICEFIELDS HWY 93 NORTH

• Bathos
• C'est Douche

Takakkaw Falls •

Bath Creek

Bow River

Mt Ogden ▲

to Field ←

TRANS-CANADA HIGHWAY

→ to Louise

N

Geographically, this is the largest area described in this book. Known as the Banff-Jasper Highway or simply "The BJ", it is 230 kilometres long and the epicentre of ice climbing in the Rockies featuring ease of access, reliability of formation, and ultra-classic routes. Travelling through two national parks and covering such a grand area, the parkway is described here in four sections. The first area (Waputik Range) extends from the Trans-Canada Highway to Saskatchewan River Crossing. North of the crossing each subsequent area covers a smaller area due to the higher volume of routes including the legendary venues of Mount Wilson, The Weeping Wall and The Columbia Icefields.

Getting There

Your journey onto this avenue of winter paradise begins two kilometres north of Lake Louise when you exit the Trans-Canada Highway onto the Icefields Parkway and head north toward Jasper. From the north end of parkway, take the main road in Jasper (Connaught Drive) south and continue through the Highway 16 intersection. The parkway can also be accessed at Saskatchewan River Crossing (110 km north of Lake Louise) via David Thompson Highway (# 11), 98 km from Nordegg. Specific details about facilities and emergency assistance are listed under each section.

Maps

82 N/9 Hector Lake
82 N/15 Mistaya Lake
82 N/10 Blaeberry River

Waputik Range

Technically, the Waputik Range describes the mountains along the west side of the Icefields Parkway from the Trans-Canada Highway north to the Howse River. For ease of description, the routes along the east side of the road are included here as well. They vary tremendously in character. Bow Lake and Mt. Murchison offer a number of classic, more moderate lines, while the peaks northwest of Bow Summit are unique in that they contain only a few routes but are some of the biggest and hardest routes ever completed.

Facilities

Because this region is geographically so close to Lake Louise, few people stay overnight in the area. Mosquito Creek Hostel, located between Hector and Bow Lakes, is popular with skiers and often crowded. Most climbers eschew Mosquito Creek in favour of the Rampart Creek Hostel farther north near Mt. Wilson and the Weeping Wall.

Emergency

Contact the Lake Louise Warden Office. Pay phones are located north of Bow Summit just south of the Saskatchewan River Bridge at the warden station and at Mosquito Creek Hostel, south of Bow Summit. A warden may be on duty at the Saskatchewan River station but in recent years it has been staffed only periodically in winter. Assistance may also be available at Num-Ti-Jah Lodge on Bow Lake, but beware, most climbers/skiers are unwelcome there. See page 272.

Hector Lake

Orion Falls ** 150 m IV, 5+

The long ski approach to this remote climb is definitely worth the effort. Climbing in this area is both spectacular and exciting. Park at the Hector Lake viewpoint 19 km north of the junction with the Trans-Canada. Ski along the trail down onto Hector Lake and make the long journey across the length of the lake (light ski gear recommended). Head into the narrow canyon at the inlet of the lake. The climb is right of centre, below the Waputik Icefield (82 N/9 388145). The climb itself is safe from avalanche hazard but the slopes leading to it are threatened by snow and serac hazard.

The crux first pitch can form with a nice groove or as a fierce featureless pillar. Easier ice leads to the top. Another steep pitch may form above. Rappel the route.

Senior Project 120 m V, 5+

Complicated and obscure is the best way to describe this route. *Senior Project* was climbed initially as part of a special course in an outdoor education program–my kind of schooling! It is a serious venture due to its long approach and avalanche and serac hazard. If you're looking for adventure, you might think about a second ascent of this line. It's probably better than most people would care to think.

Park at the Hector Lake viewpoint 19 km north of the junction with the Trans-Canada. Ski down onto Hector Lake. Cross the lake and up the east side of the drainage to Lake Margaret. Continue up the prominent snow gully at the south end of the lake. From the top of the gully is the first clear view of the first pitch;

four hours (82 N/9 430136). Low-angle ice leads to a 50-m pitch which tops out in a basin east of Turquoise Lake. The next three pitches are 0.5 km away at grid reference 425132. The traverse to these pitches is exposed to serac fall. A 20-m steep pitch leads to a vertical (crux) third pitch. The top of this funnels you into a snow slope below a rock wall with two pitons. The route finishes with a 20-m vertical pillar.

Rappel the top three pitches and traverse back to the top of the first pitch. There is a rock bulge to the right of it (unconfirmed if it is on climbers' or skiers' right), walk around to the right of the bulge into a little recess and the final rappel anchor.

Crowfoot Mountain

Crowfoot Falls 150 m V, 5

Visible from the highway the Crowfoot Glacier sports spectacular seracs making it a major tourist attraction. This climb takes the obvious flow of water ice in a deep recess right of the glacier. It's a good route but a serious place with acres of avalanche slopes on the approach and on the climb. You should probably wait for a season in which it forms early before any snow accumulates, otherwise it would be quite nerve-wracking and is not recommended if snow conditions are doubtful. Park at the Crowfoot Glacier viewpoint 33.2 km north of the Trans-Canada and 2.8 km south of the Bow Glacier/Num-ti-Jah Lodge parking lot. Walk down to the river and cross the swamps at the end of Bow Lake. Work your way over toward the glacier, keeping well right to minimize serac hazard and stay high on moraines whenever possible. The climb starts in a deep gash

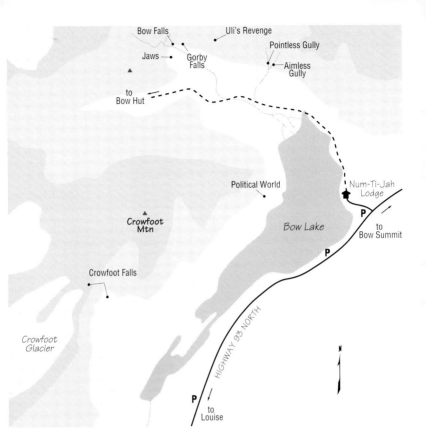

cutting the lower rock band below the obvious flow above; two hours.

This first pitch up the gash is a full 50 m of very steep ice. Continue up and left along several hundred metres of snow to the base of the obvious flow which is two pitches of beautiful ice to 80° Some very seasonal mixed routes may be found on the rock faces above the route in the late fall and/or spring. Rappel and downclimb route.

Political World ** 170 m III, 5+ R

Located on Crowfoot Mountain directly across from the Bow Lake Viewpoint about 1.4 km south of the Bow Glacier/Num-ti-Jah Lodge parking lot. Walk or ski across the lake and up the large avalanche slope to the base of the cliff. Follow a slight windblown rib in the slope to the left of the climb.

Start with a narrow pillar for 30 m leading into a gully (old bolt). Continue up snow to the right-hand of two falls (bolt) of which doesn't always form.

Kari Nagy

Traverse across steep snow covered rock to vertical, thin ice and up to the crux pillar. Continue up steep to overhanging ice for 15 m until it eases off. Continue to a bolt station on the right. A considerably easier pitch (WI 4) to the left is much more likely to freeze up. Rappel the route.

Bow Lake

The next six routes are all on the approach to Bow Glacier and Bow Hut, a popular ski touring destination. Near the north end of Bow Lake pull into the large Bow Glacier parking lot and Numti-Jah Lodge (closed in winter), 36 km north of the Trans-Canada. Park in the lot nearest the highway. Do not drive down the road toward the lodge—as a climber/skier you are very unwelcome there. The following routes can be walked to but are best approached on skis. See map page 187.

Pointless Gully * 95 m III, 4

Ski across the north end of the lake (or stick to the trail in the trees if it is not frozen) and continue up the valley for about 1 km. *Pointless Gully* is the left-hand and most obvious of two routes in the trees on the south-facing slope to the right (82 N/9 352238) about 200 m before you get to a narrow canyon. Lots of terrain above the route makes for bad avalanche hazard.

A steep pillar for starters is followed by an easy snow and ice gully to a final wide curtain. Rappel the route or if conditions permit walk off right.

Photo Opposite:
Orvel Miskiw on the last pitch of Pointless Gully.

Aimless Gully * 100 m III, 4

Located next to *Pointless Gully*, *Aimless Gully* forms in the obvious break to the right (82 N/9 353239). Watch for this break as you approach the route.

The first pitch is a technical pillar followed by a nice final curtain similar to the last pitch of *Professors*. Rappel the route or if conditions permit, walk off right.

Bow Falls *** 95 m III, 3-4

At the headwaters of the Bow River is an obvious large flow pouring over the headwall below Bow Glacier (82 N/9 348224). This route forms early (albeit poorly at first), has little avalanche hazard, is in a beautiful location, and presents a number of lines–a classic! Approach as for *Pointless Gully* but continue up the valley towards a narrow canyon. Do not enter the canyon. Instead turn to the left and follow the Bow Hut winter trail (usually broken) into the trees. Leave the trail where it enters the valley bottom again (avalanche hazard here) and contour right into the amphitheatre.

The falls begin with a broad shield of low-angle ice which can be very thin. It is a high volume waterfall and creates a large cavern (would you believe up to 10 m high!) below the ice which has been known to collapse. Fortunately no climbers have been involved in a collapse yet. Be careful. The main falls can be climbed on a number of lines with the left side offers gully type climbing, known as *Photographer's Gully*. The right side gives a steep line up varied and interesting ice. The climb ends on flat ground at a pretty lake below the Bow Glacier. To descend, traverse to the second gully to the left and downclimb back to the base of the route. If snow conditions are poor, it is best to rappel the route.

Jaws 75 m III, 4+

An aesthetic pillar that rarely forms, *Jaws* may be found on the cliff 200 m left of *Bow Falls*. This thin, narrow, ephemeral testpiece is climbed in two challenging pitches, each with a cave belay. Descend the steep gully to the left.

Gorby Falls 30-40 m III, 3

Several small icefalls known as *Gorby Falls* sometimes form on the rock about 100 m right of *Bow Falls*. They are a good alternative if there are crowds to the left. Three different lines are located in the vicinity, each with variable amounts and quality of ice. Rappel the route.

Uli's Revenge ** 80 m III, 5

The top half of *Uli's Revenge* always seems to form, but the bottom pillar rarely touches. This climb is located 500 m to the right of *Bow Falls* on the upper cliff band. Approach as for *Bow Falls*, cross the amphitheatre below that route and hike up windblown moraines left of the route. Traverse back right on a ledge to the base.

The climb is in an awesome position up a narrow, hanging icicle which starts out behind the pillar and winds to the front then continues up steep ice for another pitch. Rappel the route.

Karl Nagy sharpening the pencil on the first ascent of Uli's Revenge.
Photo Chris Goldring

Photo Opposite:
Riptide in April 1992

Inset:
Guy Lacelle on an early repeat attempt of Riptide, pitch one (1990).
Photo Barry Blanchard

Mistaya River-West Side

The following routes are located north of Bow Summit in the Mistaya River drainage on the west side of the road.

Dr. Ballards * 90 m III, 3

Park at Peyto Lake pull-out (no sign) on the west side of the road, 2.6 km north of Bow Summit. Ski down to the lake. Continue across Peyto Lake and up the drainage beyond. The route is the right-hand of two flows on the headwall below Cauldron Lake (82 N/10 312268). The similar left-hand flow is known as *Alpo*. Climb two moderate and narrow pitches. Rappel the route.

Riptide ** 225 m VI, 7 R

This unique and challenging route is not quite the "horror" it previously was, although six subsequent ascents (as of 1994) have encountered considerably more ice than did the first ascent. The route is more psychologically than technically difficult. Long sections of snow covered, hollow and/or thin ice is normal. It is best described as sustained weirdness. The longest vertical sections are at the most, 15 m, yet tool placements are difficult and screws are often in bad or plate ice. At no place can you really just go for it, and the climbing demands a delicate and thoughtful technique to the very finish. Overall, "it offers all the features of a very modern ice route and should become a classic among the harder climbs".

Park at a pull-out (no sign) on the west side of the highway 7.2 km north of Bow Summit. Cross the river and up through steep trees left of the drainage coming off the North Face of Mt. Patterson. Skis are recommended. Once in the open below the bowl, ski up the drainage (threatened by avalanches from above) staying left. A long (300 m) avalanche-prone gully must be climbed to reach the base of the route, allow at least three hours. (82 N/15 299337).

The climb is often done in five pitches, although it has been climbed in four using a 55-m rope. Bolt belays were added on the first ascent but most are difficult to find. They are located as follows: first left, second right, third centre, fourth left and fifth at the top on the left. The third pitch normally avoids some steep pillars (may be unformed) by climbing a slight gully to the right (bolt) then making a technical and exciting traverse left on thin ice back to the main falls. There are no easy sections. Each pitch is sustained with no distinct crux, although the first and the fourth pitches are a bit harder.

Rappel the route. Expect to find only the second and fifth bolt anchors. Good ice for Abalakov anchors is often hard to find; pitons and/or ice screws are recommended. The last rappel from the second bolt belay may reach the bottom if you have 60-m ropes.

Le Lézard D'Or 200 m V, 6+ /7

The reptilian reference to this variation on *Riptide* was made because the first ascentionists believed the word *Riptide* was some sort of lizard. Climb the first two and a half pitches of *Riptide*. Then, instead of traversing to the left above the bolt, follow the obvious line straight up to reach the bottom of a vertical pillar. Rappel the route. First rappel on bolts, second on pitons, third from the second belay of Riptide.

The Reality Bath 600 m VII, 6+

Located on the Northeast Face of White Pyramid (82 N/15 202435), *The Reality Bath* is undoubtedly the most dangerous ice route in the range. Two smears are often visible on this face. *The Reality Bath* is the left-hand line. Park at a pull-out (no sign) 5.8 km north of Waterfowl Lakes viewpoint. Cross the Mistaya River and ski south up the drainage and across Epaulette Lake to the face; the route should be obvious. On the first attempt during a very warm spell the seracs above the route calved twice, narrowly missing the climbers. The ascent, on the second attempt, was done in one day, perhaps one of the single most impressive feats in modern Rockies ice climbing.

The route is eleven pitches long. The first ascentionists soloed most of the route which is probably the only safe way of actually getting up. Five increasingly difficult pitches lead to a free-standing pillar followed by fragile "egg-shell like" mushrooms with little opportunities for protection. Another three steep pitches lead to a fat snow ledge and a final hard pitch feeding from the seracs. The first ascentionists attempted the seracs directly but a small degree of sanity returned and they rappelled back to the snow ledge on which they traversed right to escape.

A short insecure mixed pitch is required to reach the exit slopes. Continue on snow up the Northeast Face above the seracs to the East Ridge which leads down to a col. Then follow the valley north, back to Epaulette Lake.

Reference

Alpinism, pg. 62, 1988.

Randy Rackliff approaching the seracs at the top of The Reality Bath. What more needs to be said?

Marc Twight

Mistaya River-East Side

Wet Dream ** 60 m III, 3

This is actually up to three different ice flows. About 12 km north of Bow Summit several large drainages (Silverhorn Creek) come down from the east. These flows lie on the smaller cliff bands to the north of the main creek and have little avalanche hazard. Drive slowly and look closely–they are barely visible from the road and are most easily seen if driving south toward Bow Summit. They can be reached easily on skis (recommended); 20-30 minutes.

The gully-like, left-hand falls is the most commonly climbed, although the centre falls is often bigger. The sometimes formed right-hand is in another gully about 200 metres from the centre. Rappel and downclimb the routes.

Waterfowl Gullies 50-100 m II, 3

Directly above the road at Waterfowl Lakes is a cliff band broken by several gullies which occasionally ice up. They aren't great climbs but are close to and easily accessible from the road. The slopes are often free of snow and avalanche hazard (but not always) and the views across the lake to Howse Peak and Mt. Chephren are unbeatable. Park at Waterfowl Lakes viewpoint halfway around the lake, about 1 km north of Waterfowl Lake Campground.

The largest gully is found right above the viewpoint, but the best climbing is found in the two or three smaller gullies to the left. The crux is getting up the steep slope to the ice. Rappel and downclimb the routes.

Howse River

The Howse River is a wide, meandering river flowing east from the Continental Divide at Howse Pass (the Blaeberry River drains Howse Pass to the west). Northwest of Howse River are the Lyell Icefield and Mt. Forbes, the highest peak in Banff Park at 3612 m. Howse River joins the North Saskatchewan and the Mistaya Rivers near Saskatchewan River Crossing. So far, only one route has been explored in this massive drainage system. There is a lot of unclimbed ice in the area, but the approach mitigates against further activity, at least for awhile.

To Run and Not to Die 80 m IV, 3

This is the first of many potential routes in the Glacier Lake region. The approach to Glacier Lake is almost 12 km one way, requiring the better part of a day. Park 3 km south of the Saskatchewan River at the Mistaya Canyon Trailhead. This trail is rarely skied but is an improved access over the normal summer trail (starts near The Crossing Resort) that leads to Glacier Lake. Refer to *Ski Trails in the Canadian Rockies*, page 155, for exact details. At Glacier Lake, ski across to its west end to where the climb is visible up a 300 m avalanche-prone slope on the north side of the lake (82 N/15 075525).

Once you survive the horrible bushwhack from the lake to the base of the route, climb 40 m of 70-80° ice to a good ledge. Continue up lower-angled ice for 30 m to a rock pinnacle on the right. Another 10 m with some mixed climbing leads to the top and a tree belay. Rappel the route.

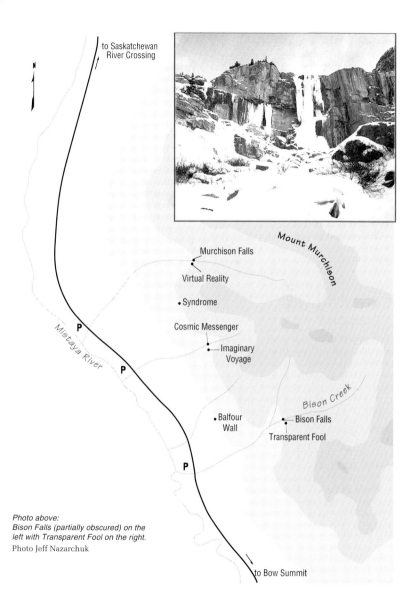

to Saskatchewan
River Crossing

N

Mount Murchison

Murchison Falls

Virtual Reality

• Syndrome

Cosmic Messenger

• Imaginary
Voyage

Mistaya River

P

P

Bison Creek

• Balfour
Wall

• Bison Falls

Transparent Fool

P

Photo above:
Bison Falls (partially obscured) on the
left with Transparent Fool on the right.
Photo Jeff Nazarchuk

to Bow Summit

Mount Murchison

North of Waterfowl Lakes is a multifaceted peak with three large cirques, each containing quality ice. All routes but two are located in one of these cirques that line the peak on the northeast side of the road. Approaches take one to two hours depending on snow conditions. Only *Murchison Falls* and *Virtual Reality* are not easily visible and identifiable from the road. Only the last pitch of these routes can be seen through the trees. The routes are described as you travel north from Bow Summit on the Icefields Parkway. See map page 195.

Reference

"Guide to Mt. Murchison, Mt. Wilson & the David Thompson", *Rock and Ice Magazine*, No. 59, pg. 70, Jan/Feb. 1994.

Transparent Fool ** 45 m IV, 5

This popular, spectacular route forms as a clear straw leaving running water visible underneath the ice. Park at the Bison Creek stream bed (no sign) 7.2 km north of Waterfowl Lake Campground and 11.7 km south of the David Thompson Highway. *The Fool* is obvious pouring over a steep headwall. Hike up the creek to where it turns into a tighter canyon. Head up the ridge to the left staying on the high ground above the canyon. Follow this as high as possible and find a safe line down the slope into the creek. Continue up the creek and turn right to the base of *Bison Falls* and *The Fool*; 1.5-2 hours. The avalanche-prone slopes on both sides of this tight canyon, and the large sunbaked gully feeding into it, make the approach particularly avalanche-prone.

A 15-m curtain leads to the pillar. Continue up the vertical and often featureless pillar for 30 m to the top. Beware of falling icicles on either side of the main pillar. Rappel or walk off.

Bison Falls 80 m III, 3

A wide curtain starts 30 m to the left and below *Transparent Fool*. **Unnamed** by the first ascentionists, this drainage is called Bison Creek. Many parties climb this as a warmup to the nasty to the right. Some folks even rappel down *The Fool* to pre-inspect or perhaps pre-place protection? Tch-Tch.

Start well below *Transparent Fool* and climb 25 m of 80-90° ice to a tree belay. Some snow is followed by 18 m of vertical ice that leads to easier ground. Descend as for *Transparent Fool*.

The Balfour Wall * 20 m II, 2-4

A variety of steep curtains and pillars are visible on a cliff band in the trees 500 m down left of Bison Creek. They have a quick approach through the trees with no avalanche hazard. This is a nice place for top roping and working technique as an alternative to more crowded areas. The amount and quality of ice are better later in the season.

Cosmic Messenger * 60 m III, 5

Spectacular views of Kauffman Peak are the main attraction for this route in the next major cirque north of Bison Creek. The route is easily visible from the road. Park in an unsigned pull-out 9.3 km north of Waterfowl Lake Campground. The route is best early in the year before deep snow increases avalanche hazard and lengthens the approach; 1.5 hours in good conditions.

Climb the first pitch 40 m up a steep pillar to a hanging belay. This is followed by an easier curtain to a pin belay on the right. Rappel the route.

Tom Fayle

Murchison Falls. *But My Daddy's a Psycho!* is hidden on the left.
The first pitch of *Virtual Reality* is formed to the right.

Imaginary Voyage 55 m III, 3

This shallow gully 20 m right of *Cosmic Messenger* is prone to spindrift, thus creating an interesting time up less than perfect ice. Rappel and downclimb.

Syndrome * 45 m III, 4

Located on the flat rock buttress between *Murchison Falls* and *Cosmic Messenger*, *Syndrome* is a rarely formed route facing the road. Park as for *Cosmic Messenger* and hike up through steep trees to the base in about an hour.

This is a worthwhile route that sports interesting technical climbing on occasionally thinner ice. A single bolt belay/rappel on top.

Murchison Falls *** 180 m III, 4+

This classic waterfall is located in the most northerly cirque just before the road starts to descend to Saskatchewan River Crossing. Park where the obvious drainage crosses the road 10.3 km north of Waterfowl Lake Campground and 8.6 km south of The Crossing. Only the top of the route is visible from the road a few hundred metres north of the parking. Beware, this approach can be very easy or very hard depending on snow conditions and routefinding; snowshoes may help. Skis are not recommended.

Start by hiking directly up the creek bed. When the creek steepens into short ice steps, move left (north) onto high ground above the creek. Continue up to the base of the route. A moonscaped hanging valley is found above the route, so there is little avalanche hazard (possible cornice); however, the open slope below the route can be dangerous.

Solo up easy ice and snow to the base of the main falls. Steep steps interspersed with easier terrain lead to the final crux pillar, a long lead on just off-vertical ice. An easy 20 m step leads to the top.

From the base of the main falls it is possible to climb a narrow gully to the left. This variation called **But, My Daddy's a Psycho!** (WI 5+) climbs one steep and sometimes bad ice pitch. Above, you traverse back right to the final crux pitch of *Murchison*.

Rappel the route. Below the final 20-m step is a fixed rappel anchor out to the right. Be careful of stuck ropes here. Continue descent on ice.

Virtual Reality *** 160 m IV, 6

A late bloomer, sometimes taking until mid-March to form completely, *Virtual Reality* is an awesome route. It rarely forms, but when it does, it is situated 10 m right of *Murchison Falls*. Keep an eye out for this one. If formed, it is not one to miss. Climb up easy ice and snow to the base of *Murchison Falls*. Head out right up another 30 m of snow to the base of the fall.

There may be any number of lines presenting themselves; pick the driest and least threatened by falling icicles. The first ascent party climbed a series of three freestanding icicles on the left side with technical hooking and mushroom sections. Many of the difficulties are created by large icicles that often hang out behind your head. Rappel as for *Murchison Falls*. Due to the large number of freehanging icicles it is not advisable to rappel this route.

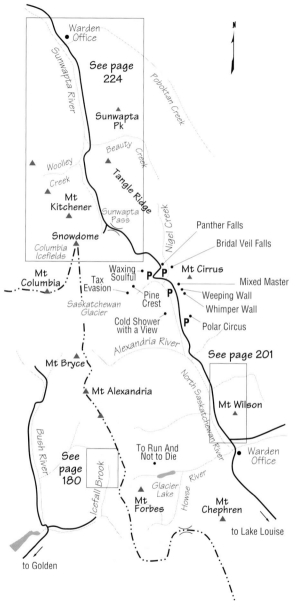

N

Warden Office

See page 224

Poboktan Creek

Sunwapta River

Sunwapta Pk

Beauty Creek

Woolley Creek

Tangle Ridge

Mt Kitchener

Sunwapta Pass

Snowdome

Columbia Icefields

Nigel Creek

Panther Falls

Bridal Veil Falls

Mt Columbia

Waxing Soulful

P P

Mt Cirrus

Tax Evasion

P

Mixed Master

Pine Crest

Weeping Wall

Whimper Wall

Saskatchewan Glacier

Cold Shower with a View

P

Polar Circus

Alexandria River

See page 201

North Saskatchewan River

Mt Bryce

Mt Alexandria

Mt Wilson

Bush River

To Run And Not to Die

Warden Office

See page 180

Icefall Brook

Glacier Lake

Mt Forbes

Howse River

Mt Chephren

to Lake Louise

to Golden

Mount Wilson

Towering 1800 metres above the highway, the South Face of Mount Wilson presents a stunning sight as you approach the Saskatchewan River Crossing from the south. Fed by a large icecap, it contains nearly two dozen routes presenting one of the greatest concentrations of easily accessible, hard waterfall climbing anywhere in the world.

Because of the sheer size and multitude of gullies, finding your designated route can be trying at best. In bad snow conditions, snowshoes offer a great advantage on the somewhat steep and timbered approaches. Skis are not usually needed or recommended due to deadfall. Most obvious lines have been opened, but occasionally the right conditions prevail to form up another freestanding "classic Rockies death climb". Most of the routes are found along the 12.3-km stretch between Rampart Creek Hostel and Saskatchewan River Crossing. The rest are situated in a small area just north of Rampart Creek. All highway distances given here are measured from the junction of the Icefields Parkway and the David Thompson Highway (DTH) as you travel north toward the hostel. See map page 201.

Reference
"Guide to Mt. Murchison, Mt. Wilson & the David Thompson", *Rock and Ice Magazine*, No.59, pg. 70, Jan/Feb. 1994.

Facilities
Besides the climbing, perhaps the best feature about Mt. Wilson is the nearby Rampart Creek Hostel which offers a great base camp to dry out, drink stout beer, and inquire about local conditions. An updated logbook of routes in the area is usually kept with the care-

taker. The Crossing Resort, just north of the junction with the David Thompson Highway, is closed from mid-November to early March. Early and late season climbers may find lodging, gas, a cafeteria, and pub (with a big screen TV for the Stanley Cup play-offs).

Emergency
Call the Lake Louise Warden Office. A pay phone is located at the warden station on the east side of the road just south of Saskatchewan River Bridge. A warden may be on duty, but the station has been closed recently. See page 272.

Maps
82 N/15 Mistaya Lake
83 C/2   Cline River

The Shining Nobodies 40 m III, 3
As you descend the hill from the south toward Saskatchewan River Crossing, *The Shining Nobodies* is visible in the gully directly above The Crossing Resort (82 N/15 163593). It is a short sunny climb located one drainage right of *Oh Le Tabernac*. If there is a good trail to *Oh Le Tabernac*, it is best to follow it to the base of the cliff and traverse right to the climb; otherwise, you can pick your way more directly.

Climb one pitch of good ice underneath a large avalanche path. Rappel the route.

Oh Le Tabernac *** 55 m III, 5+
Known for years as "Wilson Falls" the present name, a French expletive, aptly describes your thoughts when ascending this testpiece. It is the first major route found 2.1 km past the David Thompson Highway (82 N/15 156595). It is the very steep, sunny waterfall below a huge bowl. Higher in the bowl are four other quality lines. Hike or ski directly up the

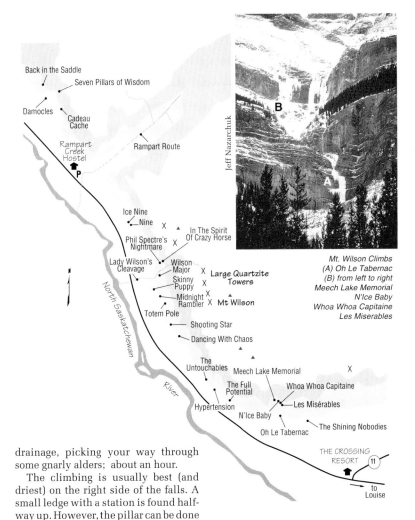

Back in the Saddle

Seven Pillars of Wisdom

Damocles

Cadeau Cache

Rampart Creek Hostel

P

Rampart Route

Ice Nine

Nine X

In The Spirit Of Crazy Horse

Phil Spectre's Nightmare X

Lady Wilson's Cleavage

North Saskatchewan

Wilson Major X

Large Quartzite Towers

Skinny Puppy X

Midnight Rambler X

Mt Wilson X

Totem Pole

Shooting Star

Dancing With Chaos

River

The Untouchables

Meech Lake Memorial

Whoa Whoa Capitaine X

The Full Potential

Whoa Whoa Capitaine

Hypertension

Les Misérables

N'Ice Baby

Oh Le Tabernac

The Shining Nobodies

THE CROSSING RESORT 11

to Louise

Jeff Nazarchuk

Mt. Wilson Climbs
(A) Oh Le Tabernac
(B) from left to right
Meech Lake Memorial
N'Ice Baby
Whoa Whoa Capitaine
Les Miserables

drainage, picking your way through some gnarly alders; about an hour.

The climbing is usually best (and driest) on the right side of the falls. A small ledge with a station is found half-way up. However, the pillar can be done in a full 50 m, creating a much more challenging ascent. A fixed belay is found in the rocks on the right side. If continuing to the upper climbs, traverse left and up small steps to the top. If not, rappel the route.

Jeff Lakes

Eric Hoogstraten getting creative on Oh Le Tabernrac.

In the spectacular bowl above *Oh Le Tabernac*, up to five separate climbs can be found (82 N/15 155600). Some confusion exists over which routes are which. From left to right they are Un-climbed (far left in a deep gully), *Meech Lake Memorial*, *N'Ice Baby*, *Whoa Whoa Capitaine*, *Les Misérables*. To reach them you must climb *Oh Le Tabernac*, then pound for 60-75 minutes to the base of the routes. All routes are descended by rappel. The quality of climbing here is worth the effort, but beware of severe avalanche potential in this sunbaked bowl and also from above. The sun and albedo have quite an effect on the ice. It can go from great plastic to melted garbage in no time. During an early ascent of *Whoa Whoa Capitaine* a climber had his tools rip through the slush. His hands came out of the leashes and, after falling 8 m, his tool caught in the ice with an umbilical cord saving a further plummet. After twenty minutes of hyperventilating and throwing up, he went on to finish the lead!

Meech Lake Memorial * 60 m IV, 4+

A wide flow of good sunny ice at the back of the bowl, *Meech Lake* is the easiest route offering moderate to steep climbing on a number of different lines. Great views of the nasties to the right!

N'Ice Baby *** 110 m IV, 5

A rarely formed route 50 m right of *Meech Lake Memorial*, *N'Ice Baby* is an excellent route offering a good compromise of excellent ice with difficult but not unrelenting steepness. 30 m of low angle ice to the base of the pillar. Climb 80-90° ice for a full ropelength to where the climb eases off towards the top.

Whoa Whoa Capitaine *** 80 m IV, 6

Two long, vertical, narrow and scary-looking columns are located on the far right side of the bowl, 20 m right of *N'Ice Baby*. Both routes are reached by a short shield of lower-angled, thin ice. *Whoa Whoa* takes the left-hand pillar. The next 60 m finds dead vertical and technical but usually good ice. Either use a semi-hanging belay atop the initial shield and then do all of the hard climbing in one pitch or start at the bottom and belay on ledges or caves about halfway up the waterfall.

Les Misérables *** 80 m IV, 6+

This testpiece is the right-hand of two narrow pillars. Even though only a few metres from *Whoa Whoa Capitaine*, this route is quite different in character and considerably harder. Unfortunately it doesn't often form and when it does, is usually cracked or broken. Climbed in two pitches, *Les Mis* offers sustained climbing throughout on extremely technical and overhanging ice. Unlike *Whoa Whoa*, you can't sneak the route with one hard pitch, it's gnarly to the bitter end. Rappel the route or traverse left and descend *Whoa Whoa*.

The Full Potential * 50 m III, 4+

The Full Potential can be identified by a spectacular icicle hanging off the rock band high above and two gullies north (left) of *Oh Le Tabernac*. Park 4.4 km from the David Thompson Highway. Approach on the right side of the gully until above some small cliff bands. Then drop into the drainage proper; one hour (82 N/15 142597).

This route is varied, sporting a free-standing pencil, 'Bourgeau-like' thin detached plate over rock, and vertical plastic. Rappel the route.

Hypertension *** 280 m IV, 5+

Hypertension, located in a large gully north of *The Full Potential*, is a very aesthetic and excellent climb. However, the bottom freestanding pillar rarely forms completely so get it while you can. The pitches above have even inspired past parties to attempt aid climbing past the overhangs. The upper pitches become visible at 4.7 km. Park at 6 km with the bottom pillar visible. Hike up through the trees to the right until it is easy to drop into the gully. Continue past a small ice step for a total of 1.5 hours (82 N/15 137601).

After climbing a 2 metre-wide pencil and thin ice for 50 m continue up snow and easy ice to a cave between two freestanding pillars. Climb a long vertical pitch above on good ice. Continue up the gully on more moderate ice for two pitches. A long sustained curtain 100 m above may form in some years and would offer a great challenge. Rappel the route.

The Untouchables

These are the three separate drips that sometimes hang down off a large cliff to the left of the *Hypertension* gully (82 N/15 135605). They have never come close to reaching the ground but perhaps some day these outrageous lines will be climbed.

Near Death

It is unknown exactly where this route lies among the numerous drips along this massive peak or if it is in fact another described line. The first pitch climbs a large freestanding pillar (see photo in *Rock and Ice*, No. 47, pg. 89, Jan/Feb 1992) to a steep but more reasonable second pitch.

Dancing With Chaos * 105 m IV, 6

A rarely formed climb, 6.8 km from the David Thompson Highway, *Dancing With Chaos* is visible through the trees on the bottom rock band. It usually has a huge broken icicle on the rock cliff above. Approach 2.5 hours up a timbered ridge to the right of the route then traverse left across rock slabs to the base (83 C/2 128616).

The first pitch is on poor ice up a steepening slab to a sheltered cave. The next 55-m pitch offers consistently vertical to overhanging technical climbing on "funky ice". With better ice it would be a more reasonable day out. Rappel the route.

Reference

Canadian Alpine Journal. Vol. 74, pg. 41, illus., 1991,

Shooting Star *** 350 m V, 6

Once thought to be the *Totem Pole* which lies farther left, *Shooting Star* has been the scene of many 'first ascents'. This most impressive climb is characterized by two narrow pillars cutting up 100-m rock bands with a large chockstone at the top. The upper part forms regularly and is obvious from the road. The lower part does not form every year and it is difficult to evaluate this bottom section from the road. The route is fed from the large gully coming off the upper face of the peak just right of the four obvious white quartzite towers looming high above and is 150 m left of *Dancing with Chaos*. Either follow the approach for that route and then traverse over to the route or park 7 km from the David Thompson Highway and ascend avalanche-prone slopes directly to the base (83 C/15 126620).

The bottom three pitches of Hypertension with an unclimbed pillar hanging above.

The first crux pitch is on a long vertical wall of poor ice. The next 50 m is on better ice 75-90° Gain 150 m of snow to a freestanding pillar. Climb the pillar and ice gully to a belay on the left. Finish above on 85° ice to an extraordinary exit under the chockstone.

Rappel the route or walk left through woods 250 m to a small gully where a short rappel can be made to the snow slopes below the upper tier. Rappel the lower tier in two rappels with a bolt set for the last rappel.

Totem Pole 200 m III, 4+

It is unknown if this route forms regularly or not because it is hidden from the road. Left of *Shooting Star* is a prominent rock buttress and to the left of that are two narrow parallel gullies 100 metres apart. The right-hand gully is *Totem Pole* (83 C/15 123624). It was originally climbed in an attempt to reach ice farther up the peak.

Rambly ice leads to a freehanging 'totem'. The first ascentionists stemmed up between the pillar and the rock wall and then traversed around to the top, a technique that made climbing the totem quite manageable. If attacked face-on, look out. Rappel the route.

Midnight Rambler ** 150 m III, 3

Park 8 km past the David Thompson Highway below the left-hand of two narrow parallel gullies. The climb is visible near the bottom of the cliff band (83 C/15 122625) as a narrow flow of good-looking ice about 800 m south (right) of the obvious cleft containing *Lady Wilson's Cleavage*. A broken off icicle looms off the cliff band above.

Climb a 50 m pitch of 80° to a snow gully and up a short vertical pillar followed by 50 m of easy snow and ice. Downclimb and rappel the route.

Skinny Puppy 50 m II, 5

Skinny Puppy is a rarely formed pillar which spills over a short cliff just 200 m right of *Lady Wilson's Cleavage* (83 C/15 119629). Walk through generally open terrain to the base.

The climbing is usually up a technical and difficult tube. However, it may fill out into a wider curtain.

Lady Wilson's Cleavage *** 300 m III, 3

This is the biggest, most obvious cleft in the entire South Face between the Saskatchewan River and Rampart Creek. Park where the drainage crosses the road at 8.9 km from the David Thompson Highway (83 C/15 111629). This ice has previously been forgotten as the approach ice to *Wilson Major*. *The Cleavage* offers a great place to get mega-miles on easy ice. Ice usually extends to the road and barring deep snow you can put your crampons on at the car. The downside is the extreme terrain trap you'll find yourself in during high avalanche hazard. Be observant of conditions.

200 m from the road starts the first substantial step of ice. Continue up countless steps with interesting climbing on ice which is wet even in the coldest temperatures. 250 m up, the gully necks down quite tightly so beware of loaded slopes above. A steeper 30 m crux pitch is found deep within the cleft and deposits you below *Wilson Major* where the cleavage widens. Rappel and downclimb route. It is possible to descend much of the route through steep bush to the right.

Wilson Major * 50 m III, 3-6

This route just visible from the road above *Lady Wilson's Cleavage* was formerly called **Unnamed**. The present title comes from the name of a large

Shooting Star as seen from the approach.

slope nearby that the Warden Service regularly bombs for avalanche control. The climb is up to 150 m wide offering lines with a wide variety of difficulty (83 C/15 121634).

The ice ranges from excellent blue plastic to wild mushrooms on the steeper sections. These lines are out of the main firing line of avalanches in the Cleavage, yet you must ascend that route to get there. Great towers of white quartzite loom on either side of the gully. A beautiful but spooky place. Rappel the route. Some trees may present themselves for anchors; otherwise, use the ice.

Phil Spectre's Nightmare 80 m V, 6

Climb *Lady Wilson's Cleavage* and continue up the gully past *Wilson Major* (one hour) to a broad curtain of icicles, 1000 m above the road (83 C/15 123636). This route takes the left-hand pillar.

Climb up technical mushrooms to a cave behind the upper pencil. From the cave, launch up 40 m of steep technical ice. The name refers to the noises made by the pillar on the first attempt.

A second, slightly harder line called ***In the Spirit of Crazy Horse*** (60 m V, 6) was taken on a chandeliered cigar to the right (climbed in protest for Leonard Peltier). It offers similar acrobatic and strenuous climbing.

Descend the obvious gully to the left or rappel the route. Once again, these routes can be very dangerous in poor snow conditions.

Nine 70 m IV, 6+ X

This climb was called ***Happy Days*** in the previous guide; however, the first ascentionists had named it *Nine*—a bit boring, but naming a route is one of the few claims a first ascentionist has. It is a radical testpiece that rarely forms. Its

twin route *Ice Nine* is found just a few metres to the left (83 C/2 112647). To approach either route, park 11.2 km past the David Thompson Highway (1.1 km south of the hostel) and hike up a fairly steep but short slope to the left, 40-60 minutes depending upon snow conditions. These routes are threatened by a large avalanche bowl above.

When formed, this route is very thin with several freestanding pillars and it usually lasts only a few days before it falls away. A serious route. Rappel off tree to the right.

Ice Nine ** 95 m IV, 6

A very aesthetic and difficult route, *Ice Nine* unfortunately forms only about every other year. Expect chandeliered and technical climbing; however, it can form thick and plastic. 1991 was such a year and it received several solo ascents. Approach as for the route *Nine*.

The first pitch climbs a free standing pillar (10 m from the wall) easing after 15 m. Depending on the exact line taken you may find a ledge to the side for the first belay. Most parties use a semi-hanging stance below the upper crux. The second 50-m, partially freestanding pitch climbs steeply but the ice improves to the top. Rappel the route.

Rampart Route * 70 m III, 3

From the hostel, hike up Rampart Creek for two hours to the route (83 C/2 106667). The creek above the hostel is an impassable canyon. Follow the orange ribbons starting near the #3 cabin to reach the creek above the canyon. Be careful about straying towards the canyon—it's a long, nasty way down. Talk to the house parent for more details.

This pleasant two pitch route is similar to *Panther Falls*, but much more scenic. Rappel the route or walk off.

Ken Wylie

Bruce and Sheila Hendricks climbing Pitch 2 of Ice Nine in excellent conditions.

Icefields Parkway 209

The next four routes are visible up an open gully 2.9 km north of the Rampart Creek Hostel.

Cadeau Cache ** 50 m IV, 5

Both the climbing and the approach to this climb look intimidating from the road, but it's worth the effort. The route forms a beautiful pillar of green ice, hence the name which roughly translates as "Hidden Jewel". It pours over a cliff to the right of *Damocles*. The best approach is to climb the first pitch of *Damocles* (WI 3), and then traverse up and right to the base. To get more climbing out of the day, it is also possible to climb the crux pillar (WI 5) and the next little step on *Damocles* and then traverse right to *Cadeau Cache*. Otherwise, thrash your way through small cliff bands and bush directly to the route (83 C/2 085682).

The route begins with some interesting mushrooms, then up the pillar on steep, excellent ice. Rappel the route.

Damocles * 300 m III, 5+

This is an innocuous-looking route but don't be fooled, it will give you everything you need. The most obvious feature of the route is the crux pillar, a 20-m, freestanding tube of hard climbing (83 C/2 081686). Park in the open area below the route. As you hike or ski up the drainage towards the climb, it will be easy to get pulled into a left-hand gully. This way has more alders and scrubby bushes and you'll need to cross back right to reach the *Damocles* gully. Get into the main gully right away for slightly easier travelling. Allow 1.5 hours if breaking trail. Remember that this gully is open and avalanche-prone.

Climb up a 40-m seepage in the gully (not visible from the road) followed by some snow. Avoid a rock step on the left and continue to the base of the pillar. Struggle up this deceptively hard pitch to a tree belay and continue up a short step to a snow gully and several more pitches of excellent ice. The route forms differently every year. Often the pillar is missing, but sometimes it is there and the small step above it is gone, barring access to the upper pitches. Rappel the route.

Seven Pillars of Wisdom ** 550 m IV, 5 R

Some years, excellent climbing may be formed above *Damocles*. It requires that you climb that route and continue above amongst spectacular quartzite cliffs for a total of seven pitches, including another WI 5 pitch at the top which can be quite thin. This beautiful route is as least as long as *Polar Circus* and more sustained and highly recommended. Rappel the route (pitons advisable).

Back in the Saddle * 90 m III, 4

The top pitch is visible above the trees only as you drive south on the parkway and as you come up the hill prior to reaching the open area before *Damocles* and *Cadeau Cache*. Park as for those routes, walk or ski into the hidden left-hand gully as mentioned for *Damocles*. Continue up the gully (a very large funnel for avalanches). The route lies in another narrow gully that branches up and right from the main gully and is not visible until below it (83 C/2 080687). The route itself is relatively safe from avalanches, however, big ones in the main gully can spill over the route. The name comes from the fact it was the first climb after big ground falls (on separate occasions) for both first ascentionists.

Climb a steepening apron to a full 50-m pitch of excellent 85° ice. Rappel or walk off right (avalanche-prone).

Weeping Wall Area

Two routes alone make this a destination for ice climbers around the world–Polar Circus and The Weeping Wall. Legendary in status, they offer unparalleled quality, length, formation reliability and easy access. Almost all the routes in the area have a sunny southern exposure and are found within half a kilometre of the road.

Facilities

Rampart Creek Hostel is a quick 30 minutes down the road. There once was a popular cook shelter and parking area near the base of Polar Circus, but they were quietly removed by the Park Service in the summer of 1994.

Emergency

Call the Lake Louise Warden Office. There is a pay phone at the warden station on the east side of the road just south of the Saskatchewan River Bridge. There may be a warden on duty, but the office has been closed recently due to government funding cuts. See page 272.

Maps

83 C/2 Cline River
83 C/3 Columbia Icefield

Polar Circus *** 700 m (500 m of ice) V, 5

The showpiece of the Canadian Rockies and a must for all climbers! The name originated from Charlie Porter who, on the first ascent, when messing with tangled equipment on a scary pitch, complained "this is nothing more than a Polish Circus!". Uncertain of the implications, Bugs McKeith later adapted this statement to the present name.

The route has lost much of its fearsome reputation and is routinely done in eight to ten hours car-to-car. It has been soloed in less than four. Beware of serious avalanche slopes, both from above and when turning *The Pencil*. Several pitches may appear unformed from the road, but the route forms without fail every year. It offers nine pitches of generally moderate ice gradually steepening until the final crux pitch. It is recommended as a must tick and also as good ground for intermediate climbers looking to cover alpine, multi-pitch terrain. Since the descent is down the way you came, it is easy to opt out if the climbing gets too desperate. Enjoy!

It is found in an obvious cleft 27 km north of the David Thompson Highway (15 km from Rampart Creek Hostel). Walk through light trees into the drainage. At the base of the first piece of ice, most parties climb up a steep slope to the left for several hundred metres. Then make an exposed traverse (avalanche-prone) right into the climb. Alternatively, ascend the gully direct on short ice steps and snow. Climb a final 70° ice step followed by 150 m of snow to round the corner and the base of the first steep pitch.

The first 50 m begins in an apron and steepens into a classic WI 4 pitch. Continue on to the second easy pitch. Walk 100 m up to *The Pencil*. Most often you will see a broken icicle looming above. As described by Bugs McKeith, "It is the most impressive single ice feature on the route, a 150 foot-long, 6 foot-diameter, totally freehanging icicle precariously suspended above a multiple mushrooming, ice pedestal." In 1991 this dynamic feature touched down (see page 99, second edition, *Waterfall Ice*) for perhaps only the third or fourth

Joseph Josephson

The upper three tiers of Polar Circus taken from the rib between the snow bowls.

time. Even with the telltale crack near the top, it was quite solid and had numerous ascents throughout the season, including a solo.

In order to turn *The Pencil* climb a short step to the right onto easier slopes above. A fixed belay/rappel station is found approximately 20 m right of *The Pencil* in the rock band. Directly above, some low-angle thin ice occasionally forms to create an interesting two pitch variation. Otherwise continue up right 200 m through some small trees (running belays) and then left to a small notch. Traverse left across a very exposed snow basin for 150 m back to the gully and the main falls. Again, beware of avalanche hazard. The upper section consists of three separate tiers, each climbed in two pitches. The first tier is 65 m of 70-80° ice to a small ledge. The *Ribbon Pitch* starts the next tier and begins vertical then kicks back to a curving gully and a fixed belay on the left. A shorter pitch above leads to a snow ledge. The final 100 m is usually climbed on the right side. A beautiful pitch up a series of grooves (WI 4) leads to a small ledge and a bolt belay. Getting off this belay usually constitutes the crux with 15-20 m of vertical ice then easing toward the top and a belay on the right. Heavy traffic often creates a pitted overhanging hook-fest on this crux section. The vast curtain to the left offers more sustained climbing but on usually excellent ice.

Begin the descent immediately; up to nine 50-m rappels. Most stations are fixed, but may be covered. Be prepared to make several stations off the ice. When rappelling the *Ribbon Pitch*, continue past the ledge and make the next rappel off the ice. 50 m takes you to a snow ledge, to bypass one short rappel.

Reference
Polar Circus, Vol. 2, pg 56, illus., 1987.

Bob-Sized 10-20 m II, 3
On the slopes 400-500 m left of *Polar Circus* are four or five smears. Often snow-covered, they may have high avalanche hazard. At times they are clear of snow and offer good introductory ice.

Cold Shower With a View 45 m III, 4
Located southwest and across the river from the Weeping Wall is a blue/green pillar high up on the ridge just left of a tremendous avalanche chute. From the Weeping Wall pull-out, cross the river and hike for three hours depending on snow conditions. Stay to the left in the

The Pencil in 1991-92.
Photo Tom Fayle

trees to avoid the avalanche gully. This route gets the sun first thing in the day so an early start may make it more enjoyable. There are commanding views of the Weeping Wall complex.

Climb a pleasant but often wet one pitch pillar. You can walk off to the right but to rappel the route would be the safest alternative.

Whimper Wall * 80 m III, 4

A dogleg smears appears out of a blank rock wall 200 m right of the Weeping Wall. Approach for the Weeping Wall, then traverse right to the base. Skis may be helpful.

Climb 74-80° for 45 metres to a snow ledge. Move the belay right to the base of the second crux pitch. Occasionally a third pitch forms. Rappel the route.

Mixed Master *** 300 m IV, 5.8 WI 5

Surprisingly, this route is located in the first significant gully 200 m left of the Weeping Wall and is only 15 minutes from the road. This highly recommended route is one of the finest mixed ice routes in the Rockies. Park at the Weeping Wall pull-out, walk down the road and hike up easy slopes to the base.

The first two pitches ascend a Scottish-style narrow ice gully into a small amphitheatre. Traverse right past a tree and up a short 70° water ice pitch to a good belay in an alcove. Traverse left on rock and up a short steep wall (5.8) onto a snow-covered ramp. Continue into the main gully and a bolt belay. Climb a low-angle thin ice pitch up a corner and some snow. The final rope length ascends a vertical ten inch wide ice vein (crux) followed by a thicker flow of steep ice. Rappel the gully direct on fixed anchors and trees, the final rappel (seventh) off ice.

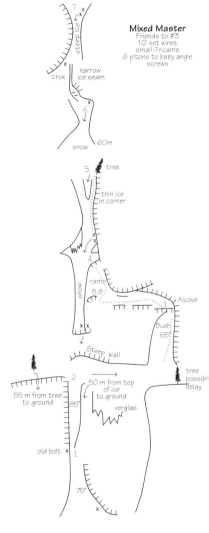

References

Canadian Alpine Journal, Vol. 75, pg 78, illus., 1992.

Tears of a Clown 30 m II, 3

From the Weeping Wall pull-out go north for 600 m. On the right side of a large recess away from the road, the route forms in a right facing corner capped by several overhangs (83 C/3 989787). The crux is 4 -5 metres of 80° ice. Rappel the route.

Team Effort 40 m III, 4

200 m left of *Tears of a Clown* in the back of the recess, *Team Effort* is found in a huge right-facing corner which offers a matrix for the ice to bond to. The crux is 10-12 metres of vertical ice which can be quite rotten due to the southern exposure. Rappel the route.

Snivelling Gully * 160 m II, 3

Named in commemoration of climbers' boyfriends and girlfriends appreciation of winter camping, *Snivelling* is a low-angle trough on the left side of the Weeping Wall. The quick approach and easy climbing ensure its popularity. In spring conditions, it can occasionally get wet avalanches oozing down it.

The first 30 m is often plagued by open water. The best variation is to climb one pitch up the *Left-Hand Weeping Wall* and traverse in on top of a large rock. The next ropelength has some 60° ice followed by snow (and open water). The final pitch offers a classic WI 3 pitch of 75-80° sometimes thin ice. Streaking up to the right are a number of steep and difficult pillars. They give quite an ambiance when climbing this narrow gully. **Snivelling Direct** * (125 m II, 5) offers very challenging climbing on a number of chandelier columns.

Snivelling Gully Descent

There are several ways to descend *Snivelling Gully*. At the top on the left side of the gully is a large obvious tree. Rappel from here onto a ledge below an overhang. Walk left to another tree and rappel onto the large halfway ledge which has a two-bolt, chain anchor just right of the rappel line. From here, rappel straight down off the ledge (left of the main gully) for 50 m to a three-bolt station which is visible from the base of the Weeping Wall. Make a 40-m rappel to the ground.

The second descent option starts from a tree to the right of *Snivelling Gully* near the top of the *Left-Hand* route. Rappel 50 m to the prominent ledge that runs across the entire Wall. In the past, parties have used a small tree on the left side of this ledge as a rappel anchor. The area around the tree has become very eroded and may no longer be considered safe. A bolt station can be found on the rock outcrop 5 m behind the tree. Make a steep 45-m rappel into the gully. From this point, it is possible to walk left on the halfway ledge to the two-bolt chain anchor described in the first descent option. This provides a clean, safe rappel line, away from open water, falling ice and crowds in *Snivelling Gully*.

To continue straight down *Snivelling Gully*, there is a two-bolt chain anchor on the left side below the halfway ledge where the gully narrows. From this anchor a 55-m rappel will reach the ground; otherwise, use a second chain anchor also found on the left side.

Lower Weeping Wall Reference

Rock and Ice, Vol 52, pg. 112, illus., topo; Nov/Dec 1992; *Polar Circus*, Vol 2, pg. 57, illus., 1987.

The classic Upper and Lower Weeping Wall. Snivelling Gully is hidden on the far left side of the Lower Wall.
A) Snivelling Direct (top only) B) Lower Weeping Wall C) Aerial Boundaries D) Teardrop/Weeping Pillar
E) Mare in Winter F) Nasty Habits G) Ice T, H) Tales of Ordinary Madness J) Common Approach Pitches to
the Upper Wall- Right Side.

Lower Weeping Wall

Undoubtedly, *The Weeping Wall* is the most famous climb in Canada. It is an impressive south-facing curtain, as wide as it is high, only ten minutes from the road, "a vertical football field" of ice offering all levels of difficulty. Avalanche hazard is *almost* nonexistent here. Snow on a prominent ledge two-thirds up the wall and snow buildup along the top of the wall have been known to release. Park at the plowed pull-out 28.6 km north of Highway 11. The climbs are obvious across the road.

The common descent for all routes is down *Snivelling Gully*. In 1992, a bolted rappel line was added on the rock wall

to the right of the *Right-Hand* route. The actual location of the bolts is not known for sure, but the first rappel is off a tree near the top of the *Right-Hand*. Three more bolt stations are in a right-trending diagonal line making for a good descent from the *Right-Hand* route and the *Upper Wall*.

Left-Hand *** 160 m II, 4

The easiest and most popular line, the *Left-Hand* has several variations. Pick one with the best ice and least people. The second pitch is the crux with ice up to 85° The third pitch up to the prominent ledge can be very thin with open water and little recommends the route in these conditions. A final step of 80°-85° leads into the trees.

Joe Josephson cranks the crux during the first ascent of Aerial Boundaries.

Central Pillar ** 160 m III, 5+

A large cave is usually found in the very middle of the Wall. *The Central Pillar* climbs up either side of the cave. Climb the initial apron, then a short second pitch to below your proposed line. A sheltered belay may be difficult to find. Pick whichever side suits your fancy. These pillars can be very chandeliered and vertical. A full pitch puts you on the prominent ledge. An easier step leads to the top.

Right-Hand *** 160 m III, 5

Again, this route has several variations, with most people sticking to the best ice. The first 60 m has ice up to 75° and leads to the prominent corner on right side. A fixed belay may be found on a small rock ledge on the right. Climb a long pitch up the corner or on the curtain to the left on steep exposed ice to the ledge. Finish up 20-30 m to the trees.

Aerial Boundaries *** 170 m IV, 5+

About 100 m right of the Lower Weeping Wall is a shallow gully topped by several large overhangs. The route rarely forms completely but is a classic.

Pitch one climbs into a small alcove on WI 4 ice. Lead out of the gully and up a strenuous pillar to a hanging belay below the overhangs. A short rambly pitch leads to a big ledge. The next pitch can be any one of a number of pillars that may form off the overhang. The first ascent party climbed a double freehanging cigar for 40 m to the second overhang. Two short WI 4 pillars lead to the top. Descend *Snivelling Gully*.

Jeff Nazarchuk scores on the vertical football field of Right-Hand Weeping Wall.

Upper Weeping Wall

Up to six independent lines of varying thickness and quality can form on the Upper Weeping Wall. From left to right they are *Teardrop/Weeping Pillar* (forms every year), *Unclimbed* (very ephemeral and anaemic), *Mare in Winter*, *Nasty Habits*, *Ice T*, *Tales of Ordinary Madness*. *Snivelling*, *Lower Weeping Wall*, or *Aerial Boundaries* must be climbed to reach them, making for a long day. Bring a head lamp–most parties end up rappelling *Snivelling* in the dark. Early season can be an endless wallow up the snow ledge between tiers; snowshoes can make the hike easier. Later in the year a good donkey trail usually becomes established from near the top of the *Right-Hand* route. An ascent of the Upper Weeping Wall is a feather in any ice-climber's hat.

The descent from The Upper Wall can be arduous and is not to be taken lightly. A number of different rappel routes have been used down the rock walls. They can be difficult to find and have caused more than one epic due to manky anchors and stuck ropes. It is recommended to rappel your route or use the following description. A bolt belay is sometimes found uncovered on the rocks near the top of *Teardrop* on the left; otherwise, use the ice or a tree back from the lip. A single bolt station is on the left in a small alcove directly below some large icicles, beware. Another rappel can be made from a cave just above the ledge. Then downclimb or make a short rappel off a rock anchor to the ground. This descent is dependent upon the quantity and quality of ice. Be prepared to make or leave up to four ice and/or rock anchors. Rappel the *Lower Wall* as for *Snivelling*. Good luck!

Teardrop ** 155 m IV, 6

Teardrop is essentially the line of least resistance up the left side of the waterfall. Reach a prominent snow ledge in two short pitches. Sometimes an interesting variation pours over the buttress just left of the main falls. From the ledge the top is a full 100 m away containing two long vertical sections, one just off the ledge and another near the top. Watch for huge icicles hanging off an overhang on the left threatening the lower pitches.

Weeping Pillar *** 155 m V, 6

A truly awesome line! The first ascent party included the *Central Pillar* route on the Lower Wall but many parties today cheat a little bit and use the *Right-Hand* route. On the Upper Wall follow a direct line up the right side. Climb good ice up to 85° to the ledge. Above, climb two 50-m pitches that are dead vertical. The crux is usually wherever you encounter the worst ice. It can be horrendously bad, going from overhanging mushrooms to sun-leached slush. However, don't despair–it isn't always in such rough shape and *The Weeping Pillar* can offer some of the most difficult plastic ice you'll ever climb.

Upper Weeping Wall - Right Side

Aside from the usually massive *Teardrop/Weeping Pillar* complex, the five remaining routes only reach the prominent snow ledge one-third of the way up the wall and only form in the best of years. To reach the snow ledge, there is a WI 4+ pillar followed by easy ice directly below *Mare in Winter* and *Nasty Habits*. The first ascent of *Tales* climbed this pillar and it has become the standard approach pitch. A wider, usually thin flow may be located 50 m

Awesome positions on the Upper Weeping Wall.

François Damilano Collection

to the right (80 m WI 4) ending in a small island of trees. This was used on the first ascent of *Nasty Habits*. The following routes are described from the snow ledge only. Note that the lengths of the routes are given starting from below the approach pitches.

Mare in Winter ** 200 m IV, 4+

This route was once referred to as "*Nasty Habits-Left*". The crux of the route is found on the pillar reaching the snow ledge. Above is a wide flow considered part of *Nasty Habits* but is considerably easier, offering three short pitches of good ice. Combine it with *Left-Hand* on the Lower Wall to create a poor man's *Weeping Pillar* with seven pitches of sustained WI 4 climbing. When formed, this route receives numerous ascents and even a few solos.

Nasty Habits 200 m IV, 6

Nasty Habits plasters the steep buttress several metres right of *Mare in Winter*. The first pitch above the snow ledge starts up a narrow smear and continues up steepening terrain to the final pillar. The second pitch may leave you wondering why you ice climb; an 85-90° pillar of scary technical ice. A third pitch of low-angle ice and snow takes you to the trees at the top.

Ice T * 180 m IV, 6

This long, narrow smear joins *Nasty Habits* near the top of the wall. The route is climbed in two long pitches and is often very thin near the bottom. The first ascentionists found it as thick as it's ever been. Nonetheless, both pitches offered steep, strenuous pillars separated by bad ice. Refer to the Rampart Creek Hostel logbook for the original and complete title.

Tales of Ordinary Madness ** 180 m IV, 5+

This route is located on the far right side of Upper Weeping Wall. Traverse under *Nasty Habits* 50 m to a narrow, blue pillar that spills over a left-facing corner. Spectacular icicles spiral off the corner to create a cavelike ambiance. The route faces more west than the rest of the wall and thus stays in shape longer. The first 30-m technical pitch is up splattered mushrooms. The final pitch goes left onto a very steep and sustained pillar of good ice. 50 metres just makes it to a big tree at the top.

Saskatchewan Glacier

Although technically part of the Columbia Icefields, these routes are approached from The Big Bend which is closer to the Weeping Wall than the main Icefields. 5.6 km north of the Weeping Wall, park in the parking lot (no sign) exactly at the corner of The Big Bend, an obvious 180° curve in the road where it starts ascending towards Sunwapta Pass. Ski up the drainage and bypass a deep canyon on the trail to the left; a ski trail is often already broken.

Waxing Soulful 50 m III, 3-5

Ski for about an hour towards the glacier and the climb is located 40 minutes up the slope on the right side (83 C/3 928804). The slope up to the climb can be horrible in deep snow. The climb lies on the south side of Parker's Ridge just before tree line and a recommended approach is to ski tour over Parker's Ridge from near the Hilda Creek Hostel. This approach is much shorter, quicker and more enjoyable provided the avalanche hazard is favourable. Use a map to locate the climb and the best ski approach over Parker's Ridge.

Peter Amann

Panther Falls.

The climb is a wide curtain with a variety of lines that start easier on the left and end in large overhanging icicles on the right. The first ascent team climbed a steep central groove. Rappel the route or continue your ski tour over Parker's Ridge.

Pine Crest 150 m III, 4+

Park at The Big Bend and ski about 1 km short of the toe of the Saskatchewan Glacier. The climb is on the north side of the valley (83 C/3 914796).

Two short pitches of easy angle ice lead to an avalanche-prone gully which can be avoided by a rock rib to the right. Climb a 50 m vertical pillar ending in the rock face above. Rappel the pillar then walk off to the right through trees.

Tax Evasion * 80 m IV, 5

Approach as for *Pine Crest*. The climb is located on the south facing cliffs just past the toe of the glacier (83 C/3 901793).

Climb very steep ice for 25 m before it eases off for another 25 m. A second pitch of WI 3 ice follows. Rappel the route.

Nigel Creek

Bridal Veil Falls * 110 m III, 3

Continue 4.5 km past The Big Bend and park at the Cirrus Mountain and Bridal Veil Falls viewpoint overlooking Nigel Creek. The top of the falls is visible across the creek from the edge of the parking lot. At the far south (right) end of the lot descend through steep trees to the creek and continue about 200 m downstream to the falls. There is large avalanche hazard from above.

This fun route consists of two, 30 m pillars broken by a 50-m snow slope. Expect good climbing on steep sunny ice. Make a 50-m rappel from trees on the left then walk off. An interesting pillar forms in a fissure to the left of the route, it usually ends after 15 m but it may form to create a wild mixed climb.

Panther Falls * 60 m II, 3-4

This climb is hidden and ends 10 m from the north end of Cirrus Mountain viewpoint. Approach Nigel Creek as for *Bridal Veil Falls*, then walk upstream 400 m. If you head down from near the north end the parking lot you will run into several steep cliffs that require a rappel or two. This is a bit of a hassle but it avoids the pound up the creek to reach the climb.

The first 30 m is of moderate angle but technical with large mushrooms and plate ice. On the second pitch are two variations, a steep chandeliered pillar on the right or an easier flow on the left. Continue up easier steps past open water to large snow covered boulders. Walk out left to the parking lot.

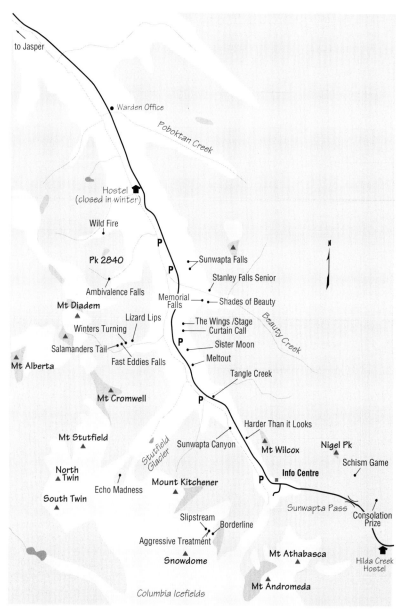

to Jasper

Warden Office

Poboktan Creek

Hostel
(closed in winter)

Wild Fire

Pk 2840

Ambivalence Falls

Mt Diadem

Lizard Lips

Winters Turning

Salamanders Tail

Fast Eddies Falls

Mt Alberta

P

P

Sunwapta Falls

Stanley Falls Senior

Memorial
Falls

Shades of Beauty

Beauty Creek

The Wings /Stage

Curtain Call

P

Sister Moon

Meltout

Tangle Creek

P

Mt Cromwell

Mt Stutfield

Stutfield Glacier

Sunwapta Canyon

Harder Than it Looks

Mt Wilcox

Nigel Pk

Schism Game

North
Twin

Echo Madness

Mount Kitchener

P

Info Centre

South Twin

Sunwapta Pass

Consolation
Prize

Slipstream

Borderline

Aggressive Treatment

Snowdome

Mt Athabasca

Hilda Creek
Hostel

Mt Andromeda

Columbia Icefields

Columbia Icefields

Considering the cold, icy alpine nature of the Columbia Icefields area, it is surprising there are not more waterfall ice climbs. Most attention is centred around the infamous *Slipstream*, as it presents an almost unparalleled amount of moderate water ice climbing with an outrageous position. For the first time ever in the winter of 93/94, the route did not form. Hopefully the ice-cap feeding the route will not change course and the route will continue as one of the greatest and most sought-after water ice routes in the world.

The weather can be atrocious at the Icefields. Always cold and often windy, many of the peaks are not visible for days on end because of all too common whiteout conditions. As an alternative to water ice, there are a number of classic alpine ice and mixed routes that have become popular winter objectives. Consult *Selected Alpine Climbs in the Canadian Rockies* for more information. In case you make the long journey to the Icefields and the longer routes on the west side of the road are in poor condition, there are a number of short ice routes along the east side that offer good diversions for your energy. And of course, there is the legendary *Curtain Call* that still repulses many.

Facilities

Hilda Creek Hostel is just south of the Icefields near Parker Ridge. This cosy spot with no phone, running water or electricity has an excellent sauna (indicative of where people's priorities lie). However, the Hilda Creek Chalet may be constructed in the next few years. The hotel and associated buildings at the Icefields are closed in winter.

Emergency

Pay phones are located on the north side of the Icefields Information Centre on the east side of the road across from Athabasca Glacier and, 17.7 km north at Beauty Creek Hostel (closed in winter). Sunwapta Warden Station (Poboktan Creek), 14.2 km north of the Beauty Creek Hostel, usually has a warden on duty and there is a pay phone in the parking lot. In a pinch try the Tangle Creek Maintenance Compound on the west side of the road, 0.5 km north of Tangle Creek. Someone from the road crew is usually there. See page 272.

Maps

83 C/3 Columbia Icefields
83 C/6 Sunwapta Peak

Sunwapta Pass

Consolation Prize 30 m III, 3

This climb is on the east side of the road directly above Sunwapta Pass and the Banff/Jasper Park boundary (83 C/3 898851). It is best visible from 300 m south of the actual pass. Climb a short steep pillar that is worthwhile only as the name implies. Rappel the route.

Schism Game 180 m III, 4

Located on the east side of the road above Wilcox campground, 2 km north of Sunwapta Pass in the fourth and deepest gully left of *Consolation Prize*, *Schism Game* is an obvious narrow pillar. Park at the campground entrance and ski through trees to the base. A WI 3 pitch is found just to the right in a neighbouring gully. Easy ice leads to a snow slope, then a short steep pitch topped by more easy ice. Walk off to the north or descend the route.

Mount Snowdome

Mt. Snowdome is famous for several reasons. It is most commonly known as the hydrological apex of North America. Water draining from its summit reaches three oceans; the Pacific, the Atlantic (via Hudson's Bay), and the Arctic. Covered by the Columbia Icefield it is nothing more than a gentle ski tour on its south and west sides. The east and north sides are a different ball of wax. Each of these sheer faces drop off the edge of the icecap for 1000 metres. They present a stunning sight from the Icefields Parkway. Climbers know the peak for its East Face where there are three routes including the infamous *Slipstream*.

The North Face has been attempted and the aspirants barely escaped with their lives. Their gully was swept by seracs only minutes after they retreated. All of the completed routes top out onto the icecap. Whiteout conditions are very common and it is required you carry a map and compass for whiteout navigation. The top of Snowdome is not a place to be fumbling around.

To descend from *Slipstream* and the other Snowdome routes, walk left along the icecap. Stay far right and away from the corniced edge. Rope up for glacier travel–the seemingly uncrevassed terrain is notorious for hiding big holes. Traverse around to the head of the Dome Glacier and a couloir leading down from the edge of the ice cap between Snowdome and its east ridge (Little Snowdome). Check out this gully while climbing the route. When in doubt while looking for the descent (remember the cornices are bigger than you think), keep traversing left, as the cornices get smaller. Traverse from the left back right directly into the couloir. Or, a rock station is located just left of the couloir at the top of a rotten cliff band but may be difficult to find. From there a 50-m rappel over steep rock deposits you in the gully. Several ice rappels lead to easier downclimbing. Once on the glacier, hastily get out from underneath the seracs. Follow the glacier out (staying right) to your skis and breathe a sigh of relief and satisfaction.

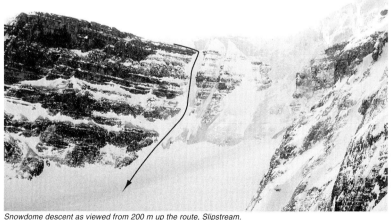

Snowdome descent as viewed from 200 m up the route, Slipstream.

Joe Josephson

Slipstream *** 925 m VI, 4+

For many waterfall ice climbers, this is the pinnacle of achievement. *Slipstream* commands an outrageous position with large amounts of relatively moderate terrain. Don't underestimate this route–it is a **very serious** undertaking–the number of lives lost on this route testifies. Not to be taken lightly, *Slipstream* offers all hazards and problems of the biggest winter alpine routes. It has the Commitment Grade VI for legitimate reasons. Be patient, wait for the right conditions and you'll be rewarded with one of the finest alpine climbs in North America. John Lauchlan described it as the "classiest route" he had ever completed.

Situated on the right side of the East Face, *Slipstream* weeps from the serac edge of the Columbia Icefields. The upper section is visible from the Information Centre near the Athabasca Glacier parking lot. Access (and the full view) is gained by driving about 1 km north of the Information Centre and parking on the flats at the bottom of a small hill. Ski up gravel flats and onto the moraines leading to the route. Park the skis near the bottom of the face and climb right of a small icefall to the prominent snow cone at the base; 2-2.5 hours.

The initial 500 m consists of rolling terrain that is often covered in snow. The first pitch encountered is the crux, a full 50 metres of classic WI 4 climbing. Then climb a snow slope (avalanche-prone) to the upper pitches. Three ropelengths of varied and sustained climbing leaves you at the final snow slope. This is one of the most dangerous features on the route, a perfect bowl in the fetch of spindrift blowing off the icecap. It is 80-90 m long and leads up to the right-hand margin of the ice cap. Once you safely make it to the edge of the glacier ice, it's almost in the bag and you're soon to be rewarded for all the toil getting to this point. The exit pitch climbs onto the edge of the serac between the east and north faces. The view down (1000 m) either side will leave your mind spinning! Either climb the ice arête or boldly traverse onto the North Face proper and climb steep water ice to the cornice and then the top. The position near the top of the route is unbeatable.

Reference
Polar Circus. Vol 2. pg 58, photo, 1987.

Lauchlan Original Finish Grade VI WI 6

On the first ascent of *Slipstream*, Jim Elzinga and John Lauchlan climbed directly over the serac barrier via a long, ferocious pillar of water ice that only occasionally forms. It is likely no one has repeated this original finish, as everyone heads right up the snow slope.

Aggressive Treatment 925 m VI, 5.8 WI 4

In the gully immediately left of *Slipstream* lies *Aggressive Treatment*. It is less a waterfall and more a difficult and serious winter alpine route. It is included here for completeness and in tribute to the exceptional climbers that completed it. The route starts at the same snow cone as *Slipstream* then heads into the gully system to the left. A bivouac was required at about two-thirds height. See the *Canadian Alpine Journal*, Vol. 65, pp. 37-8, 1982.

Borderline 800 m VI, 5

An immense piece of ice under house-sized seracs, *Borderline* hardly ever forms. "Thank God" claim the first ascentionists, as if it should compel people to climb it when it does form. The name more than adequately describes the level of risk you are taking on this adventure. *Borderline* is found two gullies left of *Aggressive Treatment*. To reach the route, climb up the snow cone below *Slipstream* and then traverse the crevassed glacier below the face. In recent years, the gully left of *Borderline* is more common to form and on occasion, has remained formed year round. This unclimbed line is swept by seracs virtually daily.

The first half of the route climbs WI 3 ice to a steep headwall. Continue up four pitches of steeper ice to the serac barrier. The first ascentionists found a complicated but easy exit through crevasses to reach the top.

Sunwapta Canyon

The following three routes are found in Sunwapta Canyon. Park 4.5 km past the Icefields Information Centre just outside the "No Stopping-Avalanche Area" sign and before the road starts going up Tangle Hill. Walk north along the river bed for about 1 km into the canyon. The climbs are visible from a viewpoint another 1.5 km up the Tangle Hill. The canyon is a severe terrain trap for rockfall and avalanches; even the smallest slide could bury you in this restricted canyon.

Photo Opposite:
The East Face of Snowdome.
From left to right: The top of Borderline, Aggressive Treatment, in very fat conditions, Slipstream.

JD 85 m III, 2

The first waterfall on the right extending from the bottom of the canyon toward the highway (83 C/6 813894) is JD 85. It is very low-angle ice with a couple of steeper sections. Continue to the highway and a point about 300 m south of the viewpoint or rappel the route.

Miller Time * 45 m III, 2

Continue past *JD* and just past a left-hand bend is a large keystone wedged into the canyon. *Miller Time* flows over either side of the keystone (83 C/6 809897). The chockstone is most commonly climbed on the left side which finds a nice pitch up to 80° to a tree belay. Rappel back to the canyon floor and climb two short icefalls on the east side to exit the canyon.

First Lead ** 55 m III, 2

This is the large falls downstream from *Miller Time* (83 C/6 808897). Remarkably it can form across the entire width of the canyon. Climb 30 m to a nice ledge belay followed by a short steep step which leads to the top and a tree belay. Rappel from trees to canyon floor and exit as for *Miller Time*.

Tangle Hill

The following routes are all found on and around Tangle Hill. This is a large hill that the road climbs over to avoid Sunwapta Canyon.

Harder Than it Looks 75 m II, 4

Drive 3.8 km north of the Icefields Information Centre and park a short ways before the road starts climbing over Tangle Hill. This route faces Snowdome and is in a shallow gully system above an "It is unlawful to feed the wildlife" sign (83 C/3 823880). A short route with an even shorter approach. The route lies in a signed avalanche area so don't stop (or climb for that matter) here in 'iffy' conditions.

The first WI 2 pitch runs onto the scree slope below the route and may be up to 45 metre-long. The second 30-m crux offers an often anaemic vertical pillar. Double rope rappel off large blocks at the top.

Tangle Creek *** 60 m I, 2

This is a classic practice and beginner's area located on the north side of Tangle Hill on the east side of the road. Park in the plowed signed parking lot on the west side of the road 7.4 km north of the Icefields Information Centre or 10.3 km south of the Beauty Creek Hostel (83 C/6 805906).

Walk across the road and start climbing in less than five minutes. Good bulgy ice with lots of variety and a number of different lines which always form. Rappel from trees.

Stutfield Glacier

The Stutfield Glacier cirque is one of the most beautifully tortured valleys within the Icefields. A flat, open plain leads to complex moraines and a multitude of hanging glaciers pouring (literally) off the icecap. In winter, the valley has a number of impressive waterfalls that stream upwards for hundreds of metres and it's disappointing that *Echo Madness* can be considered the only safe route in the area as all others are threatened by active serac fall. Someday, someone will attempt one of the several unclimbed lines in this valley. Good luck; you'll need it.

Echo Madness ** 250 m V, 4

To reach Stutfield Glacier cirque and *Echo Madness*, park at the Mount Kitchener viewpoint 1.7 km north of Tangle Creek. Head down the slope to the river. Continue up the broad valley to the truncated spur in the middle of the headwall at the back of the cirque. The route is obvious on the middle of this spur but doesn't always form.

Climb four increasingly difficult pitches. Several unclimbed WI 5 pitches may be found above but are usually rather thin. Rappel the route.

Tangle Ridge

Melt Out * 100 m III, 3

Park 3.6 km north of Tangle Creek or 6.7 km south of Beauty Creek Hostel near the "Approaching Columbia Icefields Area" and "Yield to Snowplows and Sanders" signs. The top of *Melt Out* is barely visible about 300 m south of here and it forms regularly. Walk or ski up the road cut and head up a faint drainage on the east side of the road, through trees to the base (83 C/6 784932).

Two short pitches of undulating ice lead to a low-angle final pitch. Protectable rock belays are available on the left as you climb up. Scramble down the left side or rappel the route.

Sister Moon * 140 m III, 4+

This route, capped by a large overhanging wall, spills out of a hole on the right side of a cliff. It rarely forms completely. Park along the road 4.8 km north of Tangle Creek or at the unmarked Woolley Creek pull-out, 0.5 km north. Approach through sparse trees to the right of the route; about 45 minutes. The climb is three pitches high and quite narrow near the top. Rappel the route.

Curtain Call *** 125 m IV, 6

A very experienced climber once described this climb: "On the first pitch you have to climb up these 'psycho' bobbles of unconsolidated ice two feet deep and then sacrifice an arm to put in any protection". Indeed, this is an awesome route that continues to instill fear in all its prey and one of the scariest-looking routes around. It may go several seasons without an ascent even though it forms every year. The crux, aside from dead vertical ice most of the way, is often the funky overhanging mushrooms that form near the middle of the route. Depending upon the season, they can be at the end of the first pitch or at the start of the second. The steep pillars at the bottom and at the top are often excellent ice. Park directly below the route at a lone gate along the east side of the highway, 6.4 km north of Tangle Creek. Walk or ski across the open meadow and into the trees. Continue up steep trees and an open area below the route.

Climb up an initial apron to a large ledge below two serious and sustained pitches leading to the top.

To descend, there are two options. From the top of the route traverse right into a large avalanche-prone gully which is descended easily to the base of the cliff. If the avalanche hazard is unacceptable, rappel the route.

The impressive Curtain Call in "fortunate conditions" (1989).
Photo Jeff Lakes

The Wings and The Stage * 50 m III, 3

Two wide smears are found about 200 m left of *Curtain Call* in broad concave section of the cliff (83 C/6 783955). Approach through trees between these routes and *Curtain Call*. Allow at least 1.5 hours. There is avalanche hazard from above.

The Wings are the right-hand smear with *The Stage* to the left. Both offer a number of different lines that are each a full rope length high. Rappel the routes. A bolt and piton anchor may be found left of centre on *The Stage*.

Woolley Creek

Park at a pull-out (no sign) on the east side of the road 5.2 km north of Tangle Creek. Cross to the west side of the Sunwapta River and head up a steep trail on the left side of the canyon until it drops you into Woolley Creek above the canyon. Continue up until near tree line and below the large North Face of Mt. Cromwell; two hours. The following routes are on the cliff band above the creek on the right side. The best time for these routes is early in the season (November) when you can walk to them and before the avalanche hazard rises. They probably fill out later in the year, but the climbing is most interesting when it's thin. It is unknown if they form regularly. Pitons are advisable for all routes and descents.

Lizard Lips ** 120 m IV, 4 R

Lizard Lips is the first route you come to (83 C/6 746934) and is the biggest, most obvious line. Climb a chandeliered, stepped curtain in three pitches. Rappel the route or the lower-angled gully just to the right.

Winter's Turning * 100 m IV, 3 R

100 m left of *Lizard Lips* is a break in the rockband that rises from left to right. *Winter's Turning* pours straight off this break at about half height and hits the bottom of the cliff just left of a couple of large trees. It doesn't reach the top of the cliff. It is stepped, thin climb with a short pillar two-thirds the way up. Another thin smear may exist in a cleft just right of the trees. Rappel the route.

Fast Eddies Falls * 100 m IV, 3 R

On the left side of the right-trending break from which *Winter's Turning* starts is another aesthetic smear Climb up and left on thin icicles and smears for several pitches. The route may, in some years, reach the top of the cliff. Rappel the route.

Salamander's Tail * 120 m IV, 4+

This route is in a deep gully and is the farthest left of the possible routes on this cliff band. It is impossible to see until you go slightly past it and look back into the gash about 500 m left of *Lizard Lips* (83 C/6 743933). A steep initial pitch leads to two more pitches of WI 3 ice. Rappel the route or traverse under avalanche-prone slopes to the *Lizard Lips* descent.

Beauty Creek

Shades of Beauty ** 120 m III, 4

A classic climb, easy for its grade; Beauty Creek is the major drainage north of *Curtain Call*. The top of *Shades of Beauty* is visible from the Parkway. Park in a plowed pull-out 7.9 km north of Tangle Creek or 2.4 km south of Beauty Creek Hostel. From the parking lot take the signed hiking trail next to the creek, cross an old road and continue up the drainage on the left side of the creek. Skis may be helpful for the first km but once you start gaining elevation up Beauty Creek it's easier to walk. Keep going until below the route. Hike up the slope (avalanche-prone) to the base; 1.5 hours (83 C/6 795962).

The first tier leads to a nice ledge below a 12-15 metre curtain of steep ice.

Climb this to a larger ledge. The final pitch climbs a long sustained section to a broad ledge below a rock overhang. Traverse left 50 m and rappel off a tree. Then scramble back to the base.

Stanley Falls Senior ** 45 m III, 4

Directly across the valley from *Shades of Beauty* is a pretty one pitch route that gets lots of sun and easily combined climbed the same day (83 C/6 794967).

Rambling ice leads to a steep pillar and the top. Rappel the route from the ice. Don't try to go back from the edge of the climb; water leaches from the scree and ice doesn't usually extend past the top of the climb. Good belay ledges and bulges of ice are found near the top.

Memorial Falls 50 m III, 5

This route, named in memory of Jasper resident Rick Blak who died in a caving accident, is located 200 m right of *Shades of Beauty*. This pillar rarely forms and is often seen only as a 5-10 m smear of ice at the bottom of the cliff. When formed it is easily visible from the Parkway. 50 m of steep ice leads to a scree ledge and a natural chock stone belay. Rappel from the chockstone.

Sunwapta Falls 65 m III, 3

Directly above the parking lot for the Beauty Creek climbs are two narrow canyons tucked into the trees. They lie several hundred metres apart and both contain several short pitches of rolling ice. Follow the trail as for *Shades of Beauty*. Then bushwhack more directly to the route(s). Rappel the routes or climb out of the gully and descend through trees.

Northern Icefields

Ambivalence Falls 300 m V, 3

A classically-narrow line that snakes up through the headwall at the headwaters of Diadem Creek, this climb is a beautiful line, albeit threatened by searches throughout. Park 1.6 km north of Beauty Creek Hostel at the "Tangle Ridge"/"Mt. Mushroom" viewpoint. Cross Sunwapta River and ski up Diadem Creek to its headwall; 2.5 hours.

Climb the obvious line through the headwall to the serac barrier. Traverse left to where a few metres of mixed climbing puts you onto the glacier above. To descend, travel north across the glacier (away from the obvious North Face of Mt. Diadem) until you can enter an avalanche-prone gully that brings you down to the valley floor. A large ridge line north of the gully may be a safer descent.

Wild Fire ** 180 m V, 6

A modern ice route offering difficult and sustained climbing. Park 4 km north of the Mt. Mushroom/Tangle Ridge pull-out. Ski up the first drainage north of Diadem Creek for two to three hours. *Wildfire* is located on the North Face of Peak 2840 m (83 C/6 725000).

45 m of vertical, thin, and intricate ice leads to a hanging belay. 20 m of easier ice leads to a vertical pillar and a piton belay on the right. Climb the pillar and two more easier pitches to the top. Rappel the route from pitons and ice. On the first ascent, no anchor was found at the top of the route so they rappelled off two large equalized rocks buried into the snow.

The key word found in previous descriptions of David Thompson area routes is "bushwhack". A lot of gumption is required to reach some of these climbs in heavy snow conditions. However, the area generally receives less snow than routes closer to the Continental Divide and travel is usually easy. Some approaches are a longer than average but the climbing is usually worth it and you are likely to be alone. This is the east leg of a 'Golden Triangle' (with Mts. Wilson and Murchison) formed around the Saskatchewan River Crossing which contains over one-tenth of the routes in the entire range. *Kitty Hawk* and *Nothing but the Breast* are as good as they come and should not be missed.

References

"Guide to Mt. Murchison, Mt. Wilson & the David Thompson", *Rock and Ice Magazine*, No. 59, pg. 70, Jan/Feb. 1994.
"A Mini-Guide to David Thompson Ice", Cyril Shokoples, Rescue Dynamics, 1992, 1994.
Canadian Alpine Journal, Vol. 75, pg. 76, 1992.

Getting There

From the south, follow the Icefields Parkway (Highway 93) north from near Lake Louise for 110 km to the Saskatchewan River. The David Thompson Highway junction is 300 metres north of the crossing. This same intersection is 120 km south of Jasper. Highway 11 can be reached from the Red Deer by driving west to Nordegg, about 50 km from the main climbing area and 98 km from the Icefields Parkway. The climbs are described from west to east. Distances given in the descriptions are measured from the junction of the David Thompson Highway and the Icefields Parkway and indicate roughly where to park and begin the approach.

Facilities

The Crossing Resort at Saskatchewan River Crossing is closed from mid-November to March 1. When open, there are rooms available, gas, a cafeteria and a bar. The David Thompson Resort near the Cline River is closed in winter. Climbers from the Banff area usually stay at the Rampart Creek Hostel 12.3 km north of Saskatchewan River Crossing on the Icefields Parkway. If approaching from Edmonton or Red Deer, the Shunda Creek Hostel is a short distance west from Nordegg on Highway 11 and only 30 to 60 minutes from the climbs. An updated log book on David Thompson climbs is maintained at the hostel. Nearest gas or supplies are in Nordegg to the east, Lake Louise to the south or Jasper to the north.

Emergency

Contact the Lake Louise Warden Office. Pay phones are located at the warden office on the south side of the Saskatchewan River, the Crossing Resort, the east side of the highway, 28.4 km from the Icefields Parkway, across from Cavalcade Campground (Two O'Clock Falls), at the David Thompson Resort, 43.5 km east of the Parkway, and in Nordegg. See page 272.

Maps

82 N/15 Mistaya Lake
83 C/2   Cline River
83 C/1   Whiterabbit Creek

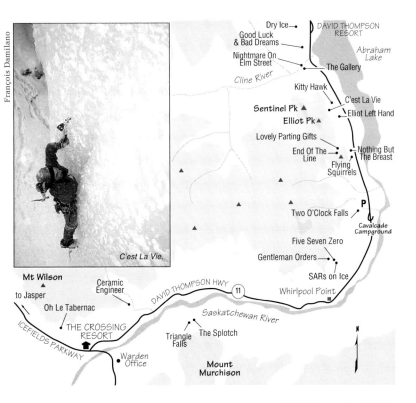

François Damilano

Dry Ice→
Good Luck & Bad Dreams→
DAVID THOMPSON RESORT
Abraham Lake
Nightmare On Elm Street
The Gallery
Cline River
Kitty Hawk
C'est La Vie
Sentinel Pk ▲
Elliot Left Hand
Elliot Pk ▲
Lovely Parting Gifts
End Of The Line ▲
Nothing But The Breast
Flying Squirrels
▲
▲
▲
P
▲
Two O'Clock Falls
Cavalcade Campground
Five Seven Zero
Gentleman Orders→
SARs on Ice
Mt Wilson ▲
Ceramic Engineer
DAVID THOMPSON HWY ⑪
Whirlpool Point
to Jasper
Oh Le Tabernac
Saskatchewan River
ICEFIELDS PARKWAY
THE CROSSING RESORT
Triangle Falls
The Splotch
Warden Office
Mount Murchison
N

C'est La Vie.

Owens Creek

Ceramic Engineer * 70 m III, 3

This climb is found in Owens Creek just east of Mt. Wilson (83 C/2 227643). Park 5.9 km from the Parkway. Hike just over 1 km northwest into the creek drainage, continue upstream for another kilometre. Several routes can be seen on the west wall 150 m above the creek. *Ceramic Engineer* climbs several pitches of easy rambling. Rappel the route.

Corona Ridge

The Splotch 60 m III, 3

Drive down Highway 11, 8.5 km from the Parkway. Two climbs are across the river on a lower buttress between Murchison Creek and Corona Creek (82 N/15 258595). Ford the river (knee-deep, and possibly frozen) and follow old logging roads. Bushwhack 1.5 hours to the base. *The Splotch* is the left-hand falls of good sustained climbing at 70-75° Rappel the route.

Triangle Falls 60 m III, 3

Approach as for *The Splotch. Triangle Falls* is 200 m to the right. Do both the same day so you never have to go back. Similar climbing to but not as sustained as *The Splotch*. Check out the smear hanging near the top of the crag. Rappel the route.

Whirlpool Point

SARs on Ice * 30 m III, 3-4

From *Whirlpool Point* itself, a series of seepages can be seen high on the ridge to the north. *SARs* is the lowest (83 C/1 369635). This small step makes an ideal approach for several other smears. Park at a large clearing just east of *Whirlpool Point* 22.5 km from the Parkway. Bushwhack to the base, about an hour.

Climb a near vertical pillar on the right with easier ice to the left. Continue on to other routes or rappel the route.

Five Seven Zero *** 100 m III, 4

Five Seven Zero is a fine climb with good views. To approach, it is highly recommended to climb *SARs on Ice*, then keep right to avoid the cliff band between the two climbs. Otherwise from *Whirlpool Point*, intercept the lower (eastern) of two parallel ridges which is followed to the base in one hour. The first crux pitch cannot be seen until you are very near the start of the climb.

Start with a 25-m, freestanding fang. Two lines diverge to the top with the left being harder with a short pillar.

From the top of the climb head south towards *Whirlpool Point*. Do not head for the ridge but traverse through the trees to a small seep coming directly from the rock (*Gentlemen, Orders*). Walk around a broad

ledge dividing that climb in half and easily descend snow and ice to the trees to eventually join the lower ridge. As an alternative, most parties rappel the top tier from trees and then traverse 25 m right to escape via *Cheater's Gully* back to the base.

Private Functions 25 m WI 2

25 m to the left of *Five Seven Zero* is a variation of its first pitch. From the top of *Private Functions*, traverse back to that route. The far right of *Five Seven Zero* can be taken to allow for a WI 2 climb throughout.

Bloodline * 25 m WI 3

In a gully 25 m left of *Private Functions* is a pillar that is similar but easier than the first pillar on *Five Seven Zero*. Traverse easily back to the main ice flow.

Gentlemen, Orders 50 m III, 2

Found just south of *Five Seven Zero* are two short pitches that are good for filling out the day after climbing the above routes. The descent for *Five Seven Zero* cuts across the middle of this climb. This and the four routes listed above can all been climbed in one day.

Two O'Clock Creek

Two O'Clock Falls ** 120 m III, 2-3

Two O'Clock Falls is easily visible behind Cavalcade Campground in the Kootenay Plains a short distance west of Two O'Clock Creek (83 C/1 388672). Just west of Cavalcade Campground is a turnoff leading to a poor road. Park at the turnoff and follow the road in the general direction of the ice. You will eventually come to a clearing. From there, look for an indistinct trail or bushwhack to the ice. **Note:** There are a number of native ceremonial lodges in this clearing; it is crucial that you do not disturb these structures.

This wide expanse can be climbed in two or three pitches offering many lines of good ice. Rappel the left-hand side or thrash down steep trees to the left.

Mount Ernest Ross

In Search of Flying Squirrels ** 400 m II, 2/3

Found 100 m left of the obvious *Nothing but the Breast. Flying Squirrels* is a shallow gully of ice recommended only when well formed and clear of snow. Park at 33 km from the Parkway and walk 30 minutes to the base.

The first 250 m or so is easy rambling. To reach an upper WI 3 pitch, suffer up another 150 m of scree to an exciting 50-m pitch that may be very thin and have difficulty with belays.

To descend the upper pitch, you may find a rappel station, otherwise downclimb the rock to the left. The rest of the way down is the same for *Nothing but the Breast.*

Nothing but the Breast *** 150 m III, 4+

This bad joke by the first ascentionists was originally rated II, 3! It sits in a fine position over the lake and is close to the road. It forms every year and is usually seen as a wide section of green icicles, or earlier in the season, a narrow shaky tube. Park 33 km from the Parkway and walk straight to the route (83 C/1 387719).

The bottom two pitches of undulating ice are not hard but are usually very thin. It is difficult to find belays. The final, near-vertical, two-stepped pillar is best done as one pitch. To descend,

either walk left staying high to avoid cliffs, then into the trees back to the road, or rappel the upper pillar off ice and walk down to a big tree on the right and make on 50-m rappel, then downclimb back to the base.

Lovely Parting Gifts * 65 m III, 3

A narrow drainage can be seen from Highway 11 between Ernest Ross and Elliot Peaks, 35.4 km from the Parkway. Follow the right-hand stream bank coming from the canyon and drop into the stream bed at the last possible moment. Clamber up some short ice steps and a boulder field to a fork where the canyon opens slightly. To reach *Lovely Parting Gifts*, take the left-hand canyon and look for this climb on the right-hand wall of the canyon just before you reach *End of the Line* (83 C/1 376733). All routes in this canyon are subject to rockfall. This long winding canyon has been the scene of at least one serious accident. Beware.

The climb fills out later in the season, getting easier. As a result it can be as difficult as WI 4 or only WI 2. A single bolt is located up and left at the top of the main ice flow. A second single bolt station is found 40 m down on a thin slanting rock ledge to the left. It is advisable to bring additional bolts for these anchors.

End of the Line * 100 m III, 3

This route is the obvious waterfall at the end of the left-hand canyon (83 C/1 375733). When approaching the route, beware of an avalanche path on the left. Allow two hours in deep snow.

The first pitch sports a bolt belay and begins at 80° then eases off. Near the top of the pitch is an interesting rock/ice chimney problem followed by a

Bruce Hendricks enjoys the sun on Nothing But The Breast.

jammed log belay (this may not be a permanent feature, so be prepared). Another less step pitch goes up for a full rope length and two bolts on the right. Rappel the route.

Mount Elliot

Elliot Left-Hand Gully ** 200 m III, 4

Formerly called **Sentinel Left-Hand** this is the left-hand of three prominent gullies on Elliot Peak. All three of these gullies are major funnels for avalanche so know the prevailing conditions. Park where blue ice on the first pitch of easily visible from the Highway 36.3 km from the Parkway. Bushwhack for an hour to the base (83 C/1 371755).

50 m of 70-80° wet ice leads into the narrow slot. Wind upwards on more moderate ice and snow to the final curtain. A wide and long pitch of steep ice eases toward the top. Rappel the last pitch from a tree to the left. Rappel and downclimb the rest of the route. Some fixed anchors may be present.

C'est La Vie 35 m III, 4+

Many avalanches have been seen to roar down this gully–hence the original name of The Grand Central Gully. C'est la Vie was first climbed only after finding a team on every other route between there and The Weeping Wall. It is the middle and largest of the three prominent avalanche gullies on Elliot Peak. It is important to venture onto the route only after the upper bowls have avalanched. The climb is located in a right-hand branch very high up and is seen from the road as a nice blue pillar (83 C/1 355757). Lots of small steps and snow climbing is required to reach the main pillar.

Park below the gully and walk through the trees. Follow the rib to the left of the drainage to the base of the cliff band in about an hour. A short ice step leads into the narrow gully which winds up to a final mixed step where the gully opens up. Continue past an ice step to a right-forking gully which is climbed past another ice step to the final pitch, a very pretty freestanding curtain of good ice. Rappel and downclimb the route. The mixed step can be rappelled (double ropes required) off a small but very sturdy tree on the left (look for sling).

Kitty Hawk *** 200 m IV, 5

The hardest and best David Thompson route, *Kitty Hawk* is one of the best climbs in the Rockies with an ambience similar to *Polar Circus* or *The Sorcerer*. It forms every year and is a true sandbag at its original rating of WI 4. The name originated from the first attempt in 1980, which ended with a leader fall on the penultimate pitch, "a real whipper" requiring an improvised rescue and several stitches. After several false starts and partner epics, the first ascentionist finally succeeded in a rope solo of the upper pitches. Later, on the descent, he broke through a snow crust and lacerated his thigh with an ice tool, requiring 26 stitches. *Kitty Hawk* is the farthest right of the three prominent gullies on Elliot Peak and is obvious from the road (83 C/1 366763). Park below the route 38.5 km from the Parkway and approach for an hour.

Climb two easy pitches into the narrow slot and the base of steeper ice. Start with a WI 3 to an unsheltered belay. A long pitch of good technical WI 4 leads to the base of the crux pillar. The next very difficult pitch climbs over large overhanging mushrooms onto a vertical pillar. From a platform above, an easier pitch leads to the top.

Rappel the route. As of 93/94 the route is littered with some very frightening single bolt anchors. Do not trust them. Adequate ice anchors can be found.

Sentinel Mountain

S'N'M Falls * 150 m III, 3

S'N'M Falls, on Sentinel Mountain, is visible from the Cline River Bridge, 42 km from the Parkway. It is found low down the rightmost indistinct gully, below which is a prominent avalanche swath. From the parking lot on the south side of the bridge, hike or ski along Pinto Lake Trail. Eventually take to the trees and work your way along scree and boulders to the base; allow two to three hours (83 C/1 343774).

Climb three pitches of undulating ice ending in a long snow gully. Cross into the trees to the right and work your way down without difficulty.

Cline River Gallery

This is a series of curtain, pillars and short nasties spreads along the south side of the Cline River Canyon and offers many lines up to a ropelength long (WI 2-5+). The approach can be as difficult to follow as the climbs are to find. Follow the Pinto Lake Trail that starts just south of Cline River Bridge. The trail begins to climb uphill at a grove of poplar trees (aspen trees). As it does so, it rounds a small knoll behind which is the first small indistinct draw. Follow the draw which disappears and then bushwhack to a prominence above the river. Follow this until *Nightmare on Elm Street* is visible across the river. Drop down towards the river and look for a dry gully immediately east of the ice and downclimb it to the canyon bottom (83 C/1 345789). Allow one to two hours.

Pure Energy ** 30 m III, 4+

Pure Energy forms consistently and usually quite well. It is the right-hand massive pillar that descends to the waters edge.

Are You Afraid of the Dark? * 30 m III, 5

Just left of *Pure Energy* is a large rock overhang separating that route from the rolling terrain and ice ramps to the left. In 1990 a thin sheet formed off the overhang and made for an exciting climb. Most years it vainly attempts to reach the ground—don't let that stop you.

Splashdown A & B 30 m III, 4+

Upstream from *Pure Energy* are two steep ice flows going right into the water. The water is rarely frozen so don't try to approach the climbs up the canyon. You will likely need no encouragement in this regard. Snow covered ice near the lip of the canyon can make it tricky getting to the top of the climbs as well. Be careful. Rappel to the base and claw your way out. These are not climbs for leading and are top roped from the rim. The ice is occasionally not well attached to the wall. They form often but in varying quality.

Cline River Canyon

Nightmare on Elm Street 45 m III, 3

Follow the major trail that starts just north of the Cline River bridge until the first reasonable-sized grove of poplar trees on the left and the trail begins to descend. Bushwhack directly toward the river and search for a clearing along the edge of the canyon. Two large trees at the edge of the canyon are marked with flagging tape above the climbs; one hour (83 C/1 347791). *The Gallery* ice climbs should be visible across the river at this point. A 50-m rappel takes you into the canyon (beware of open water). The climb is one pitch of moderate ice, steeper at the bottom.

Mount Stelfox

Good Luck & Bad Dreams *** 150 m III, 4

A David Thompson classic! This climb is located above the heli-pad between the Cline River bridge and the David Thompson Resort. Park as for *Nightmare on Elm Street* and hike for 45 minutes (83 C/1 347805). It rarely forms completely and may not see any ice whatsoever in the bowl. Beware of severe rockfall in warm temperatures.

The first crux pitch begins as a pillar for 25 m. Continue up 50 m of rolling ice. The third 50-m pitch rears to 80° ending at a nice belay ledge. The final pitch starts steep then eases off to the open area at the apex of the great funnel above. Another ribbon of ice may be present above.

A walk off is possible through the trees and off the backside toward the Cline River. Otherwise, rappel the route.

Dry Ice * 400 m IV, 3

45.3 km from the parkway is a fine route that forms almost every year. It is in the leftmost of two obvious gullies which are subject to extreme avalanche hazard. From the swamps near the David Thompson Resort, bushwhack through open forest and then poplar trees to the creek bed near the bottom of the climb; 1.5 hours (83 C/1 346835).

Climb six steps of ice with the second being the longest. Further up is a classic WI 3 pitch followed by the crux pitch. Climb two more steps then finish with a 20-m pitch. Further exploration will not reveal any further ice up the gully.

Rappel the route.

Mount Abraham

Captain's Log * 110 m III, 3

Captain's Log is located across Abraham Lake south of Mt. Abraham. Wait until the lake freezes, then cross the lake (objective hazards of ice-fishermen) into the stream bed to the base of the climb on the left sidewall; two hours (83 C/1 402854).

Climb two undulating pitches in a wild situation with lots of fossils in the area. Rappel the route.

Nordegg

Crescent Falls 25 m II, 3

The falls are formed by the Big Horn River pouring over large rock ledges. Only the upper fall has been climbed. 17.7 km west of Nordegg on Highway 11, turn north onto a difficult road. At a junction, keep left and continue to the falls. Walk down or rappel to the base. The climb is one pitch with tree belays at the top near the road.

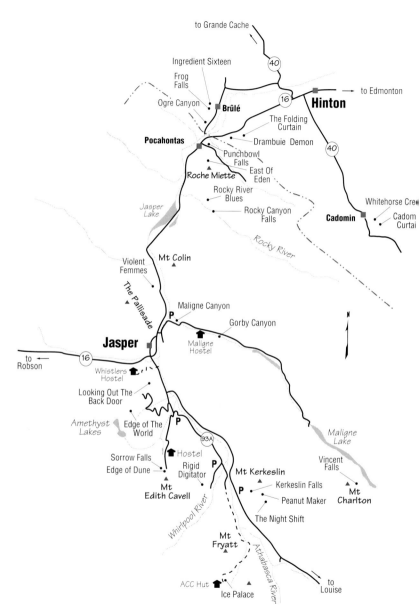

to Grande Cache

Ingredient Sixteen

Frog
Falls

Ogre Canyon

Brûlé

Hinton

to Edmonton

The Folding
Curtain

Drambuie Demon

Pocahontas

Punchbowl
Falls

East Of
Eden

Roche Miette

Rocky River
Blues

Rocky Canyon
Falls

Whitehorse Cre

*Jasper
Lake*

Cadomin

Cadom
Curtai

Rocky River

Mt Colin

Violent
Femmes

The Pallisade

Maligne Canyon

Gorby Canyon

Jasper

to
Robson

*Maligne
Hostel*

*Whistlers
Hostel*

Looking Out The
Back Door

*Maligne
Lake*

*Amethyst
Lakes*

Edge of The
World

Hostel

Sorrow Falls

Rigid
Digitator

Mt Kerkeslin

Vincent
Falls

Edge of Dune

**Mt
Edith Cavell**

Kerkeslin Falls

**Mt
Charlton**

Peanut Maker

The Night Shift

Whirlpool River

**Mt
Fryatt**

Athabasca River

to
Louise

ACC Hut

Ice Palace

242 *Jasper Area*

JASPER AREA

Although the town of Jasper is the northern Rockies equivalent of Banff, the scene here is much more quiet both in terms of the number of tourists and the amount of waterfall ice. The topography features wider valleys of a less alpine nature than those farther south. As a result, there are few climbs in the vicinity of Jasper. Access is also a problem. Many routes require a walk or ski of two or more hours. There remain several promising areas that likely hold new routes but again they require long ski tour approaches. This is a perfect area for those willing to go exploring in their quest for new ice routes.

Getting There
Jasper is reached by a 342 km drive from Edmonton via Highway 16 in about 4 hours or via The Icefields Parkway (Highway 93) from Lake Louise. Jasper is also served by Via Rail if you fancy this romantic mode of travel.

Facilities
Jasper has all amenities, including groceries, showers in the coin laundromats and 24-hour gas stations. There are many hotels but the most reasonably-priced lodging is at Whistlers Youth Hostel, 7 km from town. Drive the Icefields Parkway south 2 km to the first road on the right, Whistlers Road, and follow it 3 km to the hostel. A Park Information Centre is located across from the VIA Rail Train Station in the centre of town (Connaught Drive) and the warden office, a short distance along Maligne Lake Road, 5 km east of town. Fork left shortly after crossing the Athabasca River Bridge.

Emergency
Call the Jasper Park Warden office or the local RCMP detachment. See page 272.

Highway 93

This includes the climbs accessed off the Icefields Parkway (Highway 93) south of town. Jasper is only an hours drive north of the Columbia Icefields but the nature of the terrain changes drastically so that there are few roadside waterfalls on this stretch of highway. The large peaks on the west side of the valley probably have more than a few waterfalls hidden in them, but the long ski tour approaches will keep most of them hidden for years to come.

Maps
83 C/12 Athabasca Falls

Fryatt Creek

Ice Palace 1 & 2 100 m III, 2-3
Ice Palace sits in a superb location near the headwaters of Fryatt Creek. From here you can enjoy great views of Brussels Peak. Due to the long approach from the highway, *Ice Palace* is best climbed from the ACC Sydney Vallance Hut (83 C/12 403174). The tour begins from the Icefields Parkway 7.5 km south of the Athabasca Falls parking lot and tourist centre (closed in winter). Exercise extreme care crossing the Athabasca River– it is fast and deep. If the river is not frozen, cross the bridge at the summer trail beginning at Athabasca Falls. The hut, 13 km from the river crossing, may take most of a day to reach. Refer to *Ski Trail in the Canadian Rockies,* page 184.

The climb is two parallel smears on the headwall below the Hut (83-C/12 404177). The approach to the Hut climbs up the hill to the right of the falls. The left-hand line is longer and steeper and gives two good pitches that reach 70° near the top. Both lines exit up snow to the top of the headwall.

Mount Kerkeslin

Kerkeslin Falls *** 310 m III, 3

One of the best routes in the Jasper area, *Kerkeslin Falls* is visible from the Parkway in a significant avalanche chute on Mt. Kerkeslin. Park at Goat Lookout and walk or ski up mixed ground to the base in 30-60 minutes.

The climb consists of good ice steps separated by sections of snow. The best pitches are at the beginning and are up to 40 m high. Rappel and downclimb the gully.

Peanut Maker 100 m of ice III, 3

One drainage south of *Kerkeslin Falls* you will find five short pitches with lots of walking. Park 1.5 km south of Goat Lookout where the creek bed of this climb crosses the Highway near the old Fryatt Creek cable crossing. Continue up the drainage for 1.5 hours to the base of the first cliff band.

The first pitch climbs rolling steps of WI 2 in a narrow smooth-walled chute. After five minutes of walking, climb a second 20-m pitch in a canyon. Above is the crux third pitch offering 25 metre-high twin columns of ice on either side of a chockstone. Walk another 30 minutes to find the 20-m fourth pitch of easy ice. The fifth and final 25-m pitch is another ten minutes upstream. Rappel and downclimb the route.

The Night Shift * 100 m IV, 4

A third route, *The Night Shift*, is found on Mt. Kerkeslin in the next drainage south of *Peanut Maker* or two south of *Kerkeslin Falls* (83-C/12 452295). Park 3.3 km south of the Goat Lookout and just north of the Mt. Christie picnic area. Bushwhack to the creek bed and gain about 500 metres of vertical to reach the base of the climb; three hours.

The climb consists of two 50-m pitches, the first of which is moderately angled on the left side and steeper to the right. The second is a full runout at 80° Rappel the route.

Highway 93A

Also called the Athabasca Parkway this is a side road on the west side of the Athabasca River that gives access to Whirlpool River, the Mt. Edith Cavell Road and Marmot Basin Ski Resort. Winter access onto Highway 93A is off the Icefields Parkway, 7 km south of the Highway 16 intersection.

Maps
83 D/9 Amethyst Lake
83 D/16 Jasper

Looking Out the Back Door 210 m IV, 4

Also known as *Peveril Falls*, this route has a large avalanche-prone bowl above the climb. An early season ascent is recommended, it may be possible to check with the Marmot Basin Avalanche team for an update on conditions. From Highway 93A turn right up the Marmot Basin Ski Area Road and follow it and park at a big bend around Portal Creek. Ski up Portal Creek 7 km and the climb is above the Portal Creek campsite outhouse and is the only obvious climb in the area (83 D/9 223446).

Climb 60 m of moderate ice followed by 20 m of WI 2. Walk 200 m to a third pitch of steep WI 4. Rappel top pitch and continue rappelling or downclimb to the right on avalanche prone slopes.

Edge of the World ** 60 m II, 2

This climb makes a good early season warmup and practice area. Drive up the Marmot Basin Ski Road and park at the corner of the second last switchback before the entry gate. Walk along an overgrown cut line and followed it north 0.5 km to its end at the lip of a canyon. Rappel to the bottom of the climb (83 D/16 273510).

This is a wide tier that is climbed in two short pitches that increase in difficulty as you move left.

Fall of Dune ** 50 m IV, 4+

Mistakenly called **Going to Town**, this is the obvious flow about 50 m right of the middle portion of the Angel Glacier tongue below Mt. Edith Cavell (83 D/9 288367). Follow Highway 93A, 5 km to a large parking lot for the Mt. Edith Cavell Road (pay phone). This is not plowed in winter necessitating a long ski up the road to reach the mountain. It is recommended to stay at the Edith Cavell Hostel, 11 km from Highway 93A. Often there is no house parent, so check at the Whistler Hostel near Jasper for a key. It takes four to five hours to ski to the hostel. From the hostel, ski another 3 km up the road to the route which, contrary to a previous description, does not have a serac hazard. The views are simply majestic.

The route is one pitch of sustained ice which is usually smooth, thick and hard. Rappel the route.

Sorrow Falls * 55 m IV, 4

Sorrow Falls is another route to the right of *Fall of Dune* that offers a good way to reach the upper Angel Glacier in winter. There is a tree a the top of the climb and it is easily done the same day as *Fall of Dune*.

Rigid Digitator ** 120 m III, 3

A beautiful climb, *Rigid Digitator* offers expansive views. Follow Highway 93A to the Meeting of the Waters parking lot which is as far south as the road is plowed. Ski south on Highway 93A for 2 km then turn right up the Whirlpool River Fire Road which is followed for another 6.5 km to a summer trail head. Another 0.5 km beyond is the Moab Lake turnoff to the right. The lake is just a short distance down the hill and the climb is located to the right above the lake. Although the approach covers 9 km it gains only 110 m in elevation and takes two to three hours.

Climb a sustained 30-m pitch up and slightly right with ice to 85° Move back left and continue straight up for three more pitches. Walk off left through trees.

Maligne Lake Road

The scenic drive along Maligne Lake Road and the magnificent Maligne Canyon make this area one of the premier and most popular tourist destinations in Jasper Park. Maligne Lake Road branches from Highway 16, 5 km east of Jasper. Maligne Canyon parking lot is located 3.2 km from the turnoff. Stop at the back of the lot to access the following five routes. The *Original Route* follows the floor of the canyon while the other four are found up the canyon walls. They may be checked out from the walkways above and approached by rappelling from the appropriate bridge.

Maps

83 C/11 Southesk Lake
83 C/13 Medicine Lake

Maligne Canyon

Maligne Canyon Original Route ** II, 3

Follow the trail to the lower end of the canyon. The route is largely horizontal with five short steps of ice, the longest being 35 m in the deepest part of the canyon. It is a beautiful journey up this impressive canyon. The horizontal sections can be very dangerous and require great caution. Water levels will drop leaving ice plates suspended 3 m or more above the river. The climb exits in the parking lot.

Fall of Knight * 25 m II, 2

Found close to the second bridge, this climb is named after the demise of a certain gentleman of that name. Several body lengths of vertical ice ease off to 50°.

Solo Out 15 m II, 2

A couple of lines near *Fall of Knight* are offered on this short climb.

The Queen *** 35 m II, 4

Located just before the fourth bridge on the left-hand wall, *The Queen* is the best route in the canyon and is a classic top rope challenge. It offers steep ice that gets more difficult as it succumbs to the blows of countless climbers.

The Last Wall ** 30 m II, 2

The lowest climb in the canyon, *The Last Wall* has a variety of lines that can be climbed anywhere.

Gorby Canyon

Continue along Maligne Lake Road for 3.2 km to where the road bridges a canyon. Seepages from the canyon walls give nice WI 2 flows that are good for practice and instruction.

Maligne Lake

Vincent Falls 90 m IV, 3

If snow conditions are slow, this trip usually requires at least one night out and possibly two. It is located in a remote area at the north end of a group of five seeps on the lower slopes of Mt. Charlton just beyond Spirit Island and the narrows of Maligne Lake. Ski down the lake for 16 km through the narrows and around a sharp peninsula on the west side of the lake. The climb is easily visible from the lake. Ski or walk through brush and up a creek to the climb; 30 minutes (83 C/11 668308).

Climb a broad ice sheet to a tree followed by another pitch to a tree belay. Rappel from trees.

The following routes are found north-east of Jasper along the Yellowhead Highway (Highway 16) which follows the Athabasca River. It is the largest of the major river valleys in the mountain national parks. This valley is influenced by warmer and windier front range conditions with subsequently little snow on the approaches which are longer than average. The stark beauty of the area and good quality climbs make up for the length of the approaches. Pay phones are available at Pocahontas, 41 km from Jasper and a small cafe at Folding Mountain Campground, just east of the park gate. The Overlander Lodge, several kilometres farther east, offers a larger restaurant and lodging.

Maps

83 D/16 Jasper
83 F/4   Miette
83 F/5   Entrance

Violent Femmes 50 m III, 4+

Violent Femmes is an obscure and ephemeral climb found on The Palisade about 8 km east of Jasper above the Parks Canada gravel pit. If formed, the route is obvious and offers a steep one-pitch work-out.

Rocky River Blues ** 230 m III, 4

One of the best routes in the Jasper area, *Rocky River Blues* seems to form regularly. It can be seen from Highway 16 on the southwest side of the obvious obelisk rock peak called Roche Miette about 3 km east of the Rocky River. Park at the first pull-out northeast of Rocky River and walk up the gravel flats for about an hour. Turn left and head northeast toward the first major drainage

where the falls are situated for about another hour (83 F/4 389887). Be sure to sight the climb from the road and count which drainage it lies in—you can not see the route from the valley below.

Climb 40 m of steep chandelier ice ending in a narrow gorge. Follow snow uphill for two ropelengths to a final 100 m of thick, plastic and rolling ice. Rappel the route.

Rocky Canyon Falls * 85 m III, 3

Rocky Canyon Falls is an interesting canyon to climb in. Although the approach is long—two to three hours, the pretty scenery compensates for it. Park as for *Rocky River Blues* and continue up the Rocky River for 7 km to a canyon. The falls are located on the left (south) side near the end of the canyon. Beware of open water in narrow spots; ice shelves on the sides may allow passage.

Climb two easy WI 3 pitches of tiered ice separated by 20 m of snow. Rappel from trees.

East of Eden ** 190 m IV, 4

This classic climb in wild surroundings is an obscure route that likely has not been repeated. Park near Mountain Creek just west of Pocahontas where a ridge comes down from the north side of Roche Miette. Hike to the top of the open rib, then to the obvious saddle (two hours). Traverse southeast over scree slopes and across the starting zones of several avalanche-prone slopes to the climb in another hour. It is not known for sure if it forms regularly.

Climb an icy apron to a 10-m freehanging pencil and a rock belay. A second 40-m pitch of 70° with some steep sections ends in a snow gully and a bolt belay. The third pitch starts with a vertical 10 m step followed by pleasant, more rambling ice. Climb a 40-m pitch with short steep sections to a ledge and a bolt belay on the left. The final pitch begins with low-angle ice rising to a 15-m wall ending under a rock overhang with a piton belay. Rappel the route.

Punchbowl Falls 25 m I, 2

At Pocahontas 41 km east of Jasper and 7 km west of the Jasper Park Gate, turn south onto Miette Hot Springs Road. This beautifully sculpted waterfall is 0.8 km from the junction and offers up to half a ropelength of good practice ice.

Drambuie Deamon ** 95 m III, 3

Because of a northerly aspect, this climb forms regularly and has a longer season than most climbs in the region. It often forms by mid-November and will see better ice earlier in the season. Park near the Overlander Lodge just east of the Jasper Park Gate on Highway 16. The waterfall is obvious from the road and is located in the trees on the left-hand side of the north face of Roche a Perdix. Walk for 1.5 hours to the base.

Climb a steep 8 m wall to 60 metres of undulating ice between 45° and 60° to the base of the upper wall. A right-hand finish gives 15 m of 70° ice while the harder left-hand shows half a pitch of sustained 80° ice. Rappel the route.

The Folding Curtain * 55 m II, 2

A short distance east of the Jasper Park Gate on Highway 16 is Folding Mountain Campground. The climb can be seen to the southeast on a northeast spur of Folding Mountain and is only 30 minutes away.

Undulating ice and steep steps lead to a short vertical curtain at the top. The first ascent party climbed behind the curtain and exited through a hole onto the ice. Walk off left through trees.

Brûlé

In the flats outside Jasper Park is a large lake called Brûlé Lake. A number of climbs are found on the west side of the lake and are reached by heading north on Forestry Trunk Road 40 from Highway 16 west of Hinton. Cross the Athabasca River and turn left toward the hamlet of Brûlé. Bear left at the last house onto a poor dirt road which is rarely plowed but often blown free of snow. The next four climbs are all accessed from this road. It is about a 30 minute drive with the nearest facilities being in Hinton.

Map
83 F/5 Entrance

Ingredient Sixteen * 100 m II, 3

Follow the road past three cattle guards (Texas gates) for 3.8 km to just before the road makes a sharp left-hand turn. Hike through open timber and up the creek bed to ice seeping over rotten rock. The climb is visible through the trees.

The first pitch is classic WI 3 with near vertical pillar. The second pitch has several variations which lead to undulating ice and a basin at the top. **Note:** this route is prone to rockfall during warmer temperatures. Descend through trees on the left side. With careful routefinding, the descent can be made without rappelling.

Frog Falls 45 m II, 2

A nice practice area, *Frog Falls* is found up through the trees 6.5 km along the road from Brûlé. The climb has many steps with an overall angle of 55° Rappel the route.

Ogre Canyon Traverse 800 m II, 2

Follow the road past *Ingredient Sixteen* and *Frog Falls* 7.5 km to a wide stream bed. Just past the stream bed turn right, then right again and drive as close to the canyon as you can, roughly 8.1 km from Brûlé.

Follow the canyon throughout and eventually exit from the canyon where you find a trail on the left.

Ogre Canyon Sidewall ** 40 m II, 3

As for the traverse, this climb flows over the left side wall a short distance from the entrance to the canyon. The route is usually brittle and covered with many icicles and small overhangs ending in trees above the canyon. Rappel from trees.

Cadomin

The tiny town of Cadomin is reached either via Secondary Road 47 which branches southwest from Highway 16 a little west of Edson, or via Highway 40 which leaves Highway 16 at Hinton. Several easy climbs in the area have been popular with local climbing schools. With a little more exploring, more climbs may be found in the area.

Map
Mountain Park 83 C/14

Whitehorse Creek Seep 35 m II, 3

This is the best of the two Cadomin climbs. Drive as far south of the town toward Whitehorse Creek Campground as possible (varies with road conditions). The climb, visible 100 m before the campground, falls into McLeod River from the left-hand side of the road beyond the bridge over Whitehorse Creek. Rappel falls from above or walk along the road 0.5 km beyond the waterfall and descend through trees to gain the railroad tracks and follow them back to the base (83 C/14 775699). A straightforward and challenging WI 3 pitch, it can easily be top roped. A variety of thinner, more difficult lines form on either side of the main pillar. Finish near the road.

Cadomin Curtain 30 m II, 3

Cadomin Curtain, visible from the road, is a vertical curtain of ice which spills over a rock wall on Mt. Cadomin, east of the Whitehorse Creek campground entrance. Cross the river about 0.7 km before the campground entrance and bushwhack to the base of the climb (83 C/14 780705). The climb is 30 m of 75-80° ice. Rappel the route.

GRANDE CACHE

Grande Cache, Alberta is located at the northeastern end of the main Rockies chain. This somewhat isolated town sits at the northern end of the Chinook belt and experiences a winter climate similar to Calgary. Only two routes are reported here and they both sound to be very good. Little else is known about climbing in the area and not many climbers have made the journey. South of Grande Cache is the Willmore Wilderness Area which is the largest provincial park in the Rockies. There is an expansive amount of wilderness and unexplored terrain in the region in which you could spend a lifetime.

Getting There

The only way into Grande Cache from the south is via Highway 40 (Forestry Trunk Road). Just west of the town of Hinton (east of Jasper) on Highway 16 turn north and follow Highway 40 on a good paved road for 145 km (80 minutes) to Grande Cache.

Facilities

There are a number of motels, cafés and stores to fill most of your needs. The Grand Mountain Resort offers comfortable bed and breakfast-style accommodation (with baby sitting services!). Good primitive camping areas are located outside town near Willmore Provincial Park.

Emergency

For assistance call the Grande Cache RCMP detachment. See page 272.

Map

83 E/14 Grande Cache

Knuckle Gnasher 245 m III, 3

Start from the Gun Firing Range parking lot just south of the railway bridge. Cross the Smoky River via the railway bridge and walk upstream along an old road to a shallow, side valley. Follow the side valley toward the climb, located at the back of an overhanging amphitheatre.

Climb a vertical wall for 14 m followed by three and a half pitches of moderate ice.

Rappel and downclimb the route to the top of the vertical wall. Traverse south out of this gully.

Evergreen Gully 465 m III, 4

Evergreen is a long gully with short steep steps separated by long easy sections. Start from the parking lot of the Gun Firing Range just south of the railway bridge. Cross a road to the gully then walk or solo up minor steps to the foot of the first pitch in a deep gorge.

After the initial 9-m pitch at 70° easy ice leads to the second and third pitches which have vertical sections. Solo up to a fourth pitch which sports a narrow 6-m-high, freestanding column. More easy ice leads to a final vertical 25-m column that was not climbed on the first ascent. Walk off the right side.

MOUNT ROBSON PROVINCIAL PARK

The overwhelming feature of the area is Mt. Robson. Clearly the highest peak in the Rockies (3954 m), it is an impressive sight from any direction. The potential for frozen waterfalls on and around Robson is very high. If you are fortunate to climb here on a clear day, you'll be treated to some of the best scenery the Rockies has to offer. It is an area with high snowfalls, and avalanche hazard must be considered for every route. Waterfall climbing around Mt. Robson is combined with ski touring and requires the appropriate skills and experience necessary to be safe and enjoyable. If you don't worry about long ski approaches, go with an exploratory attitude, and are patient with the conditions, you will be grandly rewarded.

Getting There

Mt. Robson Provincial Park is located 82 km west of Jasper along Highway 16. Turn right at the Information Centre and follow a short access road (2 km) to the Kinney Lake/Berg Lake trailhead. The area is open to limited helicopter transport which could be considered if planning a trip to the north side of the mountain. Helicopter flights are available from Valemount, BC.

Facilities

The Information Centre and Robson Services gas station along Highway 16 are closed in winter and there are no other facilities available. The nearest 'civilized' services with everything you need are in Jasper (82 km) or Valemount

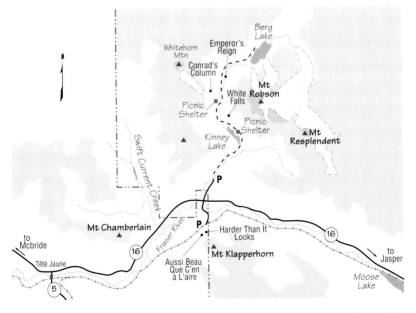

(44 km) on Highway 5, south of Tête Jaune Cache. There are camp shelters along the northeast shore of Kinney Lake and at the Whitehorn Campground, located on the east side of the Robson River, just after the first suspension bridge, near the start of The Valley of a Thousand Falls. There is an enclosed cabin/shelter with heating stoves at Berg Lake on the north side of Mt. Robson along the northwest shore of the lake, 17 km from the car.

Emergency
Valemount RCMP is probably your best bet for assistance. Otherwise try the Jasper Park wardens. There are pay phones at the Information Centre and at the Robson Services Gas Station along Highway 16. See page 272.

Map
83 E/3 Mount Robson

Mount Klapperhorn

Directly above the Information Centre on the south side of the Highway is Mt. Klapperhorn. Two prominent smears on the avalanche-prone North Face seem to form every year and both are great lines and worth the long drive to get here. With good conditions they are both climbable in a day. Opposite the Kinney Lake Road turn south, cross the Fraser River and continue up a winding road. Park at the railroad tracks and walk down (west) the tracks to below the routes. If avalanche conditions permit, walk directly up the drainage to your prospective climb(s); otherwise, follow the trees to either side. Skis may be useful depending on snow conditions. Occasionally there will be hard avalanche debris to easily walk up on.

Harder Than it Looks *** 200 m IV, 4
This is the left-hand line that offers four pitches of steep sustained climbing. Rappel the route. On a clear day you'll be treated with a massive view of the South Face and the *Wishbone Arête* of Mt. Robson.

Aussi Beau Que C'en a L'aire *** 150 m IV, 5+
This is the right-hand line. The name translates to "As Beautiful As it Looks". Climb 45 m of 85-90° ice into a small cave. This is followed by 35 m of the same quality and steepness. A short snow slope brings you to the last 15 m of moderate ice. Rappel the route.

Kinney Lake

More than 3000 metres below the summit on the south side of Mt. Robson lies Kinney Lake. A number of ice climbs are located around the lake and some are rumoured to be quite big. There are several WI 3-type routes around the lake but so far, only *White Falls* is known for sure.

White Falls * 200 m III, 3
From the Berg Lake Trailhead, ski 4 km to Kinney Lake. Continue around the lake on the right shore and head easily across the gravel flats at the end of the lake. Instead of following Berg Lake Trail to the left, go up to the right from the footbridge and follow the main drainage for about 2.5 km. The route is obvious; 2.5 hours.

The climb is done in three main pitches with ice up to 80° the second of which is hardest. Exit to the left.

Valley of a Thousand Falls

Between Kinney Lake and Berg Lake is a beautiful valley known as *The Valley of a Thousand Falls*. Again, this area is rumoured to be loaded with potentially big frozen waterfalls but only the two listed here along with some easy smears near the Whitehorn Shelter are completed. Past Kinney Lake the valley narrows. Climb up on the left flank of the valley to gain the higher Valley of a Thousand Falls. After the trail levels off, cross the first suspension bridge (11 km from the car) and carry on for just over 1 km to a second suspension bridge. An avalanche-prone slope (Emperor Hill) must then be ascended to reach more reasonable terrain leading to Berg Lake. Refer to *Ski Trail in the Canadian Rockies,* pg 216.

Conrad's Column ** 200 m IV, 5

A sustained route through a large cliff band, *Conrad's Column* is visible from the Whitehorn Shelter to the north on the left (west) side of the valley. It features a freestanding column and spectacular views of Emperor Ridge on Mt. Robson. Continue up the valley for 2 km to the base of the route, located in a right-facing corner, 100 m left of a prominent overhang and rock arch (83 E/3 882517).

Climb 45 m of thin ice to a snow ledge. Cross the ledge and climb to an ice cave on the left. The third pitch leads to a spacious belay behind the column, 40 m. Climb the freestanding column onto a good ledge, 35 m. Easier rolling ice now leads to the base of a large snow slope. Further unclimbed steps exists higher up the face. Rappel the route.

Emperor's Reign * 85 m III, 3

Emperor's Reign takes on the high volume cascade of Emperor Falls. It forms with large holes of running water and often sprinkles out over the ice, thus the play on the word "reign". Approach on The Valley of a Thousand Falls trail to the second suspension bridge and continue up the Emperor Hill for an additional 3.5 km. Take the Emperor Falls side trail to the natural clearing with a view of the falls. Descend an obvious gully on the right to reach low angle ice on the left.

Climb an easy 35 m pitch out of the gully and walk to the base proper. Move left onto deteriorating chandelier ice and continue up and finish on easier ice above. The scenery from the top of the falls is awesome. Rappel from trees.

Highway 16

The small village of Tête Jaune Cache, BC is located west of Mt. Robson at the junction of Highways 5 and 16. Although the areas northeast of Tête Jaune are technically in the Rockies, this guide does not cover any routes beyond Mt. Robson. Swiftcurrent Creek, west of Mt. Robson, has some good climbs that have been completed. These climbs and many others which have been climbed near Highway 16 toward McBride and Prince George, BC are outlined in a now out-of-print guidebook by Eric Hoogstraten called *Climbs of Passion: Rock and Ice Climbs in the Prince George District.*

FIRST ASCENT LIST

The symbol † prior to a route name indicates that the route has not been repeated. This designation has been reserved for the significantly hard (Technical Grade 5 and up) and more serious routes (Commitment Grade V and up). Obviously many of these routes have not been repeated because they are relatively new and/or rarely form.

2 Low 4 Zero, FA: Rusty Ballie, Iain Stewart-Patterson. Nov 84.

A Bridge Too Far, FA: Mike Blenkarn, Iain Stewart-Patterson, Murray Toft. Jan 82.

†Acid Howl, FA: Scott Backes, Joe Josephson. Jan 93 †FA (right side): Christophe Moulin, Richard Ouairy, April 94

Aerial Boundaries, FA: Joe Josephson, Bill Pelander, Nancy Prichard. Feb 93.

† Aggressive Treatment, FA: Dwayne Congdon, James Blench, John Lauchlan. Winter 80-81.

Aimless Gully, FRA: Troy Kirwan and party. Nov 93.

Albatros, FRA: Joe Josephson, Brian Spear (both solo). Jan 89.

Alpo, FA: Unknown.

Amadeus, FA: Dave Clay, Karl Nagy, Ray Friesen. Oct. 84.

† Ambivalence Falls, FA: Martin Garcea, Brian Webster. Mar 90.

Angel Eyes, FA: Unknown.

Anorexia Nervosa, FA: Mike Blenkarn, Bill Stark. Feb 83.

Aquarius, FA: Frank Campbell, Robert Corbeil, Steve Langley, Kris Thorsteinsson. Dec 84.

Arctic Dream, FA: Joe Josephson, Joe McKay. Mar 92. † Direct Finish, FA: Serge Angelluci, François Damilano. April 92.

Are You Afraid of the Dark?, FA: Cyril and Sandra Shokoples. Mar 90.

Arterial Spurt, FA: Unknown. Early '80s.

Aussi Beau Que C'en a L'aire, FA: Mark Aubrey, Guy Lacelle. Mar 90.

† Auto de Feu, FA: Barry Blanchard, Karl Nagy. Dec 93.

Back in the Saddle, FA: Troy Kirwan, Grant Statham. Dec 93.

Balfour Wall, The, FA: Unknown.

Bathos, FA: Frank Campbell, Bob Wills. Jan 84.

Beastiality, FA: Steve Beaulieu, Peter Corbett. 1981.

† Betty's Pillar, FA: Guy Lacelle. March 90.

Big Dipper, FA: Frank Campbell, Alan Kane. Dec 85.

Big Drip, The, FA: Frank Campbell, J.A. Owen. Mar 85.

Bill's Drip, FA: John Irvine, Chris Robinson. Oct 90.

Birthday Present, FA: Glenn Reisenhofer, Neil Winder. April 85.

Bison Falls, FA: Rusty Ballie, John Perdue. 1979.

Black Rock Falls, FA: Unknown.

† Blessed Rage, FA: Bruce Hendricks. Feb 92.

Bloodline, FA: Sheina Hughes, Morgan Neff, Cyril and Sandra Shokoples. Mar 87.

Bloody Mary, FA: Frank Campbell, Dave Clay, Karl Nagy. Dec 84.

Blue Angel, FA: Yvon Chouinard, Juris Krisjansons, Rob Taylor. Feb 77.

Blue Russian, FA: John Irvine, Chris Robinson. Oct 90.

Bob's Route, FA: Tom Hoskins. April 81.

Bob-Esque, First On-Sight Simu-Solo: James Blench, Joe Josephson, Nov 93.

† Borderline, FA: Barry Blanchard, Jeff Marshall, Karl Nagy. Jan 87.

Bored for November, FA: Mike Kietzman, Chris Robertson, Mark Stanley. Nov 93.

Bountiful Drought, FA: Adam Ferris, Mark Miller. Mar 93.

Bourgeau Left-Hand, FA: Tim Auger, George Homer, Rob Wood. Jan 74.
    FFA: John Roskelly, Jim States.

Bourgeau Right-Hand, FA: Tim Auger, Brian Greenwood, George Homer,
    Rob Wood. Feb 73.

Bow Falls, FA: Brian Greenwood, Bugs McKeith. Mar 73.

Brewer's Droop, FA: Jeff Marshall, Steve Stahl. Jan 83.

Bridal Veil Falls, FA: Benn Gadd, Martin Lesperance. Feb 80.

† Bullwinkle, FA: Allan Derbyshire, Andy Lecuyer. Jan 94.

† Burning in Water, Drowning by Flame, FA: Barry Blanchard, Joe Josephson. Dec 93.

But, My Daddy's a Psycho!, FRA: Bruce and Sheila Hendricks. Feb 94.

By Hook or By Crook, FRA: Jim Preston, Ken Wylie. Dec 89.

C'est Douche, FA: Frank Campbell, Jon Rowe. Mar 84.

C'est La Vie, FA: Ken Chambers, François Damilano, Joe Josephson,
    Brad Wrobleski. Jan 94.

Cable Gully, FA: Left, Doug Brown, Cyril Shokoples. Right, Cyril Shokoples,
    Dave Skrastins. 75-76.

Cadeau Cache, FA: Guy Lacelle, Tom Sisson. Mar 84.

Cadomin Curtain, FA: Cyril Shokoples and party. 1977.

California Dreamin, FA: Paul Obanhein, Craig Reason. Jan 85.

Campbellian Overture, FA: Joe Josephson, Stephen Ritchie. Nov 92.

Candle Stick Maker, The, FA: Frank Campbell, J.A. Owen. Mar 85.

Canmore Junkyards, FA: Dick Howe, Bugs McKeith. Feb 75.

Captain's Log, FA: Cyril Shokoples and party. Feb 87.

Carlsberg Column, FA: Jack Firth, John Lauchlan. Mar 74.
    FFA: Duncan Ferguson, Dave Wright. Feb 77.

Caroline Falls, FA: Frank Campbell, J.A. Owen, Garry Staples. Jan 87.

† Cascade Kronenbourg, FA: Remy Billon, Jean-Pierre Mottin. Mar 93.

Cascade Waterfall, FA: Unknown.

† Casino Waterfall, FA: Scott Flavelle, Dick Mitten. Mar 78.

Cedared Creek Seeps, FA: Mass Assault. 1989.

Ceramic Engineer, FA: Dave Thomson. Mar 93.

† Chalice and the Blade, The, FA: Joe Josephson, Grant Statham. Nov 92

Chalice and the Spoon, The, FA: ?

Chantilly Falls, FA: John Calvert, Trudy Kamphuis. 1978.

Christmas Present, FA: Jack Firth, Gerry Rogan, Greg Spohr. Christmas Day 78.

City Lights, FA: Frank Campbell and party. Jan 86.

Cline River Gallery, The, FA: Morgan Neff, Cyril Shokoples. Feb 89.

Coal Miner's Daughter, FA: James Blench, Geoff Powter, Sharon Wood. Mar 82.

Coire Dubh Intégrale, FA: Unknown.

Coire Dubh, FA: Bug McKeith. Dec 73.

Cold Choice, FA: Peter Charkiw, Dan Guthrie. Dec 85.

† Cold Comfort , FA: Peter Arbic. Mid '80s.

Cold Shower with a View, FA: John Miner, Jeff Steger. Feb 93.

College Boys, FA: Jeff Everett, Glenn Reisenhofer. Dec 90, FFA: Jeff Everett and partner.

Combo Falls, FA: Wayne Jones, Richard Summers. Nov 92.

Compound Gullies, FA: Unknown.

† Conrad's Column, FA: Paul O'Byrne, Matt Siska. Feb 94.
Consolation Prize, FRA: Bruce Hendricks, Stephen Ritchie.
Cool Spring, FA: John Roskelly and partner. Jan 78.
† Co-Pilot , FA: Joe Buzowski, Dan Guthrie. 84-85.
Corax, FA: Jeff Everett, Bill Kavanaugh. Jan 92.
Cosmic Messenger, FA: Joe Josephson, Karl Nagy. Dec 89.
Coughlins, FA: Tom Coughlin, William Soles. Early '80s.
Cousin It, FA: Mar 93.
Crack of Doom, FA: Lionel Ramsey, Rick Yeoman. Mar 94.
Crescent Falls, FA: Greg Grant, Cyril Shokoples. Mar 81.
† Crowfoot Falls, FA: Guy Lacelle, Jim Sanford. Mar 87.
† Cryogenics, FA: Adam Ferris, Ty Trand. Feb 93.
Crypt Falls, FA: Yvon Chouinard, Juris Krisjansons, Rob Taylor. Feb 77.
Crystal Tear, FA: Doug Brown, Daniel Smart. 75-76.
Cuckoo Falls, FA: Bernie LeBlanc, Orvel Miskiw, Marc Moquin. Dec 86.
Curtain Call, FA: Mike Weis and partner.
Damocles, FA: Bill March and party. Jan 81.
† Dancing with Chaos, FA: Bruce Hendricks, Joe Josephson. Jan 91.
† Day After Les Vacances de Monsieur Hulot, The, FA: François Damilano,
    Joe Josephson. Mar 94.
Dead Bird, FA: Karl Nagy and party.
DeMaio's DeMentia, FA: Steve DeMaio, Joe Josephson, Stephen Ritchie. Nov 92.
Dirty Harry, FA: Frank Campbell, Dave Clay, J.A. Owen. Feb 85.
Dr. Ballards, FA: Mike Blenkarn, Jeff Marshall, Iain Stewart-Patterson. Mar 83.
Dr. Heckle, FA: Mike Blenkarn, Iain Stewart-Patterson. Dec 82.
Drambuie Demon, FA: Greg Grant, Greg Horne. Dec 78.
Dream On, FA: Jean Walters, Rick Yeoman. Jan 94.
† Drip at the Centre of the Universe, The, FA: Keith Haberl, Larry Stanier. Feb 93.
Drip Dry, FA: Unknown.
Dry Ice, FA: Yves Carignan, Cyril and Sandra Shokopoles. Jan 92.
† Dunlap, FA: Rusty Ballie, Douglas Chabot. Feb 87.
Eagle, The, FA: Frank Campbell, Marion McKellar, J.A. Owen. Feb 86.
Eanee, Meanee, Minee, Moe, FA: Jean Walters, Rick Yeoman. Jan 94.
East of Eden, FA: Mike Kurth, Pat Paul. Mar 83.
Easter Bunny, FA: Brad Hagen, Greg Horne. April 81.
Echo Madness, FA: Ken Purcell, Ken Wallator. Oct 89.
Edge of the World, FA: Unknown.
† Elderly Man's Day Out, An FA: Barry Blanchard, James Blench. Sept 92.
Elk Droppings, FA: Tim Auger, Gord Irwin, Cliff White. Mar 85.
† Elk Tear, FA: Rusty Ballie, Douglas Chabot. Feb 87.
Elle and Lui, FA: Guy Lacelle, Dave Stark. Mar 87.
Elliot Left-Hand, FA: Unknown. 77-78.
Emperor's Reign, FA: Rupert Gale, Russell Kempston, Tim Thurston. Feb 93.
End of the Line, FA: Morgan Neff, Cyril Shokoples. Jan 89.
Essondale Left, FA: Steve Beaulieu, Keith Flavelle. 1983
Essondale Right, FA: Steve Beaulieu, Peter Corbett. 1983.
Evergreen Gully, FA: Dave Bedry, Greg Horne (incomplete). April 79.
Expert's Choice - Left Side, FA: Juris Krisjansons, Rob Taylor. Jan 77.
Expert's Choice - Middle Route, FRA: Joe Josephson, Steve Mascioli. Feb 94.

Expert's Choice - Right Side, FA: Brian Cusak, Juris Krisjansons. Feb 84.

Extra Lite, FA: Carlos Buhler, Mark Whalen. 1977.

Fall of Dune, FA: Rick Costea, Ken Wallator. Feb 87.

Fall of Knight FA: Unknown.

Fancy Free, FA: Scott Flavelle, Phil Hein. Jan 79.

Fast Eddies Falls, FA: Barry Blanchard, Edward Evans. Dec 82.

Faux Pas, FA: Chris Robertson, Mark Stanley. Nov 93.

† Fearful Symmetry, FA: Bruce Hendricks, Joe Josephson. Jan 92.

Fernie Pillar, FA: Unknown. c. 79-80.

Fine Line, The, FA: Bill Forrest, Bill March. Mar 81.

First Blood, FA: Barney Brown, Karl Nagy. Nov 87.

First Lead, FA: Derrick Blackthorne, Peter Jowett, John Niddrie. Feb 84.

Five Seven Zero, FA: Morgan Neff, Philip McKeage, Cyril Shokoples. Dec 85.

Fjord Falls, FA: Lionel Ramsey, Rick Yeoman. Mar 94.

Folding Curtain, The, FA: Greg Horne, Mike Taylor. April 78.

Footloose, FA: Scott Flavelle, Phil Hein. Jan 79.

Forget-Me-Not Falls, FA: Jean Walters, Rick Yeoman. March 94.

Fossil Falls, FA: Dave Chase, Dave Thomson. Mar 91.

† Fountainhead, FA: Barry Blanchard, Jeff Marshall. Jan 87.

French Kiss, FA: Juris Krisjansons. Jan 78.

French Maid, The, FA: Jeff Everett, Glenn Reisenhofer. Mar 90.

French Reality, FA: Claude Blazy, François Damilano, Philippe Pibarot. Mar 92.

Friendlier Giant, The, FA: Dave Thomson. Feb 94.

Friendly Giant, The, FA: Zac Bolan, Leslie DeMarsh, Keith Haberl. Feb 94.

Frog Falls, FA: Julie Bauer, Larry Matwie, Pat Paul. Spring 1979.

Full Potential, The, FA: Barry Blanchard, Joe Josephson. Dec 91.

Gasser, The, FA: Rick Holmes, Juris Krisjansons. Feb 79.

† Gentleman's Day Out, A, FA: Barry Blanchard, Troy Kirwan. Sept 92.

Gentlemen, Orders, FA: Morgan Neff, Philip McKeage, Cyril Shokoples. Dec 85.

Gibraltar Wall - Left, FRA: Doug Hogg, Jeff Ward. Feb 81.

† Gimme Shelter, FA: Kevin Doyle, Tim Friesen. April 83.

Glace Cherry, FA: Colleen Crowe, Allan Derbyshire. Mar 81.

Goat Mtn. Falls, FA : Unknown

God Did It, FA: Don Chandler, Phil Hein, Mike Sawyer, Albi Sole. Dec 77.

Good H'Evans Thomas, FA: Pat Paul, Vaclav Vaclavik (both solo). Mar 82.

Good Luck and Bad Dreams, FA: Dave Devin, Cyril Shokoples. Dec 91.

Good, The Bad and The Ugly, The, FRA: David Bean, Mike Blenkarn,
    Iain Stewart-Patterson. Nov 82.

Gorby Canyon, FA: Unknown.

Gorby Falls, FA: Unknown.

Graduate Gully, FA: Bill March, Tom Whittaker. Feb 85.

Grecian Formula, FA: Jeff Everett, Glenn Reisenhofer. Jan 91.

Green Angel, FA: Frank Campbell, Lewis Kaiserseder, Alan Kane, Russel Varnam, Jan 86.

Green Gully, FA: Doug Dean, Bill March, Tom Whittaker. Feb 85.

Grotto Falls, FA: Cyril Shokoples, Stuart Taylor, Brian Thompson. 75-76.

Grovelling Gully, FA: Carlos Buhler, Mike Sawyer, Albi Sole. Jan 78.

Guinness Stout, FA: Phil Hein, John Lauchlan. 1976.

Guinness Gully, FA: Jack Firth, John Lauchlan, Pat Morrow, Jim Tanner. Jan 75.

Haffner Creek Ice Flows, FA: Unknown.

Hammer Horror, FA: Chris Geisler, Dave Thomson. Feb 94.
Harder than it Looks (Icefields Parkway), FA: James Blench, Larry Stanier. Feb 89.
Harder than it Looks (Mt. Klapperhorn), FA: Doug Dean, Bill March. Mar 85.
Heart Creek Falls, FA: Unknown.
Heineken Hall, FA: Carlos Buhler and partner. 79-80.
Hello Central, FA: Chris Lloyd, Dave Thomson. April 91.
Helmet Falls, FA: Rob Mitchell, Laurie Skreslet. Mar 76.
Hers, FA: Doug Brown, Cyril Shokoples. 75-76.
High Test, FA: Peter Charkiw, Dan Guthrie. Mar 82.
Hip Wader Gully, FA: Brad Hagen, Greg Horne. Feb 81.
His, FA: Cyril Shokoples and partner. 75-76.
† Hooker, The, FA: Joe Josephson, Ken Wylie. Dec 92.
Hoser, The, FA: Mike Blenkarn, Jim Elzinga, Jeff Marshall, Iain Stewart-Patterson. Dec 81.
Hurly Bird, FA: Joe Josephson, Troy Kirwan, Grant Statham. Oct 92.
Hydrophobia, FA: Frank Campbell, Karl Nagy. Dec 86.
† Hypertension, FA: Joe Josephson, Jeff Nazarchuck. Dec 91.
I Scream, FA; Steve Beaulieu, Jean Troillet. 1981.
Ice Funnel, The, FA: Frank Campbell, Dave Dancer. Jan 87.
Ice Nine, FA: Adrian and Allan Burgess, Bugs McKeith. Dec 74.
Ice Palace (Jasper), FA: Peter Austin, James Nelson, Al Norquay, Timo Saukko. Dec 85.
Ice Palace, The (Icefall Brook), FA: Chris Lloyd, Dave Thomson. April 91.
† Ice T, FA: Scott Backes, Marc Twight. Jan 93.
Imaginary Voyage, FA: Joe Josephson, Karl Nagy. Dec 89.
In Search of Flying Squirrels, FA: Dave Devin, Cyril Shokoples. Dec 91.
† In the Spirit of Crazy Horse, FA: Barry Blanchard (half breed),
    Ken Wallator (trapped in a white man's body). Mar 93.
Indian Scalp, FA: Frank Campbell, Karl Nagy. Dec 86.
Indifferent, The, FA: John Kaandorp, Iain Stewart-Patterson. Mar 84.
Ingredient Sixteen, FA: Greg Grant, Cyril Shokoples. 80-81.
Irish Mist, FA: Allan Derbyshire, Choc Quinn. Jan 89.
Iron Curtain, FA: Carlos Buhler, Dick Renshaw. 1981.
Ivory Falls, FRA: Barney Brown, Frank Campbell, Dean Lister. Dec 88.
Jaws, FA: Dick Howe, Bugs McKeith. Nov 76.
JD , FA: Derrick Blackthorne, Peter Jowett. 1984.
Joker, The, FA: Frank Campbell, Alan Kane. Jan 85.
Jubilee Falls Left, FA: Jim Dodich Jr., Jeff Palumbo. Feb 94.
Jubilee Falls Right, FA: Doug Goodwin, Kirt Sellers. Mar 89.
Just Enough, FA: Jean Walters, Rick Yeoman. Jan 94.
Juste Pour Rire, FA: Unknown.
Kemosabe, FA: Frank Campbell, Dave Dancer. Jan 87.
Kerkeslin Falls, FA: Marc Moquin, Tom Saunders,
    Cyril and Sandra Shokoples. 1980.
Kidd Falls, FA: Barry Blanchard, Iain Stewart-Patterson. Jan 82.
† Killer Pillar, FA: Jeff Everett, Jeff Marshall, Glenn Reisenhofer. Feb 90.
Kinda Nice, FA: Colin Allison, Bruce Deaeth, Sylvain Quenneville. April 93.
King Creek Seepages, FA: Unknown.
Kitty Hawk, FA: Greg Grant. Mar 81.
Knuckle Gnasher, FA: Greg Grant, Greg Horne. April 79.
† La Goute, FA: Alain Chassie, Daniel Levesque. 84-85.

Labatt's Lane, FA: Rob Amman, Eckhard Grassman, Mike Sawyer, Peter Zvengrowski. 1975.
Lacy Gibbet, FA: Frank Campbell, John Rowe. Jan 85.
Lady Killer, FA: Steve Beaulieu, Jean Triollet. 1980.
Lady Wilson's Cleavage, FA: Unknown.
Last But Not Least, FA: Jean Walters, Rick Yeoman. Jan 94.
Last Wall, The FA: Unknown.
† Lauchlan Original Finish (Slipstream), FA: Jim Elzinga, John Lauchlan. Dec 79.
Leaky Lucy, FA: Unknown.
Les Misérables, FA: Barry Blanchard, Kevin Doyle. Jan 92.
Less Wardens the Better, The, FA: Unknown.
† Lézard D'Or, Le, FA: Claude Blazy, François Damilano, Godefroy Perroux. Mar 92.
Linda Ice-Nine, FA: Dick Howe, Bugs McKeith. Mar 75.
Lineham Cliff Waterfall, FA: Juris Krisjansons, Peter Raabe. Dec 78.
† Little Bobby On-Sight (incomplete), FA: Scott Backes, Bruce Hendricks, Joe Josephson, Marc Twight. Jan 93.
Little Devil, FA: Frank Campbell, Wayne Shakleton. Jan 83.
Little Dipper, FA: Frank Campbell, Dave Clay, Alan Kane, Kris Thorsteinsson. Jan 86.
Lizard Lips, FA: Barry Blanchard, Mike Blenkarn, Iain Stewart-Patterson. Nov 82.
Lobotomy, FA: Peter Corbett, Kirt Sellers. 1983.
Looking Out the Back Door, FA: Kevin Christakos, Ken Wallator. Dec 87.
Lone Ranger, FRA: Rusty Ballie, Juris Krisjansons. Feb 84.
Lotus Bleu, Le, FRA: Stephane Bedard, Guy Lacelle. Mar 90.
Louise Falls, FA: Jack Firth, Eckhard Grassman, Tony Mould, Peter Zvengrowski. Mar 74.
Lovely Parting Gifts, FA: Morgan Neff, Cyril Shokoples. Jan 89.
Lucifer, FA: Rusty Ballie, Juris Krisjansons. Feb 85.
Malignant Mushroom, FA: Mike Blenkarn, Bill Stark, Iain Stewart-Patterson. Dec 82.
Maligne Canyon, FA: Unknown. Prior to 1975.
Mare in Winter, FRA: Bob Cotter. Dec 91.
Marion Falls, FA: Frank Campbell, Karl Nagy, Marion McKellar, J.A. Owen. Jan 87.
† Marshall Arts, FA: Jeff Marshall, Choc Quinn. Mar 89.
Martin Creek Falls, FA: Tim Auger, Cliff White. Feb 86.
Massey's, FA: Jack Firth, John Lauchlan, Judy Sterner. April 74.
Meech Lake Memorial, FA: Joe Josephson, Jeff Nazarchuck. Dec 91.
Melt Out, FA: Dave Bedry, Tom Saunders. Mar 78.
† Memorial Falls, FA: Donna Nicholson, Ken Wallator, Brian Webster. Dec 91.
Meredith Falls, FA: Doug Goodwin, Kirt Sellers. Mar 89.
† Mexican Overdrive, FA: Dave Chase, Dave Thomson. April 91.
Midnight Madness, FA: Evan Manners, Don Peters. Jan 87.
Midnight Rambler, FA: Kev Smythe, Iain Stewart-Patterson. Nov 83.
Miller Time, FA: Derrick Blackthorne, Rob Ford, Peter Jowett. Mar 84.
Mixed Master, FA: Joe Buzowski, Troy Kirwan. Dec 91.
† Mon Ami, FA: Serge Angelucci, Allan Massin. Feb 89.
Moonlight , FA: Al Dunham, Phil Oltman. Feb 79.

Moonshadow Gully, FA: Iain Stewart-Patterson, Helen Sovdat,
  Murray Toft. Jan 81.
Mother of All Ice Climbs, The, FA: Dave Chase, Dave Thomson. Mar 91.
Mountain Dew, FA: Dick Howe, Dick Lofthouse, early '80s.
Mouse Trap, FA: Frank Campbell, Russel Varnam. Jan 86.
Mr. Jive, FA: Mike Blenkarn, Iain Stewart-Patterson. Dec 82.
Mr. Misty, FA: Dave Campbell, Jeff Everett. Mar 92.
Murchison Falls, FA: Trevor Jones, Tom Whittaker. 1977.
N'Ice Baby, FA: Robin Clothier, Philippe Pibarot. Mar 91.
Nasty Habits, FA: Jim Franken, Iain Stewart-Patterson. Nov 84.
Near Death, FA: Bill Pelander, Bill Troll. c. 1989.
Nelson Creek Falls, FA: Tom Coughlin, Bernard Ehman,
  Ward Robinson. Mid '80s.
Nemesis, FA: Bugs McKeith and partners. March 74. FFA: James Blench,
  John Lauchlan, Albi Sole. Mar 80.
Nietzsche Stick, FA: Carl Cibart, Terry Kerr, Joe Owchar, Alex Taylor. Mar 91.
Night Shift, The, FA: Ed Laporte, Ken Wallator. Jan 86.
Nightmare on Elm Street, FA: Morgan Neff, Cyril Shokoples. Feb 89.
† Nine, FA: Alain Chassie, Ken Wylie. 85-86.
No Breaks, FRA: Steve DeMaio, Ken Wylie. Feb 94.
No-One Can Stop Us Now, FA: Dave Thomson. April 90.
Nothing But the Breast, FA: Greg Grant, Dave Pors. 77-78.
† Nuclear Winter, FA: Dave Chase, Dave Thomson. Mar 91.
Oasis, FA: Andy Brown, Jeff Perren. Feb 92.
Ogre Canyon Traverse, FA: Marc Moquin, Cyril and Sandra Shokoples. 1980.
Ogre Sidewall, FA: Cyril Shokoples and party. 1980.
Oh Le Tabernac, FA: Carlos Buhler, Dick Renshaw. Jan 81.
† Olympus, FA: Frank Campbell, Al Hobson. Nov 86.
One Thin Line, FRA: Cyril Shokoples, Stuart Taylor. 75-76.
Orion Falls, FA: Laurie Skreslet, Murray Toft. 1979.
Palm Sunday, FA: Frank Campbell, Choc Quinn. Mar 93.
Panther Falls, FA: Unknown. 75-76.
Parallel Falls Left & Right, FA: Unknown. Late '70s.
Peanut Gallery, The, FA: Mike Blenkarn, Bill Stark,
  Iain Stewart-Patterson. Dec 82.
Peanut Maker, FA: Greg Horne, Ed Laporte. Jan 83.
Pencil, The, FA: Diny Harrison, Grant Statham. Dec 91.
Phantom Falls, FA: Frank Campbell, Alan Kane. Jan 85.
† Phil Spectre's Nightmare, FA: Keith Haberl, Richard Jagger. Feb 93.
Pigeon Mtn. Falls, FA: Unknown.
Pillars, The, FA: Bob Beauman, James Ross. 1980.
Pilsner Pillar, FA: Jack Firth, Eckhard Grassman, John Lauchlan,
  Peter Zvengrowski. Mar 74. FFA John Roskelly and partner. Jan 78.
Pine Crest, FA: Eric Albert, Allan Derbyshire, Jorge Visser. Feb 92.
Pipeline, The, FRA: Daren Dunbar, Joe Josephson. Jan 94.
† Pipes of Pan, FA: Kevin Doyle and party. Feb 91.
† Pipimenchen, FA: Jeff Everett, Bob Lee, Glenn Reisenhofer. Nov 92.
Pitches of Eastwick, FA: Jeff Everett, Bob Lee, Alex McConnel,
  Jim Mamalis. Nov 92.

Pointless Gully, FA: Bugs McKeith, Ian Rowe. Dec 74.
Polar Circus, FA: Burgess Twins, Bugs McKeith,
      Charlie Porter. Dec 75. FFA: Unknown.
Polish Peacock, FA: Jim Dodich Jr., Jeff Palumbo. Mar 93.
† Political World, FA: April 91.
† Popsicle Toes, FA: Dave Chase, Dave Thomson. Mar 91.
Postscriptum, FA: Serge Angelluci, Allan Massin. Dec 92.
Pretty Nuts, FA: Steve Beaulieu, William Soles. 1982.
Prism Falls, FA: Unknown. Late '70s.
Private Functions, FA: Cyril Shokoples. Mar 87.
Professors, FA: Jack Firth (solo), Eckard Grassman, John Lauchlan. Mar 74.
Punchbowl Falls, FA: Unknown.
Pure Energy, FA: Len Babiuk, Morgan Neff, Cyril Shokoples. Mar 89.
Queen, The, FA: Unknown.
Quick and Dirty, FA: Juris Krisjansons, Rob Taylor. Jan 77.
R & D, FA: Rusty Ballie, Iain Stewart-Patterson. Feb 84.
† Rad Monster, The, FA: Barry Blanchard, Jeff Marshall. Jan 87.
Rainbow Serpent, FA: Joe Josephson, Brad Wrobleski. Jan 92.
Rainy Day, FA: Todd Dempsey, Dale McKnight. Mar 93.
Rampart Route, FA: Mike Balfour, Margo Talbot, Ken Wallator (solo). Mar 93.
Raven's Call, FA: Doug Goodwin, Kirt Sellers. Feb 89.
† Reality Bath, The, FA: Randy Rackliffe, Marc Twight. Feb 88.
Red Commie Star, FRA: Glen Reisenhofer.
† Red Man Soars, FA: Barry Blanchard, Joe Josephson, Tim Pochay. Dec 93.
      FFA: Alex Lowe and partner. Dec 94.
Red Rock Canyon, FA: Unknown.
† Replicant, The, FA: Keith Haberl, Joe Josephson, Tim Pochay. Jan 94.
Ribbon, The, FA: Frank Campbell, Dave Clay, Karl Nagy. Dec 84.
Rigid Digitator, FA: Peter Austin, Timo Saukko. Jan 86.
Riptide, FA: Larry Ostrander, Jeff Marshall. April 87.
Riverview, FA: Steve Beaulieu, Tom Sacha. 1976.
Rock On and Off, FA: Allan Massin, Steve Pratt. Dec 93.
Rocky Canyon Falls, FA: Rick Blak, Ben Gadd. Feb 88.
Rocky River Blues, FA: Chris Butler, Pat Paul. Feb 85.
Rogan's Gully, FA: Bugs McKeith, Gerry Rogan. Mar 73.
† Royal Treat, FA: Dave Campbell, Jeff Everett. Mar 92.
Ross Lake Headwall, FA: Unknown.
Ruby Falls, FA: Unknown.
S'N'M' Falls, FA: Arnie MacAuley, Morgan Neff, Cyril Shokopoles (solo). Dec 88.
Sacré Bleu, FA: Guy Lacelle, Malcolm Taylor. April 83.
† Sad and Beautiful World, FA: Keith Haberl, Richard Jagger. Mar 93.
† Saddam's Insane, FA: Jeff Everett, Jeff Marshall. 90-91.
† Salamander's Tail, FA: Martin Garcea, Ken Wallator, Brian Webster. Feb 91.
Sam Goes Trekking, FA: Ken Chambers, Guy Lacelle,
      assisted by Sam the dog. April 94.
SARs on Ice, FA: Arnie McAuley, Morgan Neff, Cyril Shokoples, Bob Verret. Dec 86.
Schism Game, FA: Margo Talbot, Ken Wallator. Nov 92.
Scotch on the Rocks, FA: Tim Auger, Gord Irwin, Marc Ledwidge,
      Cliff White. Feb 84.

Scuds From Above, FA: Dave Chase, Dave Thomson. Mar 91.
† Sea of Vapors, FA: Bruce Hendricks, Joe Josephson. Feb 93.
Seagull, FA: Frank Campbell, Orvel Miskiw. Feb 85.
† Senior Project, FA: Rusty Ballie, Douglas Chabot. Mar 86.
† Seven Pillars of Wisdom, FA: Barry Blanchard, Troy Kirwan. Feb 92.
Shades of Beauty, FA: Mike Blenkarn, Iain Stewart-Patterson,
    Colin Zacharias. Jan 81.
Shampoo Planet, FA: Peter Arbic, Joe Buszowski. Nov 92.
Sharon's Drip, FA: Don Chandler, Phil Hein, Sharon Wood. Dec 77.
Shining Nobodies, The, FA: Mike Balfour, Chris Pooly, Margo Talbot. Jan 94.
Shocking Alternative, The, FA: Chris Geisler, Dave Thomson. Feb 94.
Shooting Star, FA: Andy Genereaux, Jeff Marshall. Winter 85-86.
Shower Bath Falls, FA: Steve Beaulieu, Scott Flavelle. Mar 81.
Silk Tassel, FA: Pat Morrow, Murray Toft. 1974.
    FFA: Albi Sole and partner. Dec 77.
Silver Tongue Devil, FA: Frank Campbell, Alan Kane. Dec 85.
Silverton Falls, FA: Jack Firth, Ray Gillies, George Homer, Bugs McKeith,
    Gerry Rogan, Laurie Skreslet, Rob Wood. Feb 74.
Sinatra Falls, FA: Unknown. Late '70s.
Sinister Street, FA: Dave Thomson. Mar 92.
Sinus Gully, FA: Bugs McKeith, John Lauchlan. Feb 74.
Sister Moon , FA: Karl Nagy, Glenn Reisenhoffer. Jan 92.
Skinny Puppy, FA: Eric Hoogstraten, Jeff Lakes. 1992.
Sky Pilot, FA: Barry Blanchard, Kevin Doyle. Jan 83. FFA: Unknown.
Slipstream, FA: (see Lauchlan Original Finish). FSA: Rodden McGowan,
    Larry Stanier. July 89.
† Sliver, The, FA: Barry Blanchard, Joe Josephson. Dec 93.
Snipe Falls, FA: Bernie LeBlanc, Orvel Miskiw, Marc Moquin. Dec 86.
Snivelling Gully Direct, FRA: Trevor Jones, Raymond Jotterand, Greg Spohr. 1978.
Snivelling Gully, FA: Jim Elzinga, George Homer, Bugs McKeith,
    Gerry Rogan. Nov 73.
Snowline, FA: Barry Blanchard, Iain Stewart-Patterson. Jan 82.
Solid Cold, FA: Bill Marriot, Randy Thomas. Dec 87.
Solo Out, FA: Unknown.
Sorcerer, The, FA: Kevin Doyle, Iain Stewart-Patterson. Feb 83.
Sorrow Falls, FA: Donna Nicholson, Ken Wallator.
Source, The, FA: Allan Massin, Steve Pratt. Nov 93.
Southern Wind, The, FRA: Barry Blanchard, John Tiencken Jr. Oct 92.
Splashdown, FA (top rope): Cyril Shokoples and partner. Mar 90.
Splotch, The, FA: Dave Thomson. Mar 93.
Spray River Falls, FA: John and Mary Lauchlan. Late '70s.
Stage, The, FA: Jim Fischer, Greg Grant, Don Hilaire, Tom Saunders,
    Cyril and Sandra Shokoples. Mar 81.
Stanley Falls Senior, FA: Unknown.
† Striving for the Moon, FA: Barry Blanchard, Ward Robinson. Dec 92.
Suffer Machine, The, FA: Jeff Everett, Glenn Reisenhofer. April 91.
Sullivan Falls, FA: Rick Holmes, Juris Krisjansons. Feb 80.
Sunset Falls, FA: Carmie Callanan, Frank Campbell, John Hammond,
    Peter Roxburgh. Nov 84.

Sunshine Corner, FA: Lorne Nelson, Don Peters. Mar 85.

Sunshine, FA: Frank Campbell, Robert Corbeil, Steve Langley, Kris Thorsteinsson. Dec 84.

Sunwapta Falls, FA: Bob Hiltz, Mick Locker. Mar 82.

Super Bock, FRA: Carlos Buhler, Jack Lewis. winter 82-83.

Swansea Flows, FA: Doug Goodwin, Kirt Sellers. Mar 89.

Sweet Dream, FA: Jean Walters, Rick Yeoman. Jan 94.

Syndrome, FA: Serge Angelucci, Norm Doebel. Nov 91.

T2, FA: Jeff Everett and partners. Jan 93.

Takakkaw Falls, FA: Jack Firth, Bugs McKeith, John Lauchlan, Rob Wood. Jan 74. FFA: Duncan Ferguson, Dave Wright. Feb 77.

† Tales of Ordinary Madness, FA: Barry Blanchard, Joe Josephson. Dec 91.

Talisker, FA: Rob Allan, Jeff Marshall, Glenn Reisenhofer. Feb 92.

Tangle Creek, FRA: Cyril Shokoples, Stuart Taylor, Brian Thompson. 1975.

† Tasting Fear, FA: Steve Chambers, Martin LaLonde, John Whiteman. Dec 91.

† Tax Evasion, FA: Ken Wallator, Brian Webster. Jan 90.

Team Effort, FA: James Blench, Chris Stetham, Sharon Wood. Feb 89.

Teardrop, FA: Trevor Jones, Raymond Jotterand, Greg Spohr. 1978.

Tears of a Clown, FA: James Blench, Larry Stanier. Feb 89.

† Tease, The, FA: Jeff Everett, Karl Nagy. Mar 92.

Terminator, The, FA: Craig Reason, Jay Smith. Jan 85.

This House of Sky, FA: Unknown. Early '80s.

Tinkerbell, FA: Dave Chase, Dave Thomson. Mar 92.

To Run and Not to Die, FA: Ken Larlee, Les Pesros. Dec 93.

Tom Thumb, FA: Dave Chase, Dave Thomson. April 90.

Tonsil, The, FA: Jeff Everett, Dean Lister. 91-92.

Tool Time, FRA: Adam Ferris, Jennifer Olson. Feb 94.

† Totem Pole, FA: Joe Buzowski, Peter Arbic. Mid '80s.

Touch Me if You Can, FA: Alain Chassie, Daniel Levesque. 84-85.

Trans-Canada Iceway, FA: Serge Angelluci, Allan Massin. Nov 92.

Transparent Fool, FA: Rusty Ballie, John Perdue. 1979.

Treading Water, FA: Rob Nichols, Don Peters. Mar 83.

Triangle Falls, FA: Dave Thomson. Mar 93.

Trick or Treat, FA: Frank Campbell, Peter Roxborough. Oct. 87.

Trickle Falls, FA: Barney Brown, Frank Campbell, Dean Lister. Dec 88.

Tristan's Pillar, FA: Joe Josephson, Stephen Ritchie. Nov 92.

Tube, The, FA: Bugs McKeith, Jim Tanner. Mar 73.

Tumor, The, FA: Jim Dodich Jr. and party.

Twin Falls, FA: Unknown.

Twisted Sister, FA: Frank Campbell, Karl Nagy, J.A.Owen. Nov 88.

† Twisted, FA: Paul Obanhein, Craig Reason. Jan 85.

Two Minutes for Hooking, FRA: Jim Preston, Ken Wylie. Dec 89.

Two O'Clock Falls, FA: Unknown. 1978.

Two Steps, FA: Bugs McKeith, Chris Shank. Feb 74.

† Uli's Revenge, FA: Jeff Everett, Karl Nagy. Dec 90.

Unforgiven, The, FA: Unknown.

Urs Hole Direct, FA: Rusty Ballie, Murray Toft. Dec 81.

Urs Hole, The, FA: George Homer, Urs Kallen, Oliver Woodcock. 1969.

Vanilla Ice, FA: Dave Thomson. Feb 92.

Venus, FA: Hans Braun, Frank Campbell, Paul O'Byrne, Nina Shen, Elaine West. March 93.
Vermilion Falls, FA: Unknown. Late '70s.
Vincent Falls, FA: Ian Bruce, Al Munro. Jan 88.
Violent Femmes, FA: Ken Wallator, Brian Webster. Feb 90.
† Virtual Reality, FA: Joe Josephson, Ken Wylie. April 93.
Waiting Game, The, FA: Dave Chase, Dave Thomson. April 91.
Walking Softly, FA: Douglas Chabot, David Corkett. Mar 86.
Wangle Dangle, FA: Dave Chase, Dave Thomson. Dec 92.
Water Hole, The, FA: Allan Derbyshire, Darryl Kell. Dec 80.
Waterfowl Gullies, FA: Unknown.
Waterworks (Boom Lake), FA: Dave Law. Dec 92.
Waterworks (Field), FA: Unknown.
Waterworks (Kicking Horse Canyon), FA: Brian Amies, Peter Corbett, Kirt Sellers. 1983.
Waxing Soulful, FA: Rick Costea, Margo Talbot, Ken Wallator. March 94.
Weathering Heights, FA: Mike Blenkarn, Iain Stewart-Patterson. Jan 83.
Wedge Smear, FA: Unknown.
Weeping Pillar, FA: James Blench, Albi Sole. 1980.
Weeping Wall-Central Pillar, FA: James Blench, Albi Sole. 1980.
Weeping Wall Left-Hand , FA: Bugs McKeith, Rob Wood. Dec 73.
    FFA: Duncan Ferguson, Dave Wright. Feb 77.
Weeping Wall Right-Hand, FA: John Lauchlan, Raymond Jotterand. 1979.
Welcome to Canada, FA: before 1985.
Wet Dream, FA: Diana Knaak, Bugs McKeith. Dec 75.
White Falls, FA: Peter Austin, Bob Knight. Jan 81.
Whitehorse Creek, FA: Cyril Shokoples and party. 1977.
Whiteman Falls, FA: Laurie Skreslet, Dave Wright. 1979.
Whoa Whoa Capitaine, FA: Alain Chassie, Guy Lacelle. Feb 85.
Wicked Wanda, FA: Kevin Doyle, Geoff Powter. Winter 82/83.
Wild Cougar, FRA: Daren Dunbar, Joe Josephson. Jan 90.
† Wild Fire, FA: Ken Wallator, Brian Webster. Jan 92.
Wilson Major, FA: Unknown.
Whimper Wall, FA: Left, Tim Auger, James Blench. Right, James Blench, Dave McNab. Nov 84.
Windy Corner, FA: Rob Nichols, Don Peters. Mar 83.
Wings, The, FA: Cyril Shokoples and party. 1981.
Winnebago Warrior, FA: Dave Campbell, Glenn Reisenhofer. Nov 93.
Winter Solstice, FA: Dave Clay, Mike Walsh. Dec 88.
Winter's Turning, FA: Barry Blanchard, Bob Bott, Dixon Thompson. Dec 82.
Wolverine Falls, FA: Alan Kane, Kris Thorsteinsson. Nov 87.
Wully Canyon, FA: Carmie Callanan, Frank Campbell. Jan 85.
Ya-Ha Falls, FA: Barney Brown, Frank Campbell, Karl Nagy, Chic Scott. Nov 87.
Yellow Bird, FA: Frank Campbell, Alan Kane. Feb 85.
Yoho Pillar, FA: Scott Flavelle, Phil Hein. Jan 79.

Useful Phone Numbers

Park Administration Offices

Kananaskis Country Office, Canmore	(403) 678-5508
Parks Canada Regional Office, Calgary	(403) 292-4401
BC Parks, East Kootenay Office	(604) 422-3212

National and Provincial Park Information/Visitor Centres

Waterton	(403) 859-2352 or 859-2445
Barrier Lake	(403) 673-3985
Kananaskis Lakes	(403) 591-7722
Banff	(403) 762-4256
Banff (French Language Information)	(403) 762-4834
Lake Louise	(403) 522-3833
Jasper	(403) 852-6176
Kootenay Park West Gate	(604) 347-9505
Yoho, Field	(604) 343-6783 or 343-6324
Valemount (Mt Robson)	(604) 566-9893

Alberta Forest Service

Ghost Ranger Station	(403) 932-5668
Nordegg Office	(403) 721-3965

BC Forest Service

Golden District Office	(604) 344-7500
Invermere District Office	(604) 342-4200

Travel Information

Waterton Park Chamber of Commerce	(403) 859-2303
Pincher Creek Chamber of Commerce	(403) 627-5199
Canmore/Kananaskis Chamber of Commerce	(403) 678-4094
Banff/Lake Louise Chamber of Commerce	(403) 762-3777
Jasper Park Chamber of Commerce	(403) 852-3858
Grande Cache Chamber of Commerce	(403) 827-3790
Golden Chamber of Commerce	(604) 344-7125
BC Rocky Mountain Visitor Association	(604) 427-4838

Travel Alberta

Field, BC Office	(604) 343-6446
Canada and USA	1-800-661-8888
Within Alberta	1-800-222-6501

Road Reports

Banff Road Report	(403) 762-1450
Jasper Road Report	(403) 852-6161
BC Highway Conditions	1-800-663-4997

Helicopters and Snow Machines

Challenge Enterprises, Golden	(604) 344-6012
Canmore Helicopters, Canmore	(403) 678-4802
	Fax (403) 678-2176
Canadian Helicopters, Canmore	(403) 678-2207
	Fax (403) 678 5600
Canadian Helicopters, Golden	(604) 344-5311
Yellowhead Helicopters, Valemount, BC	(604) 566-4401
	Fax (604) 566-4333

Reservations

Alpine Club of Canada Clubhouse, Canmore	(403) 678-3200
Southern Alberta Hostelling Association	
Calgary	(403) 283-5551
Banff	(403) 762-4122
Alberta Hostelling Association, Edmonton	(403) 439-3139
Canadian Alpine Centre and	
International Hostel at Lake Louise	(403) 522-2200

Avalanche and Weather Information

Public Avalanche Information Bulletin	
(Canadian Avalanche Association)	1-800-667-1105
Banff Avalanche Information (recording)	(403) 762-1460
Jasper Avalanche Information Centre	(403) 852-2356

Weather

Pincher Creek	(403) 627-3733
Banff Forecast	(403) 762-2088
Banff Synopsis	(403) 762-3091
Jasper Forecast	(403) 852-3185
Golden	(604) 344-7500

INDEX

Emergency Phone Numbers

Warden/Ranger Offices

24-hour emergency	(403) 852-6161 or 3100
Waterton	(403) 859-2224
Kananaskis Country Emergency Services	(403) 591-7767
Banff	(403) 762-4506
Kootenay (Radium)	(403) 347-9361
Lake Louise	(403) 522-3866
Field	(604) 343-6324
Saskatchewan River Crossing	(403) 761-7077
Sunwapta (Poboktan Creek)	(403) 852-5383
Jasper	(403) 852-6156

RCMP

24 hour emergency	Dial 0, ask for Zenith 50,000
Waterton (November to April)	(403) 653-4932
Pincher Creek	(403) 627-4424
Sundre	(403) 639-3655
Nordegg	(403) 845-2881
Canmore	(403) 678-5516
Banff	(403) 762-2226
Lake Louise	(403) 522-3811
Jasper	(403) 852-4848
Grande Cache	(403) 827-2222
Radium	(604) 347-9393
Invermere	(604) 342-9292
Field	(604) 343-6316
Golden	(604) 344-7580
Valemount	(604) 566-4466

Avalanche Hazard and Snow Stability

Public Avalanche Information Bulletin
(Canadian Avalanche Association)

1-800-667-1105
Toll free number not accessible from the USA
If calling from the USA call either the Vancouver or Calgary numbers

If calling from the Vancouver area call (604) 290-9333
If calling from the Calgary area call (403) 243-7253 (code 7669)

Banff Park Avalanche Information (403) 762-1460 (recording)